W9-CMJ-162

WITHDRAWN

Writing Double

WOMEN'S LITERARY PARTNERSHIPS

Bette London

Cornell University Press

ITHACA AND LONDON

First published 1999 by Cornell University Press
First printing, Cornell Paperbacks, 1999

Printed in the United States of America

Library of Congress Cataloging-in-Publication Data

London, Bette Lynn.
    Writing double : women's literary partnerships / Bette London.
        p.   cm. — (Reading women writing)
    Includes bibliographical references and index.
    ISBN 0-8014-3563-3 (cloth). — ISBN 0-8014-8555-x (pbk.)
    1. English literature—Women authors—History and criticism.   2. Women and literature—Great Britain—History—19th century.   3. Women and literature—Great Britain—History—20th century.   4. Authorship—Collaboration—History.   5. Spirit writings—Authorship.   6. Women mediums Biography.   I. Title.   II. Series.
    PR111.L66   1999
    820.9'9287—dc21   99-37635

Cornell University Press strives to use environmentally responsible suppliers and materials to the fullest extent possible in the publishing of its books. Such materials include vegetable-based, low-VOC inks, and acid-free papers that are recycled, totally chlorine-free, or partly composed of nonwood fibers. Books that bear the logo of the FSC (Forest Stewardship Council) use paper taken from forests that have been inspected and certified as meeting the highest standards for environmental and social responsibility. For further information, visit our website at   — www.cornellpress.cornell.edu.

Cloth printing   10 9 8 7 6 5 4 3 2 1
Paperback printing   10 9 8 7 6 5 4 3 2 1

For Tom

Contents

List of Illustrations ix

Acknowledgments xi

Introduction: Seeing Double 1

1 Secret Writing: The Brontë Juvenilia and the Myth of
Solitary Genius 33

2 "Something Obscurely Repellent": The Resistance to
Double Writing 63

3 Two of a Trade: Partners in Writing, 1880–1930 91

4 Writing at the Margins: Collaboration and the Discourse
of Exoticism 119

5 The Scribe and the Lady: Automatic Writing and the Trials
of Authorship 150

6 Romancing the Medium: The Silent Partnership of
Georgie Yeats 179

Afterword: Ghostwriting; or, The Afterlife of Authorship 210

Works Cited 213

Index 227

Illustrations

1. Cover, Sandra M. Gilbert and Susan Gubar, *The Madwoman in the Attic*   xiv

2. "Michael Field" (Katherine Bradley and Edith Cooper)   10

3. Jane and Mary Findlater (Drawing by Lady Jane Lindsay)   11

4. Jane and Mary Findlater   12

5. Edith Somerville and Violet Martin ("Martin Ross")   13

6. Somerville and Ross in their Studio   14

7. Geraldine Cummins   15

8. Hester Dowden   16

9. Gladys Osborne Leonard   17

10. W. B. and Georgie Yeats   180

Acknowledgments

This book has been a long time in the making, and, given its explicit subject, I am acutely aware of the inadequacy of any effort to fully acknowledge the many sources of visible and invisible support that have gone into its construction. I am grateful to Yale University Press for permission to reproduce the cover art to *The Madwoman in the Attic*, to H. W. Wilson Company for the right to reprint the "Michael Field" photograph, to Sir Toby Coghill for sharing the Somerville and Ross illustrations from his family archive, and to the Corbis-Bettman Institute for permission to reproduce the photograph of Georgie and W. B. Yeats. I am especially grateful to Bernhard Kendler of Cornell University Press for his belief in this project from its inception, and for his unflagging support and encouragement as this book has evolved through several manifestations. The readers at Cornell University Press provided thoughtful, engaged, and generous readings, and I have benefited greatly from them; in particular, I would like to thank Alison Booth for her astute commentary, and for the pressure she exerted to make the book tighter and more coherent.

For many years now, I have been presenting portions of this book, and of research related to it, at both national and international conferences, and at colloquia and research seminars at the University of Rochester; I am grateful to audiences at the International Conference on Narrative, the MLA, the Dickens Project at UC Santa Cruz, the Interdisciplinary Group for Historical and Literary Study at Texas A&M, and the State University of New York at Buffalo for encouraging me to believe in the wide interest of my quirky investments. Among those deserving special notice for arranging panels or responding to work presented in them are Stacy Hubbard, Audrey Jaffe, Deidre Lynch, MaryAnn O'Farrell, Jeffrey Masten, Richard Pearce, Bonnie Kime Scott, and Ronald Thomas.

At the University of Rochester, I am lucky to have wonderful colleagues. In the English Department, I want to thank especially Rosemary Kegl, James Longenbach, and John Michael for their friendship, support, and intellectual camaraderie, and I want to thank Morris Eaves for his continuous encouragement of this project, especially in its more bizarre and unfamiliar features, and for insisting that there had to be pictures. I am grateful to the Susan B. Anthony Institute for Gender and Women's Studies for providing a forum for conversations across disciplines; Rosemary Feal, Melanie May, Brenda Meehan, Deborah Modrak, and Jean Pedersen have provided support and intellectual sustenance at critical moments. Sharon Willis offered invaluable assistance in helping me to work my way out of an impasse over the introduction.

Over the course of many years, I have benefited from a succession of graduate research assistants—Christine Berni, Victoria Szabo, and Mary Kelkenberg—who have been both diligent and inventive in tracking down sources and ferreting out obscure information. Juliet Sloger has been an imaginative, resourceful, and tireless indexer. I could not have completed this book without all their labor. Kate Walsh, the English Department's Administrative Secretary, has also provided crucial assistance tracking down copyright owners for the illustrations and attending to other details surrounding the handling of the manuscript.

In addition, I am grateful to my family: to my parents, for their unwavering support and affection, and for their conviction that this book might interest even those who were not academics; to my sister Robin who confirmed such interest in many long and intense conversations; to my brother Joel for always being there for me; and to my nieces Elizabeth and Stephanie London for bringing home the reality of collective storytelling. Jonathan and Geoffrey Hahn deserve special recognition for putting up with my frantic states and giving me the space I needed. Finally, Tom Hahn has contributed to this book in ways that defy articulation; I am more grateful than I can say for his patience, intelligence, and supportiveness, and for the fact that he has always been my most discriminating reader. My partner in all things, he has made collaboration a living reality, so much so that I sometimes think he may have written every word of this book without my even knowing it.

B. L.

Writing Double

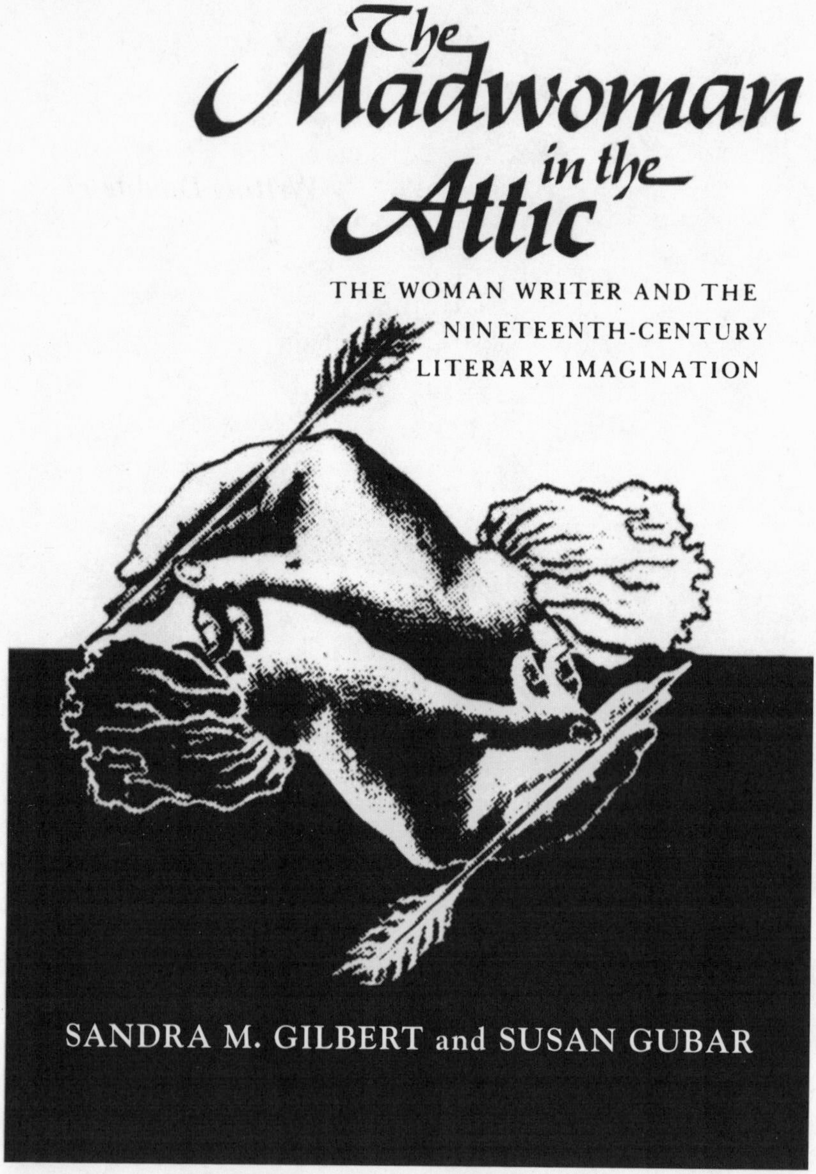

Figure 1. *Cover illustration of* The Madwoman in the Attic: The Woman Writer and the Nineteenth-Century Literary Imagination, *by Sandra M. Gilbert and Susan Gubar. New Haven: Yale University Press, 1979. Copyright © by Yale University, 1979.*

Introduction: Seeing Double

This book had its origin in what seemed to me a curious irony. Having encountered the Anglo-Irish writers Somerville and Ross some years ago in a graduate seminar, I had begun, somewhat randomly, to collect instances of women's partnership writing. Looking particularly at literary collaborations from the nineteenth and early twentieth centuries, I found myself immersed in stories of authorship with remarkably similar features. These partnerships, grounded in strong affectional, often familial, relationships between women and self-consciously insisting on their perfect textual fusion, seemed to cry out for feminist inquiry. But feminism had proved almost as silent about these partnerships as traditional literary history. The silence, moreover, had an added irony, for feminist criticism had supplied, in Gilbert and Gubar, what may be the most famous instance of women's "literary" collaboration. In what they wrote as much as how they wrote it, Sandra M. Gilbert and Susan Gubar had made double-handed writing their signature—and, by the very success of their articulation, the signature of a phase of feminist criticism devoted to the creation of a canon of women's literature.

Indeed, in what remains one of the most influential works of feminist literary criticism, *The Madwoman in the Attic: The Woman Writer and the Nineteenth-Century Literary Imagination* (1979), this image of authorship is boldly emblazoned in the two hands of the woman writer pictured on the book's cover (Figure 1). But although, at first glance, these hands might seem to signal dual authorship of the sort that went into the book's construction (a possibility reinforced by the printing of the authors' names immediately beneath this image), familiarity with the text teaches us to read the image differently: to recognize the hands as mirror images of each other. The two hands, in fact, turn out to be one—that of an author understood to be singular: *the* woman writer in the nineteenth century. That writer, Gilbert and Gubar famously argued, was inevitably divided against herself, locked in a collaboration with her own dark double. Feminist criticism, they ably demonstrated, could provide the key to decode this secret text at the heart of women's writing.

The effects of this critical construction were profound and far-reaching, for the idea of the double-handed—or double-voiced—text proved remarkably generative, ushering in a host of virtuoso readings of texts by women. But feminism's focus on the metaphorical dimensions of collaboration also had some unintended consequences, pushing women's actual collaborations even further to the margins. *Madwoman*, indeed, could be likened to the palimpsests it so forcefully illuminated, for it simultaneously introduced and erased the idea of literal collaboration— of collaborations *between* flesh- and-blood women. Indeed, the very success of *Madwoman's* formulations foreclosed another set of questions. What happens when "the woman writer" is not *one*? What happens if collaboration is understood literally? If, to return to *Madwoman's* famous cover, we imagine, two hands (belonging to two different bodies) engaged in writing, how would the scene of writing be pictured? And what alternative histories of writing might follow from this (as yet unrealized) image?

Engaged in its own remapping of the literary arena, feminist criticism had been silent about these alternative possibilities. But if earlier feminists had failed to interest themselves in the types of literary partnerships my own research was uncovering, this was no simple accident but a structural feature of the choices feminist criticism had made at a critical moment in its development. These choices, moreover, were not unique to feminism. The poststructuralist critique of authorship—most influentially expounded by Foucault, "What Is an Author?" (1969) and Barthes, "The Death of the Author" (1968)—produced no sudden surge of interest in collaborative authorship, even when these essays appeared in prominent English translations in the late 1970s.[1] And although, as critics such as Nancy K. Miller have powerfully argued, there was good reason why many feminist critics wanted to keep the idea of the individual author intact at the very moment they were demanding recognition for women's authorial achievements, feminists were not alone in maintaining this position. Even critics, moreover, who openly embraced

---

[1] Of course, to replace the unitary author with two (or more) embodied ones was not exactly what these critiques intended. But insofar as collaborative authorship, in its material practice as much as its theoretical implications, dislodges the figure of "the author," it opens to scrutiny ruling assumptions about authorship and thus enables more complex understandings of what Foucault has called the "author function."

poststructuralism's theoretical agenda did not necessarily pursue its practical implications, and when they did, they did not generally pursue them in the direction of literal coauthorship. In fact, sustained scholarship on collaboration has been preeminently a phenomenon of the 1990s, and there is as yet little agreement on the proper parameters of the subject.[2] Is collaborative authorship, for example, as some studies imply, an anomalous occurrence, of interest primarily for its exceptionality, or is it, as Jack Stillinger has argued, a common feature of most if not all authorship that passes as singular? The very fact, I would argue, that this remains a question, is testimony to our reluctance to dispense with the idea of the solitary author.

This reluctance has been especially marked when the authorship in question is of the sort we deem literary. It would seem, then, no accident that much of the emerging work on collaboration has developed in venues outside literary studies, particularly in the field of rhetoric and composition; indeed, as Andrea Lunsford and Lisa Ede demonstrate in one of the most prominent works to emerge in that discipline, *Singular Texts/ Plural Authors* (1990), it is the idea of the author, inherited from the study of literature, that has probably done the most to blind us to the fact that writing is *not* generally a solitary activity. And the higher the literary values associated with a work, the less collaborative authorship has generally been credited. What is true for academic discourse, moreover, appears even truer in the popular imagination, where the idea of the solitary author is so deeply entrenched as to leave no room for other possible configurations. In a 1996 photographic study, for example, titled *The Writer's Desk*, Jill Krementz capitalizes on a popular fascination with the scene of literary creation; out of the 110 illustrations of modern authorship that she furnishes, however, none pictures writing as anything but solitary. In fact, while Krementz's study shows the rooms in which authors write to vary dramatically, as do the authors' poses and postures—and while some write with pen or pencil, some using modern (and not so modern) technologies (typewriters and computers of various vintages)—the solitude of the act would seem the one constant.

To study literary collaboration, then, as I proposed to do—as a distinct, recognizable, and meaningful act for women—was to fly in the

---

[2] For recent discussions of collaboration, see Wayne Koestenbaum, *Double Talk: The Erotics of Male Collaboration* (1989), Andrea Lunsford and Lisa Ede, *Singular Texts/Plural Authors: Perspectives on Collaborative Writing* (1990), Jack Stillinger, *Multiple Authorship and the Myth of Solitary Genius* (1991), Whitney Chadwick and Isabelle de Courtivron, eds., *Significant Others: Creativity and Intimate Partnership* (1993), Martha Woodmansee and Peter Jaszi, eds., *The Construction of Authorship: Textual Appropriation in Law and Literature* (1994), Holly Laird, ed., "Forum: On Collaborations" (1994–95).

face of the self-evident. For common sense would argue that if women's literary collaborations had yet to find their chronicler, this was probably because they had no history to speak of—no history, that is, that would count as significant. This critique could not simply be dismissed as irrelevant. With the exception of the Brontës and the Yeatses, whose collaborative engagements I had chosen as frame texts for this study, my research had not led me to writers of canonical stature. And in the case of the Yeatses, it was only W. B. Yeats and not his wife, Georgie, who was generally recognized as an author. The collaborative authorship, moreover, in which the Brontës and the Yeatses participated—the "juvenilia" of the four Brontë siblings, the "automatic writing" of Georgie and W. B. Yeats in the early years of their marriage—did not generate the work that got these authors canonized. Produced in secret and never intended for publication, these collaborative experiments could in fact be understood as mere practice writing—apprenticeship work or anomalous outpourings, easily absorbed into more conventional career trajectories.

Literary collaboration, as practiced by men, was only slightly better documented as a self-contained subject. But as Wayne Koestenbaum and Jack Stillinger have demonstrated in markedly different contexts, collaborations often played a crucial role in the careers of male authors celebrated for their solitary genius. And here, the divergences from women's literary history are significant. For although I was looking at what was, for the most part, the same historical moment that Koestenbaum had treated in his influential study *Double Talk* (1989), I could find few examples of collaboration as famous as most of his representative cases: Freud and Breuer, Coleridge and Wordsworth, Pound and Eliot, Conrad and Ford, Robert Louis Stevenson (with his stepson, Lloyd Osborne, and with his wife, Fanny Osborne Stevenson). Even the more minor writers Koestenbaum treated were generally better known than their female counterparts—Rider Haggard and Andrew Lang, at least, if not Walter Besant and James Rice, the latter probably the most prolific and sustained of the male partnership ventures.

By contrast, the collaborative writers who formed the core of my study appeared a rather motley group, with varied and uncertain literary reputations. *Michael Field* (Katherine Bradley and Edith Cooper), a poet associated with the turn-of-the-century aesthetes, had consistently maintained in "her" own time a coterie following, and the authors were now enjoying something of a minor revival, especially as practitioners of Sapphic lyrics. *Somerville and Ross* (Edith Somerville and Violet Martin), whose popularity in the first decades of the twentieth century was enormous, had, in the intervening years, fallen in and out of political favor, but they had never completely dropped out of the canon of Irish literature. They had continued to enjoy a broad-based popular following, with one of their novels and a collection of their stories serialized on PBS's Masterpiece Theatre. *Mary and Jane Findlater*, natives of Scotland and sometime residents of England, hovered on the borders of metropolitan literary society, enjoying the friendship and respect of several prominent literary figures in the early part of the twentieth century; well-reviewed and reaching wide audiences, they wrote what was generally agreed to be accomplished fiction before, in the 1920s, retreating from the literary scene in the wake of modernism. *E. D. Gerard* (Emily and Dorothea Gerard), whose novels introduced English audiences to characters and scenes from eastern Europe, enjoyed a reputation at the end of the nineteenth century as a purveyor of the exotic; like much work, however, of the second—or even third—order, the Gerard sisters' fiction made a brief splash and then disappeared from living memory. *M. Barnard Eldershaw* (Marjorie Barnard and Flora Eldershaw), whose major literary output came in the 1930s, enjoyed a more lasting but circumscribed reputation, never really achieving a name outside the authors' native Australia, although one of their works, *Tomorrow and Tomorrow and Tomorrow* was republished as a Virago Modern Classic in the 1980s.

The circumstances of these partnerships also encouraged a certain trivialization, reproducing as they did the configurations of the family: two pairs of sisters (the Findlaters and the Gerards), an aunt and niece (Michael Field), and a pair of second cousins (Somerville and Ross). With the exception of the Gerard sisters, natives of Scotland who married Austrian army officers and moved to Poland, these were partnerships of women who chose not to marry. Their lives, like their texts, were consequently wrapped up in each other, but their relationships were not easy to define in terms of the erotic. The details of their lives thus reinforce the impression that these partnerships existed somewhere between the faintly scandalous and the quaintly domestic. These were partnerships, moreover, of women who were, or were perceived to be, decidedly eccentric—a perception often fostered by the partners. One of the last works produced by Michael Field, for example, was a collection of poems, striking for their passion and intensity, memorializing the authors' beloved pet dog. Edith Somerville was even more audacious; after the death of her partner, she claimed that Violet Martin ("Martin Ross") continued to communicate with her from the "other side," where, Martin was quick to report, she was happily united with the spirits of their dead dogs; insisting that despite Martin's death their collaboration continued much as before, Somerville maintained their dual signature for another thirty-four years.

Intrigued by this example, and with the case of Georgie Yeats in the back of my mind, I had begun to look more closely at other instances of automatic writing: writing produced by authors who believed that they were communicating with some surviving spirit of the dead who controlled their hand, forcing them to write involuntarily. For automatic writing appeared to be a logical extension of the collaborative ethos; certainly, it was widely practiced by intellectual women at the very moment others of like mind were turning to more conventional literary partnerships. What I found, however, when I began to look at the writings of respected mediums seemed quite different from the writing Edith Somerville engaged in, less closely linked than was hers to conventional literary production. Yet the writing produced by women mediums, covering a wide range of scholarly and esoteric subjects, was at least implicitly literary in nature, and, as the mediums understood it, a collaborative operation—produced in conjunction with disembodied "spirits" that dictated their words to them. Automatic writing also required flesh-and-blood collaborators. Generally, mediums produced most—if not all—of their writings in the company of others, and the productivity of the medium might depend on the presence of one or more other participants, as the case of the Yeatses dramatically illustrates (with Georgie's automatic writing prompted by W. B.'s questions).

Taking automatic writing, then, as the limit case for women's collaborative authorship, I identified another group of authors who formed the core of the second part of this study—a group, not surprisingly, even more obscure than the first. *Geraldine Cummins*, herself a novelist and coauthor of collaboratively written plays and the first biographer of Edith Somerville, was best known, as a medium, for a long series of automatic scripts on early Christian subjects—scripts that read like the narratives of biblical apocrypha. *Hester Dowden*, Cummins's friend, mentor, and collaborator in psychical research, briefly enjoyed a moment of fame when she published, in 1924, a set of scripts purporting to be communications from Oscar Wilde (then dead for twenty-three years), received by her via automatic writing. *Gladys Osborne Leonard*, investigated for the Society for Psychical Research (SPR) by Radclyffe Hall and Una Troubridge (and subject of the SPR's perhaps most extensive study), was best known for the communications of her personal familiar—a spirit named Feda, who claimed to be a fourteen-year-old Hindu girl and the great-great-grandmother of the medium. "*Mrs. Willett*," a test medium for the SPR in the 1910s and 1920s, was the subject of extensive studies involving cross-correspondence or collaborative mediumship, where several mediums working independently received messages that only made sense when read together.

As this project began to take shape around a distinct set of literary figures, the questions it raised became even more pressing. Indeed, the subjects I was dealing with could be considered not just obscure or eccentric but, in some cases, downright looney. Why did I think, then, that this history deserved more serious attention? On one level, the answer was quite simple: the history exists, and as such, deserves study. As Richard Altick has argued of this period, to study only the canonical writers would be to get a historical picture that is quite distorted—an insight particularly true for the authorship of women. In themselves, moreover, these stories of authorship had a certain fascination—if only for their curiosity value. But most important, I wanted to argue, this history provides a unique window onto the practice of authorship. And authorship, in its broadest theoretical and historical dimensions, was at the heart of this study.

Following where my examples led me, I thus found my work intersecting with scholarship on the social construction of authorship—work focused on publishing history, copyright law, and literary reception. What became clear as the project developed was that I was tracing not a history of authors or texts but the history of a practice, the history of a mode of literary production at a particular moment of its efflorescence. As a site to explore how authorship operates, literary collaboration offered a peculiar vantage; for no matter how conventional its literary products—and many of these partnerships produced perfectly conventional writing—as a *process*, collaborative authorship continued to be perceived as resolutely outside the mainstream. Indeed, as a process, collaboration was more open to scrutiny than solitary authorship. Making authorship visible in unexpected ways, literary collaboration thus put in relief the rules its own practice resisted, illuminating the very structures that necessarily excluded it from the category of authorship. In doing so, collaboration provided a platform to return to certain fundamental questions: What is an author? Who gets counted under this rubric? What forms of authorship are sanctioned and what forms marginalized at a given historical moment? What does it mean to say the author is dead? Can "dead" authors still communicate?

With these concerns in mind, I also wanted to ask a more particular question, What forms of authorship have particularly attracted women? For one of the guiding assumptions of this study was that the practices I was illuminating spoke for large numbers of women. And here the example of mediumship was especially interesting, for women were generally acknowledged to predominate in the ranks of mediums. Scholarship since the 1980s has repeatedly linked mediumship to feminine empowerment, noting the agency it afforded marginalized women; as this scholarship has also noted, mediums were often allied with various progressive movements.[3] But mediums were rarely, if ever, considered as authors, despite the fact that mediumship made many women prolific writers. By the 1910s and 1920s, these women were increasingly of the same sort (in class, education, and professional aspirations) as those who became conventional authors. To recognize mediumship as a form of authorship, then, was to recognize that women often became authors in ways not institutionally legitimated.

Feminist criticism, of course, had, for some time, been teaching this lesson. And if it had not turned its attention to literary collaboration as a historically significant writing arrangement for women, it was nonetheless asking the question, "Is collaboration a peculiarly female and/or feminist mode of production?" (Kaplan and Rose 557). Working backward from its own contemporary investments (including numerous instances of collaborative authorship), it was thus preparing the way to make women's partnership writing a recognizable subject. Holly Laird, for example, in a special double issue of *Tulsa Studies in Women's Literature* (1994–95), had begun soliciting research on what she called feminist coauthorship; the resulting forum "On Collaborations" showcases partnerships ranging from the historical and literary to the contemporary and theoretical, with "academic" collaborations by far the most fully represented. If, as some contemporary critics were arguing, "collaborative writing, particularly as a primary mode of writing, is more common among women than men" (Doane and Hodges 54), it would be reasonable to expect this pattern to extend to literary production. And it would be reasonable to expect that historical pressures would have made collaboration even more common for women at a time when authorship was not as readily available to them. Why, then, was this history of women's collaborative authorship so difficult to come by?

---

[3] See, for example, Alex Owen, *The Darkened Room: Women, Power and Spiritualism in Late Victorian England*, Diane Basham, *The Trial of Woman: Feminism and the Occult Sciences in Victorian Literature and Society*, and Anne Braude, *Radical Spirits: Spiritualism and Women's Rights in Nineteenth-Century America*. Braude offers the most forceful argument for the "overlap between the woman's rights movement and Spiritualism" (3); Basham, who looks at the occult sciences in Victorian Britain, also sees a profound link between women's engagement with spiritualism and the "Woman Question," although she is more interested in mediumship's psychological dimensions. Owen offers the most balanced and nuanced perspective on the "subversive" power mediumship afforded nineteenth-century women. For other discussions of mediumship, see Janet Oppenheim, *The Other World: Spiritualism and Psychical Research in England, 1850–1914*.

Certainly, my own sampling of authors was small, but this fact was not particularly surprising, for I had deliberately sought cases where the collaborations were most explicit; and I had sought cases where the collaborations were fully acknowledged, at least by the participants. Even in these instances, however, as subsequent chapters make clear, the authors had many incentives to keep their collaborations secret—whether they were practitioners of automatic writing or producers of more conventional literature. It would thus be safe to assume that unacknowledged collaborations must have far exceeded the acknowledged ones. And this would be even more true for the wide range of collaborative practices that fall short of full and equal coauthorship. These implicit collaborations, often grounded in acts of silent assistance, constituted a way many women entered authorship. But such collaborations generally had no place in the official record. Indeed, in the case of women, literary collaborators suffered from a double invisibility—the invisibility of collaboration and the invisibility of women's writing. Even where such collaborations were openly recognized, they tended to be represented in ways guaranteed to ensure their marginalization.

To study collaboration, then, was to study the conditions of its erasure. And these conditions had gender-specific connotations, reinforcing the idea that women were not "real" authors. Female collaborators were thus regularly dismissed as amateurs no matter how professionally they operated; their collaborations were persistently considered adolescent experiments. Their collaborations were also invariably projected by commentators as in some way secret, no matter how public the authors were about what they were doing. And no matter how sustained these partnership ventures, there was a persistent undercurrent that collaborative writing was ultimately apprenticeship for some future apotheosis where the author would be singular.

Visual representations of women collaborators further reinforced these impressions, generally underscoring the quaintness of their subjects. Designed to convey some nostalgic invocation of a bygone era, these were, above all, portraits of women *as* women. Projected as two of a kind rather than two of a trade, female collaborators were, in fact, almost never represented as engaged in writing. Instead, they were compulsively represented as twin-like in their sameness, the doubled embodiment of feminine features (Figures 2–6). Literary collaborators could thus be seen as anything but what the caption accompanying the Findlater portrait affectionately claims: "novelists of repute" (Figure 4). Indeed, the general impression these representations conveyed was that, as instances of authorship, these partnerships could not be taken entirely seriously.

Figure 2. "Michael Field" (Katherine Bradley and Edith Cooper) from British Authors of the Nineteenth Century. *Copyright © 1936 by The H. W. Wilson Company. Reprinted by special arrangement with the publisher.*

Verbal sketches of partnership writing confirm the same need to represent collaboration as spectacle—to picture the participants with appropriate props and in an appropriate setting. Thus musing on those "dear Scotch ladies," one reviewer notes of the Findlaters, "We never read a book of theirs without recalling Nora Archibald's sketch of them,

Figure 3. Jane and Mary Findlater. Drawing by Lady Jane Lindsay. From The Findlater Sisters: Literature and Friendship, *by Eileen Mackenzie. London: John Murray, 1964.*

sitting down together at the big table to write, each undisturbed by the other's rustling and fluttering" (*The Dial*, 14 June 1917, 527). And offering his "tribute to Ireland's most celebrated literary partnership," Sir Patrick Coghill, Edith Somerville's nephew, recalls the authors' attic studio (Figure 6): "It was, to my mind, a place of singular and hideous discomfort, and there the two would sit, huddled in rugs and surrounded by two or three fox terriers" (4, 7). Notably, these descriptions invoke the material conditions in which women write only to domesticate both the settings and the practitioners; indeed, they invoke a scene of writing in which writing barely figures, upstaged by the homey apparatus of creature comforts or obscured by the side show of feminine flutter. As with other representations of women's collaborations, these descriptions thus capture the ambiguous status of these literary partnerships: both engaged and not engaged in *real* writing; both professional work and invisible (domestic) labor; both private practice and public spectacle; both the embodiment of authorship and the dismantling of it.

Figure 4. Jane and Mary Findlater, "novelists of repute." From The Findlater Sisters: Literature and Friendship, *by Eileen Mackenzie. London: John Murray, 1964.*

Figure 5. Edith Somerville and Violet Martin ("Martin Ross"). Photograph for interview in
The Minute *(1895). From the Coghill Family Archive. Reprinted by permission of Sir Toby*
Coghill.

In the case of mediums, the dilemma was even more striking, for the
collaborative authorship that the idea of automatic writing evoked was
precisely of the sort that could not be pictured without marking the
medium as irredeemably wacky. In these portraits, then, the solitary
figure of the medium stands in for her invisible collaborators, her other-

Figure 6. Somerville and Ross in their studio. From the Coghill Family Archive. Reprinted by permission of Sir Toby Coghill.

worldly gaze signaling the unrepresentable (Figures 7–9). But even if one puts authorship out of the picture, there remains considerable resistance to taking mediums seriously. Consequently, portraits of mediums were required to do double duty, simultaneously projecting their subjects as "normal," even as they played off the expectation of the exotic. For a medium who was famous for her automatic writing, the signs of her authorship were likely to be erased or subsumed in the costume of exoticism. The portrait of Hester Dowden (Figure 8), for example, is one of the few to include the tools of the trade of a practicing medium. Posed with a ouija board "traveler," the medium is removed from her writing; she does not hold the pencil but rests her hand on an instrument that points the letters of "her" words out to her. This depiction of

Figure 7. Geraldine Cummins. Frontispiece to Unseen Adventures, *by Geraldine Cummins. London: Rider, 1951.*

Figure 8. Hester Dowden. Frontispiece to Far Horizon: A Biography of Hester Dowden, *by Eric Bentley. London: Rider, 1951.*

Figure 9. Gladys Osborne Leonard. Frontispiece to My Life in Two Worlds. *London: Cassell, 1931.*

Hester Dowden thus allows for double-handedness by detaching writing from our ordinary understanding of it. Indeed, the hand of the medium, reflected on the polished surface of the table, invokes another hand pushing the traveler from the other side—a hand that, within the discourse of automatic writing, may or may not belong to the medium. Reminding us of what cannot be figured, such representations make explicit the larger resistance to collaborative authorship. For they expose what other images only hint at: that collaborative authors are not what they seem to be—that they are not really authors and not really collaborators.

Given this history, I was faced with a number of problems as I embarked on this project. How could one recognize—and represent—women's literary collaborations as a practice of authorship? And what would it mean to take such practices seriously? These questions, moreover, were not merely rhetorical. For even as a growing body of scholarly work on collaboration was beginning to be published, women's collaborative authorship had remained, as Holly Laird suggests, undertheorized (*"Forum: On Collaborations"* 236). And this was true not only because male collaboration had received more systematic study but because collaboration itself was still an unstable category. This project, then, involved a number of key methodological considerations—the most fundamental being to decide what would count as collaboration for the purpose of this study. For as the scholarship on collaboration makes clear, collaborations often take place in ways that are not readily visible. As any student of the subject would immediately recognize, an authorial signature is not an accurate index to a collaboration's existence. Collaborations, indeed, frequently exist even where two authors don't name themselves as such. Collaborative authors, as my own examples demonstrate, often deliberately choose a singular (often composite) signature to protect their writing arrangements from public scrutiny—even public ridicule (Michael Field, E. D. Gerard, M. Barnard Eldershaw). And where the collaborations are less all-encompassing than the ones I focus on, we have no way of knowing how many authors pass off collaborative creations as solitary achievement—whether as an overt act of appropriation or as a mutually approved resolution to some private negotiation. In the case of Gertrude Stein and Alice B. Toklas, for example, Toklas's contribution to Stein's literary work has become an occasion for speculation, although the exact nature and extent of that collaboration remains open to question. In the case of the contemporary Native American writers Louise Erdrich and Michael Dorris (acknowledged collaborators in certain instances), the authors themselves first opened the subject, publicly insisting on a fully shared writing practice even in their ostensibly single-authored pieces. Distinguishing between individual conceptualization and collective revision, they designated as "author" the one who composed the first draft of their books, while insisting that every word in the final draft was collectively agreed upon.[4]

As these instances suggest, collaborations exist in a range of "authorial" activities not necessarily named authorship: acts of assistance and inspiration; acts of mentoring or mutual influence; acts of revision or editorial input. Seen in this larger context, "collaboration" plays a more central role in the history of women's authorship than might at first appear evident, taking in such examples as Marianne Moore and Elizabeth Bishop, H. D. and Bryher, Virginia Woolf and Vita Sackville-West, Vera Brittain and Winifred Holtby. It includes the Brontë sisters, not just in their juvenilia, where collaboration was a constitutive feature, but in the novels they wrote and published in close consultation with each other. As Betsy Erkkila has demonstrated, even such a celebrated recluse as Emily Dickinson—the epitome of a singular, individual, even eccentric writer—produced her writing in dialogue with female friends and family, among whom she circulated her unpublished poetry. As Erkkila and others have argued, there is, in fact, a potential history of suppressed collaboration in the ordinary and extraordinary stories of women's literary friendships.[5] And there is a history of literary collaborations that never saw fruition—as in Jane Carlyle's abortive partnership with Geraldine Jewsbury or in the novel Vita Sackville-West began to write with her lover, Violet Trefussis.

We confront an even larger picture if we consider women's participation in acts of authorship even more resistant to recognition—acts most commonly found in cross-gender writing relationships. As interest in Dorothy Wordsworth, for example, suggests, women's authorial contributions to an established male author's corpus are often subject to appropriation or trivialization as something less than real authorial input. Indeed, given the historical power of prescriptive gender coding, it would seem nearly impossible to gauge the acts of authorship women engaged in as sisters, daughters, wives, and lovers. And these gendered roles were not infrequently reproduced in women's professional rela-

---

[4] See Kay Bonetti, "An Interview with Louise Erdrich and Michael Dorris" 80. For other discussions of this collaboration, see also Hertha D. Wong, "An Interview with Louise Erdrich and Michael Dorris," and Louise Coltelli, "Louise Erdrich and Michael Dorris."

[5] Betsy Erkkila, in *The Wicked Sisters: Women Poets, Literary History, and Discord*, constructs precisely such a history, documenting the complex and contradictory collaborations that structure the poetic tradition in women's writing. Her examples include Emily Dickinson, Elizabeth Barrett Browning, the Brontë sisters, Marianne Moore, Elizabeth Bishop, Adrienne Rich, and Gwendolyn Brooks.

tionships. Elsie Michie, for example, has shown how even established authors like Elizabeth Gaskell suffered a loss of autonomy at the hands of male editors—especially famous author-editors such as Dickens. Yet there is another even less told story of women's authorial agency as editors and readers, as they served in these capacities for publishing houses as well as for friends and family.[6] Women's more complex authorial engagements, however, have tended to be dwarfed by the dominant model of spousal collaboration that defines most cross-gender writing arrangements—a model that relegates women to the roles of helpmeet and amanuensis. Trained to read these roles as ancillary, we lack the vocabulary to describe them otherwise. Even in writing partnerships where both the man and the woman have an authorial identity, the imputation of collaboration turns out to be more compromising for women. Indeed, it has traditionally been used to discredit women's authorship. The suggestion, for example, that Percy Shelley qualifies as a coauthor of *Frankenstein* carries the imputation of Mary Shelley's incompetence—if not authorial impropriety.[7] In fact, however recalcitrant the subjects, we seem most comfortable with the model of collaboration subsumed in the rubric, "The Genius and Mrs. Genius" (as Stacy Schiff's 1997 *New Yorker* article dubs the Nabokovs). Certainly, this role as auxiliary to genius was one Georgie Yeats famously occupied, although as Chapter 6 demonstrates, it is one she both embodied and complicated, opening to question the authorship masked in other women's comparable positions. The model, moreover, whereby wives are perceived above all as rendering emotional support and editorial and secretarial assistance has also been reproduced in lesbian couples: Gertrude Stein and Alice B. Toklas, Radclyffe Hall and Una Troubridge, Amy Lowell and Ada Russell.

This broader history of collaboration informs my investigation. But in choosing my literary examples I have concentrated on instances where the presence of two hands can be unambiguously recognized; where collaborations are acknowledged and not readily susceptible to hierarchical ordering. In this, my strategy is the reverse of Stillinger's: he concentrated on authorial practices ordinarily thought of as singular. I argue that an emphasis on women's authorship demands a methodology different from one appropriate for a history of authorship implicitly male-centered. For the hidden collaborations in which women so often participated are implicated in a gendered history that makes it difficult

[6] See, for example, Linda Fritschner's account of Geraldine Jewsbury's work as a publisher's reader.

[7] James Rieger makes precisely this argument in the Introduction to his edition of Mary Shelley's *Frankenstein* (1818 edition).

for us to read these authorial practices in their full and rich complexity. From a conventional point of view, indeed, these collaborations are only too easily dismissible.

I begin my book, then, with more comprehensive, open, and egalitarian writing relationships because they force us to take seriously the notion that the scene of writing might look quite different from what we generally imagine it to be—that it might, for example, be inhabited by two or more bodies. These literary partnerships contribute to a more expansive understanding of how and where authorship actually takes place, and in particular, how women have historically entered this practice. These most concrete instances of collaboration, I argue, literalize—and hence render visible—practices that inform a range of historical writing arrangements; thus they allow us to see as authorship what often does not pass as such. They provide new ways to think about larger collaborative structures, including those that are generally considered to be merely "assistance." One important implication of this book, then, is the starting point it provides for a much larger inquiry into the structures that have marginalized women's writing by privatizing or domesticating it: family authorship, secret or coterie writing, writing as entertainment. For these practices, as my own examples demonstrate, have stories to tell infinitely richer than the narratives we've inherited.

In structuring my book, my strategy has also been different from Koestenbaum's, whose focus on male collaborations emphasizes their transgressions of sexual propriety. My book is also different from Whitney Chadwick and Isabelle de Courtivron's study of creativity and intimate partnership; encompassing an array of twentieth-century artistic and literary unions, *Significant Others* (1993) takes as its defining unit, "the couple"—people "who have shared a sexual as well as creative partnership" (9). But this definition does not readily fit most of my examples. Indeed, with the exception of the Yeatses, it is not clear whether any of the partners I consider actually shared a sexual relationship. But it is also not clear that the category of romantic friendship, so important in earlier studies of women's companionate relationships, can adequately explain these collaborations—not only because the sexuality of these relationships remains open to question but because the romantic friendship rubric, with its emphasis on personal self-fulfillment, does not sufficiently address the professional components of these unions.

This is not to say that these partnerships are without interest for contemporary gay and lesbian studies—but the interest generated by these partnerships is in part in their resistance to easy categorization. In fact, it could be argued that the indeterminacy of their boundaries facilitated their existence by allowing women's collaborative practices to remain

at once more pervasive and more invisible than analogous male proceedings. Their equivocal location, moreover, on both sexual and professional spectrums, has left them a problematic site for feminist inquiry, both in its earlier ventures and its current manifestations. With
the exception of Michael Field, for example, they have attracted little
attention as a possible site of lesbian writing. But the imputation of
lesbianism—if only through vague innuendo—has followed women's
literary collaborations throughout their reception history. And this history has its own claims on the feminist critic.

Moreover, for the collaborators themselves, however they consciously
circumscribed their relationships, their partnerships afforded a site to
enact and extend their connection to other women, and these connections are well worth studying. The categories Koestenbaum identifies,
then, as central in male collaborations—homosocial bonding, homo-
erotic expression, homosexual panic—are not irrelevant to the consideration of women's collaborative writing, however differently they
operate there. These issues, in fact, emerge throughout this book, receiving particular attention in Chapter 2. But, not surprisingly, this book
is something other than *Double Talk* rewritten with female players. For
it seems evident that, given women's historically different relationship
to the structures and institutions of authorship—and the structures and
institutions of sexuality—their collaborations will not tell the same stories as those of their male counterparts. They require other histories and
other theories. In particular, they require an interpretive structure that
can illuminate those stories that have been ignored or displaced in traditional literary histories. The stories, then, that have most claimed my
attention are those surrounding collaboration as a site of intellectual adventure and professional recognition—the stories, still waiting to be
told, of the complicated acts of professionalization that collaboration
facilitated.

The most striking departure in this book, though, from other work
on collaboration—and what might seem counterintuitive given my
professed emphases—has been my decision not only to include mediumship as a practice of literary collaboration but to allocate it so much
space. One of my central claims, however, is that mediumship constitutes a practice of authorship that shares crucial features with other
contemporaneous modes of literary production. In particular, it shares
with other instances of collaborative authorship an uncertain place on
the public-private continuum. The examination of mediumship, and of
the automatic scripts produced through its mechanisms, thus illuminates other practices of secret or coterie writing. But mediumship also
constitutes a practice squarely, if problematically, located in the dis-

course of professionalism. Indeed, one of the informing paradoxes of this book has been the realization that what looks like an amateur practice often turns out to be deeply professional. But the professional authorship mediumship fosters calls into question authorship's more ordinary manifestations, as Chapter 5 explicitly demonstrates. For more dramatically than other forms of collaborative authorship, automatic writing destabilizes certain cherished assumptions about authorial activity. It thus counterpoints the conventionality of much collaborative writing; at the same time, it underlines what makes collaborative authorship appear so threatening. If, then, we take seriously that collaboration poses a challenge to traditional views of authorship, we should not be surprised to see that challenge materialized in practices that do not look the same as those of the solitary author. The inclusion of mediums in this book thus reminds us of the uncharted territories of authorship.

Even if one grants that mediumship involves an authorial dimension, its status as *collaborative* authorship raises some sticky questions. Mediumship, in fact, could be considered as the antithesis of collaboration—what cannot be explained as collaboration *with the living*. But looked at this way, mediumship poses a double problem: if one credits a medium's self-representation of the matter, is a medium an author at all or merely a transmitter—an amanuensis or secretary? But if one doesn't credit that the dead speak through us, does automatic writing reflect more than a metaphorical union—a collaboration with one's own psyche? What seems worth noting here is that for the authors in question the writing they produce requires the articulation of a collaborative structure, whether or not one credits its autonomous reality. Moreover, these fundamental distinctions founder in the medium's peculiar practice: an amanuensis, for example, may be no different from an author. In this respect, mediumship may be of interest precisely because of the way it literalizes things, for it pushes to the limit our common understandings of the creative process, forcing us to rethink familiar concepts like inspiration, influence, and agency. Mediumship, moreover, invites us to rethink the author's relationship to the past and to the cultural heritage that speaks through him—or her. It thus at once underlines and defamiliarizes our conventional understandings, raising the specter that all authorship can be understood as always already mediated, always already collaborative. Automatic writing can thus be seen as at once the most idiosyncratic instance of authorship and as the most representative.

Mediumship, then, finds its place in this book as a site where the practice of writing receives distinctive articulation. It also proves a site of particular interest from the perspective of women's literature, providing, among other things, a ground to rethink the "metaphorical" or "spiritual" collaborations that have been so important to feminist literary history. For one of the dominant traditions in feminist criticism has been to highlight the internalized struggles of women authors with female predecessors and the female literary tradition, even at the expense of attention to women's material partnerships with other women. Mediumship's unrelentingly literal representation of such struggles thus sheds new light on some of the leading tropes of feminist criticism; in particular, it allows us to see both the limits and possibilities of the specific ways feminism has embraced "collaboration" as a self-definition. The tropes that feminism fastened upon in the 1970s (and that continue to govern a sizable body of scholarship) did not emerge out of nowhere. In *A Room of One's Own* (1929), for example, Virginia Woolf had asserted that "we think back through our mothers if we are women" (79). And Woolf's effort there at historical reconstruction entailed the raising of ghosts of both real and imaginary women. Indeed, in the essay's famously rousing conclusion, Woolf figures the modern woman author as medium, as she invites her audience, through their collective writing, to give body and voice to Shakespeare's "dead" sister. In "Professions for Women," Woolf returns to this theme, representing the professional author as at once trance writer and exorcist, doing battle with the phantoms that prevent women from writing (241).

Historically, as such accounts remind us, women frequently projected their own authorship as a mediumistic exercise, representing themselves as no more than a vehicle for some larger imaginative power. Notable examples in the nineteenth century include Mary Shelley, Charlotte Brontë, and Harriet Beecher Stowe—to name just the most prominent. And twentieth-century writers did not completely abandon this fiction; Virginia Woolf, for example, repeatedly celebrates the author's trance-like condition, while Alice Walker signs her novels "A.W., author and medium." The conceit, however, is not necessarily gender-specific, as the case of James Merrill dramatically illustrates. Woolf herself admits that the condition is not peculiar to women: "I suspect that this state is the same both for men and women" ("Professions" 239–40). Yet Woolf installs the trance-writer image in a way that is inevitably self-referential, and inevitably gendered: "I want you to imagine me writing a novel in a state of trance. I want you to figure to yourselves a girl sitting with a pen in her hand" (240).[8] The image of the "girl" who,

---

[8] In *Orlando*, moreover, Woolf's portrait of the artistic consciousness, it is as a "girl" writing in the nineteenth century that Orlando experiences authorship as automatic writing.

"for minutes, and indeed for hours . . . never dips [her pen] into the inkpot"—of the woman author who does not write at all or does not write by her own volition—has a gender-specific history, ranging from the idealization of woman as muse to her degradation as an instrument of a Svengali. And this history, more often than not, was used to discredit women's writing by undercutting female agency.

Attention to mediumship, then, as this book proposes to study it—as a serious writing practice for women—at once returns us to this history and reinterprets its possibilities. For what seems most striking about early twentieth-century automatic writing is the complexity of its operation, which allows it to serve as both a site of cultural empowerment and a site of cultural complicity. As perhaps the most vexed site of collaboration for women, mediumship thus seems a particularly apt place to reopen the question of collaboration's relationship to feminism. This is one of the questions with which Woolf closes her essay on "Professions for Women." Once women have a room of their own, she maintains, they must decide how they will occupy their new quarters: "How are you going to furnish it, how are you going to decorate it? With whom are you going to share it, and upon what terms?" (242). If for Woolf, the terms are not self-evident, the fact of shared relationships, both personal and professional, appears a given. Woolf's questions, then, might prompt another set of considerations: Is authorial collaboration necessarily feminist? What feminisms does it support (or undermine) at different historical moments? With what ghosts do we commune in our modern understanding of the subject?

Settling on the types of collaborations I wanted to study thus left me still in largely uncharted territory. For partnership writing was entrenched in methodological quandaries. The questions literary collaborators reported as most frequent and persistent—Which hand held pen? (or, put another way, Which is the *real* author? Who did the actual writing?)—were, by general consensus, not very productive. Nor were the equally pervasive but more specific attempts to pin down the collaborators' precise division of labor. As Susan Leonardi remarks, "Anyone who has ever written, or even cooked, with someone else knows that this is not how it works" (Leonardi and Pope 259)—an insight confirmed by other scholars and practitioners of collaboration. In the case of mediums to ask, Which hand held the pen? or to try to divvy up authorial labor turns out to be even more frustrating, for as most mediums understand it, the hand that holds the pen is no more than that: an instrument or appendage for some disembodied entity that writes through them. The very existence of these putative authors, however, cannot be empirically verified, nor do questions such as, Is there really a dead spirit communicating? necessarily lead anywhere useful. For mediums, moreover, who wrote through the ouija board, the planchette, or through direct voice communication (where the medium speaks aloud what the "spirits" dictate to her), the actual transcription of the communications—the literal writing of the message—was often performed by a person other than the medium.

Yet these questions of proprietary responsibility remain of interest, if for no other reason than their persistence. They remind us of the extent to which nonsolitary authorship is practically inconceivable. For in an economy where seeing is believing, the imagination of authorship requires certain props, furnishings, and settings not readily supplied in collaborative structures. The question, Which hand held the pen?, then, reflects both a fundamental disbelief in collaboration and a certain prurient interest—a desire to make collaboration rend up its bodily secrets. As Edith Somerville complains, the public seems unable to transcend "this difficulty of two minds, and two hands, and only one pen" ("Two of a Trade" 185). The questions partnership writing most frequently generate thus play into the voyeurism that has generally surrounded collaborative writing, and mediumship more particularly. Collaborative writing (especially as practiced by women) has always invited the gaze even as it resists visualization; it has always invited attention to writing as something bodily.

How, then, does one negotiate the fascination of collaboration without simply replicating its status as curiosity or aberration? What questions must one ask to tell collaboration's stories? For if collaborative authorship has yet to receive its due recognition, this is in part because we remain so limited in our tools for representing it. Part of my project then has been to invent a new set of questions, to develop a method to render collaboration readable. And this project, I am arguing, has more than local interest: it goes to the heart of authorial identity. For if collaboration cannot secure authorship in the hand that writes, it raises far-reaching questions about how and where authorship can be located: Is there an author before the pen makes a mark? How does one assign authorship to what is figured as *talk*? What happens to the notion of text as personal (or professional) property when even the authors cannot distinguish their contributions—cannot determine the boundaries of their identity?

One way to approach these questions has been to examine the ways collaborators themselves represent their practices. As Chapter 2 illustrates, literary collaborators, particularly at the turn of the century, produced a discourse about their art with remarkably coherent features; in widely dispersed instances, and without knowledge of what others were up to, the parties to discrete partnerships articulated a strikingly common ethos, stressing above all the conversational nature of their exchange, the seamlessness of the resulting product, and the absolute mutuality of their personal and professional relationships. As the collaborators generally put it, even they could not tell who wrote what or which hand was which. As Chapter 4 demonstrates, the discourse surrounding automatic writing was every bit as formulaic, from the ways mediums discussed their surrender of agency to the parade of cultural *Others*, in all their stereotypical trappings, that mediums insisted served as secondary mediators or "control" spirits for their writings.

Collaborators, however, are not necessarily the final authority on their own proceedings. Indeed, they often share with the larger public a resistance to acknowledging the full implications of their undertaking. Marjorie Barnard, for example, despite a substantial career as a collaborative author, maintains the position that writing unions such as hers must be exceptional: "I think collaboration (in creative work) is impossible, but now and then it happens" (qtd. in Dever 70). She and other collaborators, when describing their writing arrangements, frequently reintroduce hierarchical relationships even as they celebrate their absence. Many—if not most—collaborative authors represent their joint writing as no more than a minor variation on conventional authorial practices. The utopian features that collaborators regularly articulate in their unions can thus be considered both informative and suspect. My interest, then, in the terms that literary collaborators have most relied on to describe their writing is not necessarily to endorse them as reality. Rather, it is to ask, What does belief in a certain set of features make possible? What interests are served, for example, by the story of collaboration's seamlessness? Or to turn to the example of automatic writing, my question was not whether mediums really talked to the dead but what the structures of automatic writing facilitated for them? What do these instances of collaborative authorship tell us, I wanted to ask, not only about "alternative" writing practices but about forms of authorship considered mainstream?

In treating these stories of partnership writing, I do not, then, want to gloss over what is problematic or contradictory about them. As I discuss in Chapter 4, the sameness these literary partners celebrate was often at the expense of others—as understood in terms of "race," class, or nation. It seems no accident that so many of these unions were writing *from* the borders of British national identity and writing *to* its center, producing a kind of "ethnic" literature (Irish, Scottish, Australian, Eastern European) for English consumption. It seems striking, moreover, that these partnerships, both literally and figuratively, were so often family matters, dependent on a full compass of common assumptions and experiences. It thus seems important to consider what happens to those, as it were, not one of the family: what, in other words, must be excluded to perfect these unions? These exclusions, as Chapter 4 goes on to illustrate, are even more explicit in the practice of mediumship, with its theatrical exoticism. In particular, in the discourse of "controls" (spirits who invariably crossed lines of race, class, gender, and nationality), mediumship both enacted and regulated a fantasy of communication with the Other—a fantasy that ultimately served a self-contained group of like-minded men and women. Like the literary collaborations considered here, mediumship was thus a site for a certain kind of middle-class solidarity.

Even on these terms, however, collaborative authorship remains vexed and vexing. Neither the collaborations of the self-consciously literary authors or those of the practitioners of automatic writing, for example, lend themselves unambiguously to triumphant feminist narratives of middle-class empowerment. Rather, both can be seen to reinforce as much as contest gender stereotypes. And these contradictions prompt some of the book's underlying questions. What is the interest for contemporary feminism of partnerships so locked in the domestic and familial? Why should we concern ourselves with writing practices that so relentlessly announce themselves as amateurish? Why unearth these particular practices from their historical obscurity? For as this book demonstrates, the history of collaboration does not fulfill (or fulfills only imperfectly) our utopian wishes for it. And this is a place where my work diverges from other, more idealizing feminist scholarship—both on women's collaborations and on the practice of mediumship. For example, I remain considerably more circumspect than most recent critics about the extent to which mediumship provided an "authentic" voice for women and a vehicle for an emerging feminism.[9] But, then, most earlier work concentrated on nineteenth-century mediumship. By the 1920s, where I concentrate my attention, the turn to mediumship carried different valences for women; so a new question was raised, Why would women choose this "career" when other socially approved avenues of professionalization were now more readily available to them?

Part of my argument here is to suggest that in looking at the experi-

---

[9] The cover of Braude's *Radical Spirits*, for example, offers the following synopsis, almost as if it were part of the book's title: "How séances and trance speaking empowered a generation of American women to claim their own voices." Basham argues that nineteenth-century mediumship gave women a vehicle to speak the unspeakable, a medium she ultimately associates with "the menstrual voice" (131)—a kind of biological authenticity.

ence of early twentieth-century women, we need a more complicated narrative about their access to intellectual authority and professional recognition. In the case of authorship, this has meant looking seriously at the continued hold—even the new attraction—of literary practices one might expect "modern" intelligent women to reject as outmoded. But how does one disentangle these practices from an established history that writes them off as marginal, curious, or eccentric? In undertaking this project, I have worked from the assumption that this history itself needs to be interrogated. For this reason, I begin and end this book with stories of collaboration already fairly well known in traditional literary history. The Brontës and the Yeatses offer classic instances of how collaborative authorship gets marked as an oddity, redeemable only as apprenticeship for more "serious" writing. They thus supply the terms we've inherited for taking—or, in effect, not taking—collaboration seriously. Standing, as it were, as bookends to this study, these chapters provide a context for reading the less-known authors whose stories occupy the book's middle chapters. But the book also promotes the counterargument that the practices of the noncanonical writers at its center open to new understandings the eccentric output of the canonical figures that anchor the investigation.

Having said this, however, I should make clear that this book is not a bid for canonizing any of its writers. Some, like Somerville and Ross and Michael Field, have already been the subject of certain recovery efforts and might, within standards already recognized, be potential candidates for inclusion in other new and established canons. Others, like the mediums who figure here, would not be contenders for canonization by any conventional standards of literary value. What they wrote, after all, was undeniably weird stuff. I would not want to claim, for example, that such classic texts of automatic writing as *Psychic Messages from Oscar Wilde* or *The Scripts of Cleophas* (the alleged chronicles of a first-century Christian) should be required reading in the ordinary course of literary study. Nor for that matter would I want to make that claim for the Brontë juvenilia or the Yeatses' automatic writing—although recent editions of these works make this exercise possible. Indeed, the new availability of these Brontë and Yeats materials gives my project added urgency. For it prompts some of its underlying questions: In what ways might these texts interest us? How should we go about reading them?

On one level, my answer is quite simple. If these works have interest, it is decidedly not *as texts*, in the sense of self-contained aesthetic units, and not as hidden keys to the author's biography. Their interest lies, I would argue instead, in what they illuminate about the writing process. My own project follows from this premise, even where the texts at hand might make more traditional claims on our critical faculties. Readers of this book, then, will not find much close reading of the collaborative literature produced by these unions, even in the case of its most famous instances. Rather, the book proposes, as a historical and theoretical exercise, to read *practices* of writing and their reception history. Consequently, the book is not organized around an author-text model, and it does not put forward new texts to be added to some pre-existing canon. As Woodmansee and Jaszi argue, too often such canon expansion projects leave unchallenged the idea of the unique author who is the sole and original creator of his or her literary product (Introduction to *The Construction of Authorship* 9). They thus leave little room to explore other ways authorship has been practiced. This book engages in a different kind of historical recovery project, offering what Woodmansee and Jaszi might call "role models for alternative writing practices" (9). By this, however, I do not necessarily mean that we should think of historical instances of collaboration as practices to be emulated in their particular configurations; but they can be seen as models for wider authorial possibilities, proof that authorship has been—and can be—configured differently.

The chapters of this book are thus organized topically, even for the frame chapters that would appear the most author-oriented. Chapter 1 on the Brontë juvenilia, for example, concentrates on the topos of the juvenilia as a form of secret writing. Looking at the various ways this secrecy has been deployed in the construction of the Brontës' popular and academic reputation, I propose an alternative approach to the juvenilia as an intervention into professional authorship—an intervention that asks us to rethink the very category of private publication. Chapter 6 focused on the Yeatses, considers the way a husband-wife partnership complicates collaborative structures. As a wife and medium, the author of automatic scripts and the typist/editor and literary caretaker for her husband, Georgie Yeats brings together many of the authorial roles this book investigates. Reading these roles against a history of collaboration and a history of mediumship offers us, I argue, a more historically specific and complex way to read Georgie Yeats's unvoiced claims to authorship.

The main body of the book structures itself as a set of linked chapters, with a common group of writers weaving their way through them. Chapters 2 and 3 track a group of literary authors who wrote collaborative fiction at the turn of the century, while Chapter 5 focuses on a group of early twentieth-century mediums. Chapter 4, forming a bridge between them, juxtaposes the work of these two different constituencies. All of these chapters, however, share common, often interlocking, interests: secrecy, professionalism, sexual and national identity. Chapter 2, for example, which uses responses to turn-of-the-century literary collaborators as its point of entry, opens out into a discussion of the treatment of collaboration in two distinct phases of feminist literary criticism; tracking the way responses to literary collaboration have regularly become displaced onto questions of sexuality, this chapter demonstrates a persistent link between homophobia and the resistance to double writing. Chapter 3 moves from these theoretical investments to look more closely at collaboration as a historical and material practice. Pursuing the issues of professionalism first raised in the discussion of the Brontë juvenilia, I look at a later group of "family" collaborators, exploring the paradoxical ways their professional partnerships became implicated in a gendered discourse of amateurism.

Chapter 4, focused on collaboration's implication in exoticism, looks at both the regional writing of traditional literary partnerships and the pseudo-scholarly writings of early twentieth-century mediums. Comparing the cultural Others through which mediumistic exchanges were enacted to the "native informants" that the partnership writers relied on, I explore the middle-class solidarity these writing practices fostered. Taking a copyright case involving two mediums as its point of departure, Chapter 5 lays the groundwork for reading mediumship as an authorial practice. Looking at especially "literary" instances of automatic writing (scripts purporting to be communications from famous literary authors, for example), I explore the complex ways automatic writing both questioned and commented on what it means to be an author. This chapter thus returns us to a set of questions posed in Chapters 1 and 3 about the professionalization of authorship and the place of alternative writing practices.

As this overview indicates, the writers treated here have widely divergent reputations, and the nature and availability of materials about these unions vary accordingly. For the Brontës and Yeatses, we have a wealth of materials, both primary and secondary (although in the case of the Brontës, the materials are not equally available for all four siblings). Among the writers treated in Chapters 2–4, Somerville and Ross are by far the most well documented; but for the Gerard sisters, there is almost no critical commentary outside contemporary reviews of their novels. In the case of the mediums treated in Chapters 4 and 5, materials are available from a variety of sources: case studies in the journal of the SPR, published and unpublished scripts of mediums, autobiographies and biographies (often written by disciples), newspaper accounts, and reports by skeptical investigators. But there is virtually no history of representations of mediums as authors. I have thus had to piece this narrative together out of what might appear to be "anecdotal" sources; I have had to construct the text that I then commented on.

The particular choices I have made, however, in presenting my stories are not simply a function of availability of materials. I have, for example, in avoiding close textual readings, made a deliberate decision to displace questions of value and judgment. For me, this has been a necessary strategy to refocus attention from products to processes, from personalities to practices. Similarly, I have deliberately retained a "neutral" stance in relation to the mediumistic activity I treat, bypassing the questions my audience may see as most pressing: Did mediums really speak to the dead? Did they believe that they did? What do I believe was really going on there? But for me the problem posed itself somewhat differently: What voice should I adopt in relation to my materials if I did not want to prejudge the outcome? The "safe" response was clearly to affirm my skepticism, "Of course, I don't believe in these bizarre phenomena," and to proffer the plausible alternatives (unconscious plagiarism, for example). But I wanted to see where taking these practices seriously, in their own terms, might lead us. In other words, I did not want to foreclose prematurely the possibilities of what such practices have to teach us. In keeping with this book's argument, then, I have attempted to read these varied collaborative practices in ways that point to a fuller understanding of what counts as authorship; such an exercise, I argue, opens new possibilities for reading authorship's past and practicing its future.

1

Secret Writing

The Brontë Juvenilia
and the Myth of Solitary Genius

In what was to be the first (and only) joint appearance of the Brontës as acknowledged authors, Charlotte and Anne traveled to London in July 1848. The secret authors of, on the one hand, the wildly popular *Jane Eyre* and, on the other, *Agnes Grey* and *The Tenant of Wildfell Hall* (the latter only just published), they arrived, unannounced, at the office of Smith, Elder & Co. to discuss what they described as "a private matter." In a confidence they insisted go no further than Charlotte's publishers (who until that time had known Charlotte only as "Currer Bell"), they admitted, for the first time, the secret of their identity—a secret of gender as well as number: "We are three Sisters," they told George Smith and William Smith Williams. While the third sister, Emily, the author of *Wuthering Heights*, declined to accompany them, their revelation necessarily included her; for the literary works of the yet unknown Brontë sisters, published under the pseudonyms Currer, Ellis, and Acton Bell, were popularly believed to be the work of a single author—albeit an author of indeterminate gender. Provoked by the unscrupulous fanning of this belief by Emily and Anne's publisher, Charlotte and Anne set out for London, determined to prove they were separate persons: "We have both come," they declared, "that you might have ocular proof that there are at least two of us."[1]

---

[1] Quoted in Winifred Gérin, *Charlotte Brontë: The Evolution of Genius* 363. Claiming that "to the best of his belief" the novels of Currer, Ellis, and Acton Bell were "all the production of one writer," Anne's publisher, Thomas Cautley Newby, had sold early sheets of *Tenant* to an American publisher, passing it off as the latest work of Currer Bell (Juliet Barker, *The Brontës* 557), thus prompting the sisters' visit to London. Newby's actions had an added irony, as he had previously rejected "Currer Bell's" first novel, *The Professor*, when he accepted the work of her siblings. So persistent, however, was the belief that the three Bells constituted a single author that Charlotte was forced to add an official disclaimer to the third edition of *Jane Eyre*. Only after the deaths of Emily and Anne, did Charlotte acknowledge their authorship publicly.

In thus declaring their separate identities, the sisters upheld a venerated principle of literary propriety: every text has an author and every
author has a singular identity. One had only to look at them, they implied, to recognize the self-evident truth of their claim: they were the
separate authors of separate novels and not some corporate entity. For
the Brontës, however, such a declaration had its own peculiar ironies—
not the least of them being that their first novels were produced in close
collaboration with each other. These novels, moreover, were not the sisters' first literary efforts. For long before their individual works attracted
public notice, the Brontë siblings shared the open secret of their *joint*
writing venture, a series of literary collaborations practiced and sustained to an extent unprecedented in our knowledge of literary history.

From 1826, the date of the earliest extant Charlotte Brontë manuscript—a 16-page miniature booklet illustrated with tiny water-
colors—to 1848, the date of Emily's last recorded reference to her fantasy kingdom, Charlotte, Branwell, Emily, and Anne Brontë produced a
voluminous literature that they shared exclusively with each other.[2]
Charlotte's "Catalogue of my Books," a list of the works she had written
by August 1830 (Charlotte was fourteen at the time), gives but a hint
of this massive undertaking: twenty-two volumes that included plays,
poems, tales, literary reviews, translations, little magazines, and multivolume novels—all carefully hand-printed in minuscule script and
most bound and illustrated in miniature volumes.

The product of intense partnership with shifting affiliations, Charlotte's "publications" were matched by those of her siblings.[3] Branwell,
who was Charlotte's most regular writing partner, was, by the age of
seventeen, the author of "some thirty named and distinct volumes of
tales, poems, dramas, journals, histories, literary commentary, etc. and
of almost as many fragments" (Gérin, *Branwell Brontë* 41); his juvenile
productions, in fact, may well have exceeded the combined published
writings of his sisters (Collins xiii). And Emily and Anne, although their
prose manuscripts do not survive, were no less industrious than their
older siblings.

---

[2] Christine Alexander dates this manuscript, written for Charlotte's sister Anne, as
c. 1826–28 (*An Edition of the Early Writings of Charlotte Brontë* I : 1). Accounts by both Charlotte and Branwell place the origins of the juvenile "plays" in 1826, the date of a gift to
Branwell of a set of twelve toy soldiers; few manuscripts, however, survive from this period. The earliest manuscript from the plays is Branwell's "Battell Book" (1827). It is possible that in the early stages of the partnership (1826–29), the "plays" were performed
rather than written.

[3] Initially, all four children participated in a single project, while the works produced after 1833–34 paired Charlotte and Branwell in one saga (Angria) and Emily and Anne in
another (Gondal). Critics have speculated about possible partnerships between Charlotte
and Emily and between Emily and Branwell.

Until well into the twentieth century, however, little was known about these secret writings. Mrs. Gaskell, after perusing some of the manuscripts, felt compelled to rewrite about forty pages of her *Life of Charlotte Brontë* (1857); she remained, however, notoriously nonplused by these "quantities of fragments," pulling back from any serious treatment of them. In 1895 Clement Shorter purchased a parcel of the manuscripts for Thomas James Wise. Wise's purchase, however, only added to the mystery. For Wise, a known forger of first editions, was less than scrupulous in his treatment of the texts, publishing them privately in poorly transcribed, heavily abridged, expensive limited editions, and selling off the manuscripts as collector's items—cut up, regrouped, and bound in fancy morocco casing. Not until the 1930s and 40s did critics begin to rediscover these materials, and the juvenilia was quickly hailed as the long-lost key to the Brontës' genius: "the conclusive answer," Fannie Ratchford suggests, "to most of the long-studied, much discussed Brontë problems" (*The Brontës' Web of Childhood* xiv). But to break the code and decipher their meaning, critics had first to recognize the juvenile texts as, in fact, secret writing—writing to which, aside from the author-siblings, only Mr. Brontë was privy.[4] Penetrating the surface obscurity to unlock the secret world beneath, Ratchford was the first to uncover what she famously called "the Brontës' web of childhood," "the drug-like Brontë dream."

This history, linking the juvenilia to secrecy, transgression, and even pathology, has had a decisive impact on subsequent constructions of the Brontës—for the general reading public and for the academy. Thus although the extant juvenile material—a mere fraction of the prodigious childhood literary output of the Brontë siblings—far exceeds the lifetime publications of the three Brontë sisters, it continues to occupy an ambivalent place in the stories we tell of the Brontës' genius. If long years of silence have been replaced by a spate of fascinated retellings, these tellings represent the juvenilia selectively, emphasizing above all else its psychosexual dimensions and its function as fantasy. Even the latest critical development—a focus on the colonialist aspects of the project—might be seen as a variation on these themes, examining as it does the cultural components of the children's collective fantasy.[5]

---

[4] While most critics now assume Patrick Brontë knew of his children's literary activities, there is no evidence that he actually *read* any of their juvenile manuscripts. No one outside the family, moreover, was admitted to their secret. Although Charlotte apparently told Mary Taylor (and possibly other school friends) about the tiny magazines she produced with her siblings—even offering to show them to her—she later retracted this promise.

[5] See Firdous Azim, *The Colonial Rise of the Novel*, and Susan Meyer, *Imperialism at Home: Race and Victorian Women's Fiction*, for readings of the juvenilia in terms of colonialism.

Only since the late 1980s have critical editions of any of the early
manuscripts been seriously undertaken, facilitating the counter argument that the juvenilia's interest rests largely in its status as conventional literary apprenticeship. Both arguments, however, might be seen
as overdetermined, shaped as they are by the need to find evidence of
what makes the Brontës "the Brontës." Moreover, in the absence of a
body of material shared by a wide scholarly community, commentators
have had to rely on, at best, a small fraction of the manuscripts; and they
have had to rely, as Alexander points out, on the pioneering work of a
handful of critics—work that is not always fully reliable (*Early Writings* 4). Indeed, Ratchford, who saw in the juvenilia both a hallucinatory
obsession and a full anticipation of Charlotte's future artistry, can be
said to have established the poles of all subsequent discussion. Wider
availability of complete and reliable editions, however, such as is now
becoming possible, will not necessarily extricate the juvenilia from
these overdetermined readings; for the very project of publication demands the editing out of many, if not most, of the features that mark the
juvenilia as at odds with established authorial conventions.

Like everything else, then, that belongs to the Brontës, the juvenilia remains caught in the paradoxical discourse of normality and aberrancy;
it remains caught, moreover, in the conventionalized ways these categories have been conceived to produce a narrative of now numbing familiarity. "It is certainly not rare to meet children who live in a happy
world in which everything happens to suit them; but it is unusual to see
four children share the possession of this marvelous world and collaborate to write its extraordinary story" (Maurat 48). "Now, it is not extraordinary that a group of gifted children should evolve an elaborate
play-world, with sustained characters, to which they remain devoted
for a number of years. . . . What was extraordinary about the Brontës'
games was that they produced an extensive and precocious literature . . .
a fantasy world which for all of them, at various times, became a substitute for life" (Lane 18). Upheld as the mark of the Brontës' psychological regression and literary precocity, these early collaborative works
establish the Brontës as simultaneously unique and exemplary—as at
once like and unlike "any normal children" (Barker, *The Brontës* 150).

Indeed, in the seemingly endless quest to identify what precisely
is distinctive in the Brontë children's extended participation in self-
constructed fantasy kingdoms, critics have seized on those features that
might be marked as excessive: the duration, intensity, productivity, and
shared framework of these productions. But what gets lost in the narratives that have assumed greatest critical currency is the evidence of an
extensive authorship that resists proper categories. Authorship, in fact,

tends to drop out of the picture, subordinated to the "secret world" with inviolable boundaries (Moglen) in which "the four young Brontës lived, moved, and had their being" (Ratchford), to the "burning clime" (Gérin) that absorbed so much of the young authors' energies. In the critical narratives that most generally represent them, these collaborative worlds prove something more (or less) than literary creation.

In these renderings, secrecy becomes the defining feature of collaborative production, and it remains fundamentally linked to escapism and transgression. It remains linked, moreover, to adolescent expression— a configuration that, as subsequent chapters will demonstrate, later "adult" collaborators would also find themselves caught in. John Maynard, for example, unflinchingly identifies the juvenilia with "the world below," where fantasy could freely follow "the contours of adolescent emotions, whether those of schoolboy adventure or schoolgirl romance" (13), where, to follow Ratchford, the Brontës could collectively produce their teenage diary (*The Brontës' Web* xiv). Maynard, indeed, takes this argument to its limit, representing the juvenilia as a type of cottage pornography industry—a "workshop" for exploring sexuality, facilitated by the unique conditions of private publication and circulation (40–41). Charlotte herself may be said to have inaugurated this line of thinking with her cryptic allusion, in her earliest juvenile writings, to the "bed plays" she composed with her sister Emily; distinguishing these works from "our three great plays that are not kept secret," Charlotte explains, "Bed plays mean secret plays; they are very nice ones" (Alexander, *An Edition* I:5). It may be no accident, then, that Gaskell transcribes "bed plays" as "best plays," her normalizing tendency only underlining the suggestion of the illicit (Gaskell 117).[6]

For anyone, then, approaching the juvenilia today, it comes embedded in the history that has determined what makes these texts interesting. When Alexander argues, for example, that, "What is remarkable about the juvenilia is not that Charlotte had a creative childhood, but that the imaginary world of that childhood should have continued to preoccupy her for so long," she does more than promote the common image of the Brontës as writers who, from their earliest efforts, succeeded in elevating adolescent crisis into a powerful, informing mythology. She fixes their *authorship* within this developmental trajectory: "The hypnotic attraction of Angria had stunted her development as a writer of realistic fiction" (*Early Writings* 246). If, however, one reads the

---

[6] Emily and Charlotte shared a bed and presumably invented the plays as a kind of bedtime story they told each other; Barker insists that the bed plays "were simply secret because they excluded Branwell and Anne, not because they had any sexual element" (151)—but her comment, like Gaskell's, invites speculation about what she dismisses.

juvenilia as an authorial practice with its own distinctive features, we might wonder why those features prove so relentlessly tied to the condition of (prolonged) adolescence, literally to the realm of juvenile production. Indeed, Alexander's comments raise the question (insistently mooted in most critical assessments) of what it means to label as "juvenilia" writings sustained by authors well into their twenties—indeed, for three of the participants, writings sustained until the end of their (admittedly brief) lifetimes. Such associations, moreover, prove a common trope in later representations of women's literary collaborations, fixing them as distinctly amateur activities. For the Brontës, then, as for their successors, collaborative work could thus be readily dismissed, as Collins points out, as a kind of "charming, rainy-day, activity" (xviii).[7]

Yet in the insistent professionalization of what Mrs. Gaskell once referred to as "this wild weird writing" (119), the Brontës could be seen to claim for themselves both a public and private space for their work as something more than juvenile pastime. For in exemplary fashion, the Brontës transformed what many children do (create imaginary worlds, engage in elaborate literary constructions) into a practice so sustained as to command professional recognition yet so extensive as to enter the realm of the transgressive. As several critics have demonstrated, the production of an extensive juvenilia is not in itself without precedent, as the examples of Hartley Coleridge and John Ruskin might indicate. A shared literary practice, moreover, has its analogues in other "literary" families—most notably, the Rossettis, the Arnolds, the Alcotts, the Kiplings, and the Stephenses (the family of Virginia Woolf and her siblings). Even the miniature size of these works does not make them distinctive. As Barker suggests, "For whatever reason, bright children at this period were drawn to writing little books and inventing fictitious kingdoms" (153).[8]

What would seem to distinguish the Brontë practice is a quality of excess, a refusal of limits—whether in the size, scope, duration, or range of their productions. More particularly, I want to argue, the Brontë prac-

---

[7] Charlotte herself inaugurates this tradition in her famous account of "The Origins of the Islanders": "It was one wet night in December, we were all sitting around the fire and had been silent some time, and at last I said, 'Suppose we had each an Island of our own. . . .'" (Alexander, *An Edition* I:6). For similar narratives in accounts of other collaborative authors, see Chapters 3 and 5.

[8] Alexander cites Hartley Coleridge (*An Edition* I:xix), while Barker mentions Ruskin, who, at the age of seven, "wrote over fifty pages of a little book, measuring only fifteen by ten centimetres, in a minuscule print similarly modelled on book print" (Barker 153). Winnifreth notes the popularity of writing "as a means of entertainment" in artistic families in the Victorian age (Winnifreth, *The Brontës* 25). For other examples of family collaborations, see Chapter 3.

tice is distinguished for the intensity of its investment in the profession-alization of authorship. As Gérin observes, "Everything that went to the making of books, the writing, illustrating, editing, sewing, and binding into paper covers, constituted the children's chief delight" (*Charlotte Brontë* 29). Everything that went into the publishing, sale, and review of books finds its way into their narratives, with their knowing allusions to market conditions: to booksellers and stationers, compositors and printers devils, the buying up of copyright, the publication of uniform editions versus cheap editions in numbers. In reproducing almost fea-ture by feature *in miniature*, however, the markings and mechanics of authorized publications like *Blackwood's* (with everything from book re-views, serial fiction, and art criticism to instructions for booksellers and advertisers), the Brontës entered a realm that at once professionalized their work and reinforced its marginalization.

Critics, however, have proved determined to read the "juvenile" pro-ductions developmentally, as an aberrant practice that gains its interest only retrospectively. Although they come to this conclusion from a va-riety of directions, they ultimately agree that the juvenilia is of interest only because recognizable authors of genius emerge at its termination.[9] It is on these grounds that Ratchford extols the juvenilia as the key to all Brontë mythologies and Winnifreth dismisses the juvenilia as unworthy of interest. And it is on these grounds that a host of critics have combed the juvenilia for evidence of a literary apprenticeship. Alexander, in fact, in bringing forth a complete edition of Charlotte Brontë's early writings, invokes precisely these arguments to justify publishing works never meant for publication—works that are "at times embarrassingly crude" but nonetheless "represent a unique record of the apprenticeship of a major English writer" (*An Edition* I:xxiii). Indeed, such reasoning ulti-mately justifies her decision to publish these works without Branwell's companion pieces, for Charlotte's version, she explains, is the one, "that is important to any study of the later novels" (I:vii).

While few have dismissed what Winnifreth calls "these juvenile novelettes" with quite his bluntness—"What is remarkable about the Brontës' juvenilia in view of their later eminence is that so much of what they wrote is so bad" (*The Brontës* 25)—even the staunchest promoters of the juvenilia feel compelled to cite its lapses: its haphazard, inconsis-tent, or absent punctuation; its idiosyncratic spelling; its confusing mul-tiple plots, disjointed narrative, and multiplication of characters; its lack of chronology. As I have been arguing, moreover, even the most sym-

---

[9] Azim is one of the few critics to counter this tendency, as well as the concomitant prac-tice of treating the juvenile work outside its collaborative framework.

pathetic accounts of the Brontës' early writing practice rely on terms like "retreat," "escape," "apprenticeship" (if not "addiction" and "obsession"), presenting the Brontës' extensive literary investment in imaginary kingdoms as a stage to be passed through and put behind in what Winifred Gérin has called (in her now classic biography of Charlotte Brontë) the "evolution of genius," in the path to psychic wholeness and artistic achievement.

These narratives, I want to suggest, ultimately pathologize not only the Brontës' web of childhood but the collaborative enterprise that underwrote it. For the Brontës, for better or for worse, wed their fantasy lives to collaborative performances. In the participatory creations that claimed all the Brontës, collaboration was the necessary mode for generating and sustaining, as well as recording, ongoing collective fantasies. Not surprisingly, then, the narratives that track the Brontës' professional development celebrate the renunciation of collaboration as much as the renunciation of fantasy. Thus Helene Moglen stresses the crucial place of Charlotte's independent juvenile stories (as opposed to those produced in conjunction with Branwell) as a bridge between the "fantasies of the child-woman and the consciously self-exploring art of the adult" (47). And Gérin represents Emily and Anne's separate collaboration (the development of Gondal) as "a declaration of independence" from the older children, "a first positive step from tutelage" (*Emily Brontë* 23), a journey presumably completed in the emergence of the discrete authors of individually penned novels.

The evolutionary model of artistic genius favored by the Brontë critics thus colludes with the normative narrative of authorship as single-handed production. In the Brontës' case, however, this narrative involves a paradox, for the Brontë sisters have been simultaneously lionized as individual authors and as a collective entity: the Brontës. In fact, the myth of genius the Brontës popularize depends in part on the collapsing of the single/collective distinction; it depends, that is, on our recognition of the Brontës as, in Harold Bloom's words "unique literary artists whose works resemble one another's far more than they do the works of writers before or since" (1). Even Barker, who dedicates herself to debunking Brontë myths, insists that no single Brontë can be seen out of this context—hence her decision to write a collective biography (xviii). As Helena Michie has argued, however, the emergence of the Brontës as published writers put an end to their "experiment in sisterly unity" (*Sororophobia* 55). Indeed, if to name the Brontës inevitably invokes images of the remote parsonage where the three sisters penned their novels, that parsonage, in our collective imagination, is inhabited by beings who write *separately* in the common drawing-room, each poring over her own writing desk. Even those critics most attentive to the collaborative structure of the Brontës' early writings ultimately absorb them into narratives of singular authorship. Carol Bock, for example, while insisting that the juvenile productions were, quite *literally,* "collaborative performances" (1), slips only too easily into designating Charlotte *the* author, the sole referent for the authorial designation "Brontë." In fact, having established the early plays as "the product of joint authorship" (1), Bock subordinates the sibling coauthors to Charlotte's "readers," a kind of participatory audience. And like other readers of the later juvenilia, she pathologizes Branwell to establish Charlotte's superior authorial credentials.

Yet it is precisely this view of the author's singular identity that the juvenilia most insistently resists—whether in Emily and Anne's assertion of a fused identity (an assertion that subordinates any authorial distinction between Emily and Anne to their absolute separateness from anyone outside their world of two) or in the competitive rivalry that underwrites Charlotte and Branwell's Angrian productions, where one author typically appropriates the other. There is some internal evidence, moreover, to suggest that even these standard pairings may overstate the separateness of the two collaborative enterprises—enterprises that began in a four-way partnership, conducted in oral performance as well as written saga. Although more is known about and more survives from the collaborations of Charlotte and Branwell, Emily and Anne's collaborations—with their characteristic features of a twin-like sameness—would appear to fit more closely a gender-specific pattern of double writing. For the intensely protected privacy of their world binds their exclusive isolation to the conditions of their creativity, to a space that had to be preserved if they were to keep on writing. Like the literary collaborators who would emerge at the turn of the century (see Chapters 2 and 3), they thus promoted a sense of the seamlessness of the collaboration, a union so complete as to make the mechanics of transcription seemingly irrelevant. If as Gérin suggests, "By the time they were in their late teens they knew every turn in the plot, every physical trait of each character" (*Emily Brontë* 28), to attribute authorship to separate pieces of the narrative could have little meaning for them. Much as Charlotte could say of her early bed plays with Emily, "Their nature I need not write on paper for I think I shall always remember them" (*An Edition* I:5), the nature of the partnership of Emily and Anne would seem to transcend articulation.

Certainly, Emily and Anne promoted the myth of their own indivisibility, jointly signing even their diary papers, written for each other (sometimes when Emily and Anne were separated geographically) at four year intervals on their birthdays. Composed single-handedly in the first person singular (with the author clearly identifiable by contextual markers), these papers nonetheless frequently bear a dual signature, as in "Emily Jane Brontë—Anne Brontë." The papers, moreover, our only source for the lost Gondal writings, document the individual authorship of segments of the saga. The dual signature thus stands as a radical assertion of absolute union—even in the face of obvious evidence to the contrary. Emily's and Anne's nearly indistinguishable handwritings and the uncanny resemblances in both phrasing and content in papers written apart from each other—indeed, papers sealed until the designated time for their opening, four years after the date of composition—further testify to the continuity of a collaboration that cannot be contained by mere material circumstance.

Emily and Anne's collaboration, then, might be defined by a refusal to acknowledge division—between the authors but also between fantasy and reality, between an account of daily life and the happenings in an imaginary kingdom. Emily's diary paper for 1837, for example, alludes without formal break or distinction to Anne's writing of a poem in the parsonage drawing room, Emily's concurrent writing of the first volume of the life of a Gondal character, the presence of Tabby (the Brontë family servant) in the kitchen, the preparations of the Emperors and Empresses of Gondal for a coronation, Queen Victoria's ascension to the throne, and the whereabouts of Northangerland and Zamorna (the central characters in Charlotte and Branwell's Angrian cycle). While such crossing of lines is not unique to Emily, the persistence of this pattern and its unchanging articulation over the course of the partnership make the Gondal practice distinctive.

The diaries testify, moreover, to the lack of a break between the writing and "play" of Gondal and Emily and Anne's mature writing. In contrast to Charlotte's much touted renunciation of fantasy ("Farewell to Angria"), written at age twenty-three,[10] Emily's diary paper for her twenty-seventh birthday celebrates her continuing engagement, with Anne, in the shared fantasy. Recording her first overnight journey with Anne "by ourselves together," Emily details the Gondal writings that occupy them, describing the Gondal adventure they perform and the Gondal characters they impersonate. Projecting four years ahead (as the

---

[10] Although Charlotte clearly announces her desire "to quit for awhile that burning clime where we have sojourned too long" in favor of a "cooler," more "sober" region (quoted in Helene Moglen, *Charlotte Brontë: The Self Conceived* 59), the definitiveness of this break remains open to question. As Barker illustrates, Charlotte has obviously not completely abandoned this material in the work she produces after 1839.

birthday papers did ritually), both she and Anne speculate on the collaboration's outcome. For Anne, for example, writing in 1841, the fate of Gondal is her first thought for the future: "How will it be when we open this paper and the one Emily has written? I wonder whether the Gondaliand [sic] will still be flourishing, and what will be their condition" (qtd. in Ratchford, *Gondal's Queen* 191). And four years later neither sees an end to the fantasy. Thus Emily imagines herself at thirty-one slipping out with Anne to peruse their papers, while Anne ponders the slow pace of their writing: "We have not yet finished our Gondal Chronicles that we began three years and a half ago. When will they have done?" (194).

Only months after these diary entries, Charlotte's discovery of Emily's manuscript notebook would launch the sisters' first foray into professional authorship—a collection of poems bearing a triple authorial signature, *Poems by Currer, Ellis and Acton Bell* (1846). Emily's outrage at this unlicensed intrusion has been memorialized in Charlotte's 1850 "Biographical Notice of Ellis and Acton Bell" (315). And Emily's response, Barker argues, was not unreasonable, for Charlotte's reading of the poems (not to mention her suggestion of publishing them) was a violation of the secrecy of Gondal (479). In fact, although Emily had earlier divided her poems into two notebooks—one labeled "Gondal Poems," the other untitled—there is little evidence to suggest that the poems in the latter were *not* connected to the fantasy saga. If, as has been generally accepted, then, the decision to publish (prepared for in the siblings' earlier decisions to collect, edit, and assess their work) marked the turning point in the Brontës' sense of themselves as authors, for Emily and Anne their commitment to professional authorship did not correspond with a relinquishment of earlier authorial practices.[11] Nor would this seem to be the case for Branwell, whose professional overtures coincided with a continuing engagement with Angria. Branwell, in fact, as Barker acknowledges, was repeatedly reworking his Angrian materials, and he signed his published poems with the names of Angrian characters when they appeared in the *Halifax Guardian*, the *Bradford Herald*, and the *Leeds Intelligencer* between 1841 and 1847. Even Charlotte, in selecting poems for this collection, represented herself

---

[11] In December 1836, Charlotte and Branwell embarked on what Gérin has called "an assault on the literary establishment" (*Charlotte Brontë* 108), a course of letter-writing to prominent literary figures. Charlotte's letter to the poet laureate, Robert Southey—prompting his much quoted response, "Literature cannot be the business of a woman's life"—dates from this period, as do Branwell's unanswered letters to the editors of *Blackwood's*. Emily and Anne's first dated poems also belong to this period, as does Branwell's collecting and transcribing of his earlier poetry.

through her Angrian writing, although later, after becoming an established author, she would dismiss these works as "chiefly juvenile productions" (qtd. in Barker 481).

Publication might, then, as the siblings recognized, require the excision of references to Gondal (and Angria), but this was merely to bowdlerize what remained "Gondal" writing. Yet it remains open to question whose needs were served by these strategic excisions: the sisters' need for privacy or the public's need for conventional poetics. Disputing the common tendency to separate Emily's most celebrated poems (and her much acclaimed novel) from her "juvenile" writings, Ratchford has argued that "all of Emily's verse, as we have it, falls within the Gondal context" (*Gondal's Queen* 32); indeed, she argues, the very last words Emily composed belong to the Gondal saga—a claim supported by Barker, who not only declares *Wuthering Heights* to be "Gondal through and through" (501) but speculates that at the time of her death, Emily was deeply engaged in the writing of a second Gondal novel. Such representations suggest that in Emily's case, at least, the distinction between juvenilia and literature proper is purely arbitrary.

Representations of the Charlotte–Branwell collaboration, by contrast, tell a different story: a story of rivalry and gender difference, of hierarchical authority and struggles for literary independence, and of a pronounced break between the juvenilia and the work of mature authorship. Far from the seamless union of the Emily and Anne partnership, this collaboration, apparently from the start, meant different things for Charlotte and Branwell. From the start their partnership writings announced authorship as a site of contestation. Even before the formation of Angria (in the writings of the Glass Town saga), each relied on a host of narrators who defined themselves as authors and struggled with each other for literary authority. Indeed, their juvenilia is filled with displays of authorial one-upmanship, and although both Branwell and Charlotte employ exclusively masculine spokesmen (where they do not write in their own person), there is, almost from the first, an implicit gendering of this authorial rivalry.

When Charlotte takes over *Branwell's Blackwood's Magazine*, for example, she changes not only its name but its editorial direction, pushing the journal away from the dry subject matter she associates with Branwell toward "lighter" topics: tales of magic and the supernatural. In *The Liar Unmasked* by Captain Bud, a response to one of Charlotte's slanders of his chief authorial figures, Branwell exposes the effeminate style of writing he associates with Charlotte's (masculine) writers; accusing Charlotte's author, Lord Charles Wellesley, of patent falsehoods, Captain Bud declares his writing at once degraded and feminized: a form of gossip fit only for hysterical women readers of the sort Charlotte favors (Alexander, *An Edition* I:xvii). Responding to these accusations in *The Poetaster*, her only full-scale drama, Charlotte (in the person of Lord Charles Wellesley) continues her attack on masculine pretension, crudely parodying in her title character Branwell's chief poet, "Young Soult, the Rhymer."[12]

Given this self-conscious rivalry, it is perhaps not surprising that Charlotte and Branwell do not appear to have literally written together, although the cryptic signatures, "UT" and "WT" in the early manuscripts ("Us Two" and "We Two"), are sometimes taken as indicators of places where Branwell had a hand in Charlotte's writing.[13] In fact, where dual signatures appear in these manuscripts, they link not Charlotte and Branwell but Charlotte and her fictional personae. Typically, Charlotte double signs her compositions—as in "THE POETASTER / A DRAMA BY / Lord Charles Wellesley / CHARLOTTE Brontë" or "CB Captain Tree" and "Captain Tree C Brontë"—suggesting yet another locus for the collaboration that makes this fiction possible. But if Charlotte and Branwell did not actually *write* together, this is not to deny the collaborative nature of their writing project. For they clearly wrote *for* each other and *from* each other's writings, borrowing incidents, characters, and plots and cross-referencing their works extensively.

As Alexander has argued, with the development of Angria in 1834, the partnership intensified, and Charlotte and Branwell more closely approximated each other in the *content* of their stories. Where earlier, she contends, brother and sister had "co-operated on the basic outline of the plot," now they "wrote increasingly about each other's characters and assumed a knowledge of each other's latest productions" (*An Edition* II.2:xiv). Their partnership, in fact, more distinctly takes on the features of a serial collaboration, each manuscript responding to or building on earlier manuscripts—of each author's own or of the partner's. With Charlotte's departure in 1835 (when she returned to Roe Head to serve as a teacher), their collaboration could thus be preserved at a distance, with each keeping the other apprised of the latest developments in their saga.

---

[12] It is probably no coincidence that the publication of *The Poetaster* coincides with the period of Branwell's most intense preoccupation with the writing of dramatic poetry: *Lausanne: A Dramatic Poem* (December 1829), *Caractacus: A Dramatic Poem* (26 June 1830), and *The Revenge: A Tragedy in 3 Acts* (18 December 1830)—all by "Young Soult."

[13] See Alexander, *An Edition of the Early Writings of Charlotte Brontë* I:xxi. As Alexander admits, however, the use of these initials to signal collaborative works was not consistent; at times they seem to point to sole authorship by either Branwell or Charlotte. In the later juvenilia, while Charlotte and Branwell sometimes "contribute" to each other's narratives, their separate authorship remains clearly identifiable.

Most discussions of Angria in the critical literature have focused on its thematic elements, registering the changing tenor of the collaboration through the character and plot developments: civil wars, political intrigues, marriages, adultery, illegitimate offspring, and increasingly complex personal and political relationships. But even as the characters and plots become more complicated and absorbing, questions of authorship continue to inform the narratives. Charlotte's prefaces, for example, increasingly become spaces to question (and complicate) the nature of authorship. In *A Leaf from an Unopened Volume*, Lord Charles Wellesley, who appears on the title page as the work's editor, immediately disclaims responsibility for the text that follows, representing his role as mere "amanuensis" to some mysterious and nameless author; indeed, even this role, he suggests, is performed involuntarily, making the work appear like a specimen of automatic writing: "I, mechanically as it were and despite of my own opposing will, was compelled to put in black and white the narrative which follows" (*An Edition* II.1:325). In *The Green Dwarf*, Lord Charles represents himself in a more conventional editorial capacity, presenting to the reader a tale he attributes to Captain Bud, one of Branwell's chief authors, while in *The Scrap Book*, he appears as a compiler. In the "Letter to . . . Ardrah" (included in *The Scrap Book*), Zamorna (previously known as Arthur or the Marquis of Douro) adamantly denies rumors that he had a hand in the writing of the stories of his private life published by his brother, Lord Charles Wellesley, or in the poems printed in his name by that same author (II.2:320–21). In *The Spell*, Lord Charles further questions the premise of solitary and stable authorship, inventing an imaginary twin and secret collaborator for his older brother, with the result that the writing of one cannot be distinguished from that of the other (II.2:234–35).

As these examples demonstrate, in Charlotte's hands, questions of authorship have become increasingly an internal matter. In place of the rivalries with Branwell's chief authorial figures that characterized the earliest phase of their partnership, the writings of this period reveal intensified rivalries between *Charlotte's* authorial personae. In prefaces, for example, to *The Foundling* (1833), *The Green Dwarf* (1833), and "A Peep into a Picture Book" (1834), Captain Tree and Lord Charles Wellesley carp at each other incessantly, debunking each other's characters and ridiculing each other's writings. Indeed, so intense is this rivalry that neither the details of plot nor the characterization of personalities in any given story can be considered reliable, subject as they are to change with a shift in authorship in the continuation of the saga.

Charlotte's manuscripts, moreover, betray a continued fascination with the type of secret writing the Brontës themselves engaged in.

Alongside references to public authorial performances, her manuscripts regularly cite more eccentric practices—practices that underline the text's materiality. In "The Bridal" (1832), for example, Charlotte's author, Captain Tree, invokes the text as collector's item. Led to the inner recesses of the Marquis of Douro's palace, he discovers a rare manuscript—a manuscript identified with the origins of Glass Town— concealed in a "beautiful casket" enclosed in the duke's "cabinet of curiosities." Written "on a roll of vellum, but much discoloured and rendered nearly illegible by time" (*An Edition* I:341), the condition of the manuscript anticipates the fate of the Brontës' own tales of origins. In *My Angria and the Angrians* (1834), Lord Charles introduces a piece of "found" poetry, describing it in terms that find an uncanny echo in Mrs. Gaskell's retreat from Charlotte's "wild weird writing": "It is an odd, wild fragment. Interpret it for me who can" (II.2:278). Like the Brontës' own juvenile manuscripts, this one also is a pastiche of genres.

The manuscripts Charlotte produces, then, in collaboration with her brother seem to yield a number of competing stories about authority and authorship. Critical representations of the juvenilia, however, have focused on a single narrative: Charlotte's early adulation of Branwell, followed by her later unhealthy dependence on him. Thus while Branwell can be seen at first to spur Charlotte's creativity (Gérin, *Charlotte Brontë* 78), by the end of the partnership, his influence has been recast as destructive. Not surprisingly, then, most commentators linger on Charlotte's Roe Head diary, where Branwell appears as the mainstay of her existence: "I got a letter from Branwell. . . . I lived on its contents for days." And they focus on her helplessness in the face of his tampering with her plots and characters: "I wonder if Branwell has really killed the Duchess. Is she dead is she buried is she alone in the cold earth on this dreary night with the ponderous coffin plate on her breast under the black pavement of a church in a vault closed up, with lime and mortar. . . . I hope she's still alive" (qtd. in Gérin, *Charlotte Brontë* 107). While Barker stands pretty much alone in defending Branwell's position, insisting on his consistently superior artistic instincts, she, like most other critics, assumes the true story of collaboration to be one of dominance: of one partner imposing his will on the other. Given this picture, the story of Charlotte's struggle for literary independence—her achievement of a single, independent voice—becomes implicated in the familiar story of escape from crippling gender plots, *the* story Charlotte was to memorialize in her subsequent literary career. To become an author, the story goes, Charlotte had to reject not only fantasy (as dramatically explicated in her "Farewell to Angria") but her "long partnership in writing with Branwell" (Alexander, *Early Writings* 210).

Moglen offers the most extreme version of this argument, suggesting Charlotte's need to, in effect, annihilate Branwell in order to free herself from "the artistic and personal infantilism by which Branwell had been trapped" (58), to free herself from the "incest of the imagination" (39) in which both of them were locked. If not quite as explicit, virtually every accepted narrative of Charlotte's artistic development follows a similar trajectory, reducing the once dominant Branwell to, at best, a slender influence on the emerging adult writer. But if Charlotte's artistic independence and psychological well-being demanded a break from Branwell's inhibiting masculine influence, the result was to situate Charlotte more conventionally as the single-handed author of novels with an appropriately feminine voice, subject, and theme: romantic love and sexual domination. In fact, the more Charlotte is seen to write independently (as critics agree she did in the novellas she composed from 1836 to 1839), the more romantic love emerges as her sole authorial interest.

In the accounts of Charlotte's artistic evolution, however, these narratives, which Gérin calls "the novelettes of passion," become the mark of her superior artistry—the sign that "Charlotte has done with juvenilia" and can emerge "as an adult writer for the first time" (*Charlotte Brontë* 117).[14] Masculinity, as embodied in the world of politics and wars that Branwell celebrated, comes to occupy a regressive place, both psychologically and artistically. Gérin, for example, casts that world as child's play (78), whereas Moglen credits Charlotte with the more sophisticated fantasy: "But while Branwell's fantasies were still concerned with martial accomplishments, political intrigue, and the building of empires, Charlotte fantasized about . . . courtships and, increasingly, about seduction and adultery" (217). In this rendering, Branwell's masculine interests become the mark of intellectual stagnation, the sign that where Charlotte has progressed, he is stuck on the same themes. When these themes reappear in Charlotte's later work, they are cast as a literal setback (Alexander, *Early Writings* 210).

Moreover, as Charlotte enters what her biographers see, unproblematically, as her literary maturity, her singular productions both restore and gender conventional literary hierarchies. In particular, they privilege realism over fantasy, teleological or sequential narrative over episodic or digressive writing, and ultimately, the novel—especially the domestic novel—over chronicle or miscellany. Charlotte's turn away from Branwell's ruling interests, then, can be seen to entail a turn from

---

[14] Barker is one of the few critics to be skeptical of this development in Charlotte's writing, associating Charlotte's "one great subject" with the crude romantic fantasies of "any teenage girl" (190).

his pre- or antinarrative techniques: his fascination with catalogs, sur-
veys, lists, battle rosters, architectural plans, maps, and so on. Implicit
in this model of literary development is the assumption that mature authorship requires such a stylistic adjustment, in Charlotte's words, the
need to relinquish her taste "for ornamented and redundant composition" (*The Professor* xxiii). Her choice of "the social" as her sphere of interest assumes a shift to an observational poetics—writing from experience as opposed to writing from pure imagination (or from other
imaginative literature). This shift, however, recognizes as "experience"
only that which is considered gender appropriate; and it promotes as
the mark of artistic maturity a confessional model of authorship. Thus
Moglen calls "Henry Hastings" the "forerunner of the mature novels"
because it is "the first of her stories in which Brontë models her heroine
on herself" (55), and Alexander celebrates "Mina Laury" because Charlotte makes herself the narrator (*Early Writings* 165). Barker, indeed, argues that it was Charlotte's ability "to draw on personal experience
to flesh out her characters and scenes" that enabled her, in *Jane Eyre*,
"to transform this unpromising rehash of Angrian material into one of
the greatest novels ever written in the English language" (510). Adopting a style that not only replaces fantasy with realism but turns fiction
into autobiography, Charlotte's "mature" writing, then, leaves the genius of the *woman* author tied to a particular version of self-expressivity.
It leaves her tied, moreover, to writing that appears increasingly conventional—not only in substance and style, but in material packaging.

Ironically, then, the professionalization of the female author requires
the domestication of her literary work (the repudiation of "wild weird
writing") as a precondition for entering into the normal circuits of
publishing—circuits she can most effectively enter by disguising her female identity. For the path from private to public that produces Currer,
Ellis, and Acton Bell in the place of Charlotte, Emily, and Anne Brontë
turns (gender) back on itself. With this in mind, we might read the story
of the Brontë collaborations differently—as a practice that shortcircuits
the networks that control the profession of writing and restrict access
to those who fall outside accepted norms of age, class, gender, and geographic locality.

In an essay on open secrets, D. A. Miller argues that "secrecy would
seem to be a mode whose ultimate meaning lies in the subject's formal
insistence that he is radically inaccessible to the culture that would otherwise entirely determine him" (195). Critical efforts at understanding
the Brontës' secret writing have emphasized the psychological components of this radical inaccessibility. But attention to the material features
of these productions—the microscopic hand-printing, the miniature

size, the binding with meticulous hand-stitching—suggests an inaccessibility to the modes of literary production that these works both appropriate and mimic. In secretly replicating the dominant modes of literary production on a miniature scale, the Brontës resist the determinant structures they would seem to enlist, recasting public practices in an insistently private mold. Indeed, they redefine writing as the ultimate cottage industry. Thus, for example, their much touted hand-printing, explicitly designed to imitate the available print technology, functions simultaneously as the means to preserve their secrecy, rendering their texts virtually unreadable for those outside their secret society. For, on one level at least, it is the openness of this secret writing—its familiar markings of accessibility—that most insistently declares its radical inaccessibility; in other words, what makes their productions most resemble "real books" (their material packaging) is precisely what excludes them from this category. Moreover, if the sheer volume of such secret writing would seem to defy the conditions of secrecy, it also sustains the juvenilia's status as preeminent literary mystery, leaving the critic, like Mrs. Gaskell, unsure what to do with it.

In fact, for Gaskell, the juvenile writings that make up the "curious packet" that comes to her in a confidential exchange continue to declare their mysterious depths through their surface inscrutability: "I have had a curious packet confided to me, containing an immense amount of manuscript, in an inconceivably small space; tales, dramas, poems, romances, written principally by Charlotte, in a hand which it is almost impossible to decipher without the aid of a magnifying glass." And Gaskell transmits this secret not by deciphering it but by reproducing its opacity, suggesting that it is the surface itself that most baffles credibility: "No description will give so good an idea of the extreme minuteness of the writing as the annexed fac-simile of a page" (111–12). With the emergence of modern textual editions of the juvenilia, this gesture has been reproduced in virtually every introduction, as if the editors felt compelled to provide "ocular proof" of the impenetrability of their materials; along with the requisite photographs and facsimiles, these introductions ritually trot out the old magnifying glass chestnut, if only to do it one better: "The aid of a magnifying glass, and occasionally a microscope, is necessary to decipher the earliest manuscripts" (Alexander, *Early Writings* 3).[15]

[15] Alexander, for example, while silently correcting minor errors, includes photographs to illustrate idiosyncratic spelling and punctuation (*An Edition* I:xxiii). Robert G. Collins includes reproductions of "specimen manuscript sheets" to illustrate "the sort of thing that was there to be deciphered," as well as examples, in the Notes, of "the original form of the text" to illustrate Branwell's convoluted syntax (*The Hand of the Arch-Sinner: Two*

Ultimately, however, the Brontës' biographers and editors prove committed to the normalizing narratives of authorship as we know it. Gaskell thus copies from the packet Charlotte's 1830 "Catalogue of my Books"—amounting, Gaskell claims, to twenty-two volumes of sixty to a hundred pages each—"as a curious proof how early the rage for literary composition had seized upon her" (112), and she evaluates the works as "of singular merit for a girl of thirteen or fourteen" (114).[16] An alternative reading, however, might construe this rage differently, not as confirmation of precocious creativity but rather as a declaration of professional credibility. For the rage may be less for composition per se as for the trappings of authority, for what would confirm her "early awareness of her role as an author" (Alexander, *Early Writings* 232). In fact, Charlotte's preface to *The Adventures of Mon Edouard de Crack*, written near the beginning of her juvenile writing career, anticipates Anthony Trollope's notorious confession of the mundane requirements of *professional* authorship:

> I began this book on the 22 of February 1830 and finished it on the 23 of February 1830, doing 8 pages on the first day and 11 on the second. On the first day I wrote an hour and a half in the morning and an hour and a half in the evening. On the third day I wrote a quarter of an hour in the morning, 2 hours in the afternoon and a quarter of an hour in the evening, making in the whole 5 hours and a half. CB (Alexander, *An Edition* I:134)

Yet in the interest the Brontë juvenilia has generated, its place as professional practice has commanded considerably less attention than its status as a peculiar instance of fledgling genius offering unique insight into the formation of the creative imagination—insight into, in Ratchford's words, "the story of genius at its strangest" (*Gondal's Queen* 12). This professional place, of course, remains ambiguous, for even if, for example, the obsessive documentation in the dating and signing of manuscripts proves, quite literally, a profession of authorship, it is a profession that declares, through its own isolation and excess, its radical difference from the practices it mimics. Thus the hour-by-hour, day-by-day timetables of production and the proliferation of multiple signatures that characterize the juvenile writings certify the amateur status

---

Angrian Chronicles of Branwell Brontë xlvi). All modern editions, moreover, display a repertoire of "scholarly aids" (diagrams, lists of characters, etc.) without which even their newly readable editions might remain baffling.

[16] Barker argues that Gaskell, like later biographers, conflates Charlotte's earlier and later juvenilia, thus fostering the impression "that the childhood writings were much more sophisticated than they actually were" (864n48).

of these professional inscriptions, as does the collaborative structure within which they function. Yet in their sustained engagement with the mechanics of production, the Brontës' eccentric literary practices assume public interest, exhibiting their ties to the professionalization of writing they both refuse and legitimate.

Ironically, in publishing the juvenilia and thus granting it professional stature, modern editions may have the unintended effect of limiting the scope of its significance. For the juvenilia's interest rests in part precisely in its status as unpublished (and unpublishable)—at least as publication is conventionally conceived. The logic, in fact, that informs most critical editions—to "provide an accurate clear text for the widest audience with a minimum of editorial intervention" (Alexander, *An Edition* I:xxiii); to produce "a work readily available in form and meaning to any intelligent reader" (Collins xlii)—turns out to be at exact odds with the logic that determined the juvenilia's original production—to preserve the texts for the narrowest possible audience of siblings. In other words, to make the juvenilia accessible is to deny a constituent feature of its identity—hence the need to "normalize" the texts to make them readable. Implicit in these normalizing procedures—comprehending size, format, typeface, grammar, punctuation, spelling—is the assumption that the secret of these works resides within their covers, that what is inside the manuscripts is more important than their material casing. The production of readers' editions thus inevitably locates the interest of the manuscripts in their status as *texts*. But what if we were to read these manuscripts differently?

From another perspective, one might argue that the original, untranscribed manuscripts widely dispersed in private collections, museums, and libraries—even the often "corrupt" limited editions, published and sold privately to connoisseurs and collectors—maintain an understanding of the juvenilia largely lost in the production of critical editions. Yet these same critical editions may be our best source for competing understandings of the juvenilia's interest. For in the stories they insistently tell—in introductions, footnotes, appendices, diagrams, photographs, facsimiles—of what goes into the making of a modern edition (what is preserved, eliminated, or corrected), they remind us of what they cannot comprehend: the juvenilia's status as object, as collaborative undertaking, as alternative writing practice not appropriatable to the historical conditions of the nineteenth century literary marketplace or the established categories of contemporary literary criticism.

Among the understandings of the juvenilia most in need of recovery is a closer attention to its function as miniature, for although the minute size of the early manuscripts is probably their most immediately striking feature, it is also among the first components to disappear in the production of textual editions. As Susan Stewart has argued, the presence of the miniature book alerts us to a counterhistory of the book often overlooked in conventional literary history: a history of the book as object—and, more particularly, "as an object of person, a talisman or amulet" (41).[17] Like other miniatures, then, the Brontës' personally imprinted and jealously guarded manuscripts stand as a kind of "materialized secret" (Stewart 61). In fact, many of the most distinctive features of the juvenilia—its insularity, its secrecy, its insistent association with both fantasy and the diminutive world of childhood—find articulation in the theory of the miniature. Indeed, what has been upheld as peculiar to the Brontës in their juvenile writings—their near complete absorption in an alternate world of reality—may be endemic to the mode of production through which they articulated their imaginary universes. For as Stewart has argued, the miniature negates the outside world, replacing it with an "other" time and space, subject only to the requirements of individual fantasy (65–67). True to form, that space is, for the Brontës, associated with childhood; like other miniature books, moreover, as has been true throughout the miniature's history, the Brontës' miniatures are books for children. The Brontës, however, in their productions, consolidate competing understandings of the miniature as children's literature—transforming it into literature *by* as well as for children. In the infinite regress typical of miniatures, they project not only worlds within worlds (the original Glass Town, for example, spawns a set of satellite Glass Towns, each presided over by a different sibling) but within these worlds, recorded in their juvenilia, characters who write their own juvenilia.[18]

As historical practice, the Brontë juvenilia might be profitably read against the production of other contemporaneous miniatures—productions that enjoyed a certain popularity over the course of the nineteenth century only to be, like the juvenilia, dismissed as the stuff of children or relegated to the status of collector's item. These miniature books included compilations of various sorts—chapbooks of fairy and folk tales, miniature bibles, almanacs (typically including poems and engraved illustrations), and translations of Omar Khayyám and other Orientalist writings. In their content and makeup, these popular works suggest that the Brontës may have modeled their manuscripts on other

---

[17] In the early Brontë juvenilia, the texts were literally conceived as "props" or objects—reading material designed to scale for the toy soldiers.

[18] *Visits in Verreopolis*, for example, is represented as a two-volume work, written by the Honourable Charles Albert Florian, Lord Wellesley, Aged 10 years (Alexander, *An Edition* I: 316).

miniatures, as well as on the mainstream literature they miniaturized.[19] Whether or not such mimicry was intentional, the Brontës' little books participate in practices endemic to their mode of production. Like other miniatures, for example, they affirm labor and craft, announcing themselves as unmistakably made by hand. If the production schedules they obsessively display sometimes read like a parody of work—"I wrote this in the space of one hour" (Alexander, *An Edition* I : 179)—they nonetheless confirm labor *as value*, albeit on a child's scale. Moreover, if all children's writing—any pre-published text for that matter—enjoys a necessary relationship to the handmade and the amateurish, the lengths the Brontës went to professionalize their work invite us to view their labor as a professional practice in its own right (or, more accurately, the mimicry of such a practice—i.e., the mimicry of a mimicry).

From this perspective, the requirements of the miniature might help explain characteristic features of the Brontës' juvenile writings. The near delirious quality of descriptive excess—the catalogs, lists, and unrelenting detail—speaks to the need, shared by all writings of the miniature, to illuminate a world not ascertainable to our ordinary senses (Stewart 46). Similarly, the Brontës' much celebrated hand-printing—handwriting designed to resemble print typeface—can be seen to announce the location of the miniature book as, in Susan Stewart's words, on "the interface between the manuscript and printing" (39). Minute writing, indeed, is a practiced skill, "emblematic of craft and discipline" (38); its deployment in the Brontës' hands thus speaks to their sense of their writing as literal apprenticeship. It also speaks to their desire to invest their works with personal value and meaning, to multiply "the significance of the total object" (Stewart 38). Indeed, as a mode of production, the miniature affirms the unique and authentic, qualities that have attached to the Brontës with special persistence. It may not be, then, so much of a stretch to suggest that the miniature afforded the Brontës a space to assert their uniqueness, a space to declare themselves little writers of genius. In fact, in their earliest juvenile writings, the Brontë children literally announce themselves as such, appearing in their own works as the four Chief Genii or Chief Geniuses.

In the modern editions of the juvenilia fit for mass production and consumption, however, the labor associated with the miniature trans-

---

[19] As conscious mimicry of established literary formats, the Brontës' works were inherently miniaturizing operations—a feature most evident in their imitations of other hoaxes or "imitations": e.g., *Tales of the Genii*, the poems of Ossian, etc. According to Susan Stewart, "the miniature book frequently served as a realm of the cultural other," a place "to collapse the significance of the Orient into the exotica of a miniaturized volume" (*On Longing: Narratives of the Miniature, the Gigantic, the Souvenir, the Collection* 43). The Brontës' choice of colonial subjects might then be part and parcel of their miniaturizing function.

fers to the editor. Indeed, the editor becomes, of necessity, a miniaturist—i.e., an expert in miniatures. Ironically, though, the labor these editions celebrate is the labor necessary to erase the most obvious markers of the manuscripts as miniatures—to translate the miniature writing into readable text. Alexander, for example, opens her monumental edition of Charlotte Brontë's early writings with an extended comment on the labor of transcription (*An Edition* I:x). And Collins, in his edition of two of Branwell's chronicles, relates the "daunting physical task" of getting through even a single page of Branwell's minute handwriting—writing that in an ordinary hand might fill up to ten pages (xliv). Admitting that "the necessity for reconstruction involved hundreds of minor but time-consuming decisions" (xlvii), Collins documents in excruciating detail the editorial principles he followed and the co-workers he enlisted. Where in the heyday of the miniature, printers would, Stewart claims, "vie with each other to print the smallest book as a demonstration of craftsmanship for its own sake" (39), now the editors of history's most famous amateur miniaturists vie with each other to decipher the smallest, most difficult hand and to display the most labor-intensive text. Thus Collins, for example, insists that Branwell's "microscopic" handwriting is significantly more difficult to decipher than Charlotte's (xlvi), while Ratchford puts in her bid for the special difficulties of Emily's manuscripts: "Replete with weird names of unknown persons and places and set down in minute, gnarled, and crabbed hand-printing, many of them on mere scraps of paper, they tantalized and defied would-be transcribers and editors for almost a century" (*Gondal's Queen* 11).

Indeed, so daunting have seemed the demands of the juvenilia that whole careers have been given over to it. Ratchford, whose early work facilitated the recent burgeoning in the juvenilia industry, admits to devoting "a quarter of a century" of her life (with impasses of years' duration) to the reconstruction in *Gondal's Queen* (1955) of a part of Emily and Anne's Gondal cycle—a commitment that exceeds by a considerable margin the seventeen years she attributes to the epic's original development (*Gondal's Queen* 25). "[L]ured on by distant landscapes, stirring events, mystical experiences, and the 'wild, melancholy and elevating' music of Emily's verse" (37)—and working without even a real manuscript—Ratchford testifies to both the labor and romance of getting into her subject; indeed, to edit Emily Brontë properly, Ratchford implies, she had to reincarnate her: "I spent uncounted hours in concentrated effort to think Emily's thoughts, and feel Emily's emotions after her" (24); "I have reconstructed in part two lost Emily Brontë novels; and I have glimpsed *Wuthering Heights* in the making" (37). From a modern scholarly perspective, Ratchford's naive admissions smack of amateur enthusiasm. But to dismiss Ratchford too easily is to under-estimate not only the influence of her scholarship but the degree to which the competing interests of the amateur and professional—the en-thusiast and the scholar—make,up the Brontë phenomenon, nowhere more than in the production and reception of the juvenilia. *Gondal's Queen* stands as eloquent testimony to this fact. For although it rep-resents itself as "A Novel in Verse by Emily Jane Brontë," the work consists of a selection of Emily's poems—transcribed, glossed, and as-sembled in chapter form by Ratchford—with chapter titles and "narra-tive prose links" also supplied (and written) by her. Certainly, no rep-utable modern editor would claim, as Ratchford does, to produce an "edition" with no manuscript to back it—*Gondal's Queen*, indeed, has no autonomous literary identity apart from Ratchford's "reconstruction"—but Ratchford's practice raises questions relevant to other editions of the juvenilia that also understand themselves as reconstruction projects.

In particular, it raises the question of the nature and extent of an edi-tor's contribution to a text that requires so much work to see publica-tion. Ratchford's edition, in fact, rewrites the historical circumstances of Gondal's production, for in Ratchford's *Gondal*, Anne does not par-ticipate. *Gondal's Queen*, then, replaces the Emily-Anne collaboration (to which they both contributed prose and poetry) with Ratchford's prose contributions to Emily's poetry, making Ratchford, in effect, Emily's new writing partner. But even more modest claims like those of Collins—"One necessarily became (though to a judicious and limited degree) the copy-editor/proof-reader whom Branwell never had" (Collins xlix)—cast the editor as collaborator, a necessary facilitator if not full coauthor. These modern editor/collaborators generally have little room for the real historical collaborators, the Brontë siblings, they, in some sense, re-place; indeed, the requirements of the scholarly edition militate against the inclusion of extraneous "authors."

Of course, the total disappearance of Emily and Anne's prose manu-scripts means no complete picture of Gondal will ever be possible. There is no way to measure the extent of Emily and Anne's participation in the early plays and Glass Town saga. Even where manuscripts are available, however, without some major shift in critical paradigms, we are not likely to see editions that do justice to the Brontës' extensive col-laboration, even to the extent that we have materials to reconstruct it.[20]

---

[20] The closest thing we have to a truly collaborative edition of Charlotte and Branwell's manuscripts is the much maligned Shakespeare Head edition of the juvenilia, edited by T. J. Wise and A. J. Symington (1936–1938)—a work that does not pretend to complete-ness. Much of Branwell's work, moreover, remains in "the form of facsimiles of undeci-phered manuscripts, thus remaining virtually illegible to casual readers" (Collins xli).

For the price of publication of the Brontës' early writings remains, as it was when they published their first novels, recognition of the Brontës as separate, individual authors. Alexander, for example, in undertaking a complete edition of Charlotte Brontë's early writing, assumes what may not be entirely self-evident—that Charlotte constitutes an authorial unit. From such a perspective, however, Charlotte's early writings can be deemed "complete" without the inclusion of Branwell's contributions to their joint venture; Branwell, indeed, as a coauthor, can be reduced to a running footnote to Charlotte's autonomous productions.

Given the current state of editorial theory and practice, and given the fact that each of the Brontës has his or her own following, future editions of the juvenilia are likely to proceed from similar assumptions.[21] Indeed, editors (and their audiences) inevitably approach the early manuscripts with professional investments in their favorite Brontë (often at the expense of one or more of the others). Thus Collins attributes Branwell's lack of due recognition to the attention already given to his more famous sisters. So strong, he suggests, are critical prejudices that in spite of the fact that "for at least a dozen years," Branwell was an "incredibly prolific writer, turning out hundreds of thousands of words of prose narrative, as well as poetry," he continues to be seen only as a wasted figure who burned his young life out with drugs and alcohol, much to the consternation of his sensitive sisters; indeed, Branwell's best poetry, Collins argues, "has been misattributed to Emily because of its merit" (xiii). For Collins, then, one of the first tasks of the editor is to demonstrate that Branwell's work warrants an edition, that, as an author, Branwell is worthy of study apart from his relation to his gifted sisters. Inevitably, then, it is in Collins's interest, in producing an edition of Branwell's juvenilia, to sever Branwell's writings from Charlotte's.

Collins, however, does more than extricate Branwell's texts from Charlotte's corpus; he distinguishes them both formally and stylistically, in what amounts to a reverse valuation. While admitting that Branwell's writing "is inferior by almost all the traditional criteria with which we judge serious fiction" (xiv), he credits Branwell alone with anticipating "certain aspects of twentieth-century fiction" (Collins xvii). Unlike Charlotte, Collins contends, Branwell did not write mini-novels:

[21] The problems posed by the juvenilia rehearse central questions highlighted in editorial theory: the competing requirements of critical and facsimile editions. Recent developments in editorial theory and practice, however, open the way for alternative possibilities through hypertext editions. Jerome McGann, for example, has argued that hypertext facilitates the marriage between facsimile and critical editing—a marriage that, in the case of the Brontës, would serve the dual need of allowing one to "read" the juvenilia as text without losing sight of its materiality. But the question remains whether juvenilia, as such, can command the resources for a hypertext edition.

he "did not write tales" (xiv); he "did not write formal novels" (xiv). "He is, simply enough," Collins explains, "the author of fictional chronicles" (xiv)—works whose structure is inherently episodic and digressive. But Collins's claims underplay the extent to which Charlotte's companion texts were also something less than conventional. Indeed, if Branwell's "novels," as represented in the juvenilia, were "at odds with the highly structured and largely domestically pointed English novels of the mid-nineteenth century" (Collins xvii), so were Charlotte's, notwithstanding the claims of Charlotte's modern promoters. Most of Charlotte's works self-consciously appear, in fact, as odds and ends and fragments, as miscellaneous collections of pieces in prose and verse, as loosely connected tales and prose extravaganzas.[22] These hybrid genres, favored by both Branwell and Charlotte, reflect something more than the peculiar disposition of their authors; they exist, in part at least, as a function of their collaboration. For in the type of interactive, serial publication Charlotte and Branwell practiced, individual manuscripts do not appear as self-contained units; rather, they acquire meaning cumulatively (and in response to another's contributions), often requiring retrospective reshaping. Constantly subject to another's fancy, they are, by definition, unfinished—developing on principles neither linear nor chronological.

Ironically, Collins's desire to see Branwell's work "in a parallel form" to that of his sisters would "normalize" his work in much the way their early work has been normalized. Indeed, there is a price for editorial correctness; the better the edition the more it erases the manuscripts' resistant features and the more it invites the type of formal analysis least able to appreciate what is most distinct to this writing. These features— the gaps, incoherence, and obscurity; the inconsistent names for people and places; the absence of appropriate spelling and punctuation; the wild stylistic vacillations—have often been read as signs of the pitfalls of collaboration. And read in conventional terms, they do appear as stylistic lapses. These same features, I am arguing, however, might be seen as positive indications of a style of authorship that refuses to be regulated—that announces itself, as Stewart says of the miniature, as an "affront to reason" (40). From this perspective, we might read the juvenile collaboration not as a limiting condition but as an enabling vehicle for a form of writing that resolutely stands outside the mainstream.

The "weird names" for unknown persons and places, for example,

---

[22] A mere sampling of titles illuminates this fact: *A Fragment*; *Arthuriana or Odds & Ends, Being a Miscellaneous Collection of Pieces in Prose & Verse*; *Corner Dishes, Being A Small Collection of Mixed and Unsubstantial Trifles in Prose and Verse*; *The Spell, An Extravaganza*; *The Scrap Book. A Mingling of Many Things*.

that have so baffled readers—with characters frequently appearing under multiple names, nicknames, and aliases as well as numerous titles and honorifics—might be read as more than childish extravagance. For they signal a world that works by its own logic, refusing the authority of the proper name and the structures that follow from it. Indeed, on all counts, the names appear anything but proper—so unfamiliar, in fact, that the authors themselves recognized that they could not publish their works without excising them. The names stand, moreover, as a refusal of propriety—a refusal to fix a single name to a single person; instead, names proliferate in a seemingly arbitrary manner, without even the collaborators necessarily adopting the same names for shared characters. In addition, at least in the case of Gondal, the practice of naming marks a resistance to patrilineal inheritance, for as Ratchford indicates, "by some obscure Gondalan convention father and child did not always bear the same family name" (*Gondal's Queen* 24). Corroborated by a closed circle of initiates, these practices intimate an alternative set of conventions: an alternative order of property and relationship, an alternative system of signification. Revising one of the fundamental components of language competence, these experiments in nomenclature stand as prototypes of a private language—a private order of meaning.[23] As Charlotte says of their collaborative undertaking, it constitutes *a system*—something we might now see as akin to the visionary system Yeats was to elaborate for his poetry: "all the mighty phantasm that we had conjured from nothing to a system strong as some religious creed" (qtd. in Gérin, *Charlotte Brontë* 104).

Like Yeats's *A Vision*, the juvenilia shares features with other alternative writing practices, often of a collaborative nature, that begin to appear with some frequency toward the end of the nineteenth century—most pointedly, automatic writing. Like the miniature, these practices assert their radical inaccessibility, promoting "a fiction which exists independent of human signifying processes" (Stewart 57)—sometimes independent of voluntary agency. Thus Charlotte begins an entry in her Roe Head diary, "I am just going to write because I cannot help it" (qtd. in Gérin, *Charlotte Brontë* 103); she *writes*, moreover, like a trance medium, with eyes closed and pen proceeding as if of its own impetus. In fact, some of the peculiar difficulties of Charlotte's manuscripts—the words running together, the slanting script—are typical of such meth-

---

[23] The juvenilia, in fact, contains its own secret language or dialect, the "Old Young Men's Tongue," invented by Branwell, and adopted, at some point, by all the siblings—a language apparently reproduced by holding one's nose while speaking Yorkshire dialect. As the juvenilia developed, however, Charlotte increasingly rejected this language, relegating it to the primitive outreaches of Glass Town.

ods of composition. Similarly, Branwell displays a capacity, shared by many mediums, for performative or ambidextrous writing; as Gérin notes, he could write "equally fluently with both hands—at times with both hands at once, and in moments of bravado in Greek with his right and in Latin with his left" (*Branwell Brontë* vi). Such analogies extend beyond the material act of composition. Charlotte's account, for example, of her immersion in Angria—an immersion shared by her brother—reads exactly like the testimonial of a professional medium, as Chapter 4 will demonstrate: "I remember I quite seemed to see with my bodily eyes a lady standing in the hall of a gentleman's house as if waiting for someone. . . . I most distinctly heard the front door open and saw the soft moonlight disclosed upon a lawn outside. . . . I hear them speak as well as she does, I see distinctly their figures—and though alone, I experience all the feelings of one admitted for the first time into a grand circle of classic beings" (qtd. in Gérin, *Charlotte Brontë* 105–6). Like the mediums who succeed her, Charlotte claims to write of things beyond her knowledge and experience: "I know nothing of people of rank and distinction, yet there they are before me . . . ." And like many middle-class women who took to mediumship, she practices a secret writing—"I cannot write of them except in total solitude I scarce dare think of them" (qtd. in *Charlotte Brontë* 106)—that receives its validation from a small group of fellow practitioners.[24]

Like automatic writing, the Brontë juvenilia can be profitably linked to earlier, seemingly outmoded, forms of authorship: to the preservation of manuscript culture in the age of print technology. In this light, the need to preserve manuscript features (a goal at odds with the priorities of most modern editions) takes on new significance. For the errors and lapses that editors are most quick to correct might be read in this context as signs of authenticity: the mark of writing that emerges in a flood of inspiration. The "errors," indeed, affirm the writing's immediacy. The absence of punctuation, for example, as with automatic writing, signals writing that comes with extraordinary speed, overriding conventionalized distinctions and boundaries. Literally, there are no stops—between words, thoughts, sentences, speeches—with all running into each other. The mass of words, moreover, typically crammed

---

[24] Even after the publication of *Jane Eyre*, Charlotte continued to describe her writing as a form of mediumship; in a letter to G. H. Lewes, for example, she speaks of the "Influence" that overtakes the creative writer, dictating the words she produces. Charlotte's descriptions of the juvenilia, however, provide the fullest articulation of this theory of creativity. Speaking of her characters with the familiarity of friends—establishing, as it were, her own psychic friends network—she locates her writing within the common practices of mediumship.

into a single page, often overtaking the margins, suggests both discipline and abandon, writing that tests the limits of its borders. Refusing to be contained, it is writing that resists assimilation into the conventional structures of authorship.

This resistance, I want to argue, may ultimately be what is most interesting about the juvenile manuscripts. For as a distinctive practice of authorship, they challenge certain fundamental assumptions about the nature of literary production: that authorship is solitary; that its progress can be mapped developmentally, by genre choice and stylistic fluency; that it supports fixed hierarchies (e.g., written versus oral, work versus play); that it receives its necessary validation in the public marketplace; that there is a meaningful distinction between writing and publishing. Indeed, one of the juvenilia's more radical claims would seem to be that within the closed system it designates, public authorship and private authorship are, in effect, the same; for as long as the Brontë siblings shared their literary practice, to write their manuscripts *was* to publish them, as Collins notes of Branwell (xlviii–xlix). A criticism attentive to these resistant features might, then, create a space for the serious study of other writing practices that stand outside the mainstream.

Our desire, however to fit the juvenilia into preexisting categories (whether to dismiss it as "weird" or to accommodate it to the requirements of the type of public authorship the Brontës ultimately achieved) has limited our ability to read it for the full range of stories it has to tell. These stories include the story of the coexistence, in a given historical moment, of diverse practices of authorship—including authorial practices that have not generally been recognized as such. Ironically, of course, it is only because the Brontës have come so fully to exemplify our modern understanding of authorship that we can turn to them for archival evidence of competing authorial practices. For the Brontës' fame—their unimpeachable position as writers of genius—is the primary, if not only, reason the juvenilia has commanded so much scholarly attention. It provides the ultimate rationale for engaging a wide body of readers in the serious study of writings that would otherwise be dismissed as amateur or whimsical. It explains, moreover, how we come to have such an extensive body of material to work with. For the "juvenilia" of lesser writers stands much less chance of being preserved— let alone published.

At the same time, the force of the Brontës' stature as recognized authors has largely determined our traditions for reading their earliest writings—traditions that reinforce, by regulating or reforming resistant features, our most cherished suppositions of what counts as authorship.

This tendency is by no means trivial, for the history of the Brontë juvenilia is, in large part, the history of its reception. Recognizing this fact, we might profitably ask not only what the study of the juvenilia tells us about the Brontës but what it tells us about the history and practice of authorship. What can it tell us, for example, about the ordinary (and extraordinary) structures through which authorship is entered at different historical moments? What does it illuminate about writing as we know it? What alternative practices of writing does it open to our understanding?

Critical treatments of the juvenilia have tended to foreground only certain understandings of the Brontës' practice of secret writing; in doing so, they have foreclosed other possible understandings of such modes of writing—as performed by the Brontës and by a host of ordinary people, writers without established claim to genius. In the practice of these often obscure writers, as future chapters will demonstrate, we have material for a counterhistory of authorship and its critical reception. In this light, we might treat the case of the Brontë juvenilia not as unique but as exemplary—exemplary of writing that, more often than not, is only secret because absent from history. Whatever, then, one may decide about their literary merit, the Brontës' early "publications" have considerable untapped interest for the historian of culture and the literary critic. Among other things, they reveal a good deal about what goes into (and out of) the normative narratives of literary production— the very narratives that have, in effect, enshrined Charlotte and Emily Brontë as solitary geniuses.

2

"Something Obscurely Repellent"
The Resistance to Double Writing

Explaining the decline in the critical fortunes of the poet "Michael Field," after the secret of "his" authorship was publicized—the discovery that Michael Field was not a man but two women—Mary Sturgeon, Field's biographer, speculates, "Or it may be that something in the fact of a collaboration was obscurely repellent; or even that their true sex was not revealed with tact to sensitive susceptibilities" (*Michael Field* 29). While Sturgeon's tactful formulation posits the scandal of collaboration and the scandal of gender as discrete, equally plausible narratives for her subject's literary obscurity, the story she tells suggests that the two are not unconnected. For in her tribute to Michael Field as a singular literary entity that made its mark on the world of letters in the 1880s and 1890s, the "true sex" of the partners is not so much revealed (tactfully or otherwise) as put into question by the very success of the collaboration. Thus while the individuals who make up this corporate entity can be readily identified as Katherine Bradley and Edith Cooper, an aunt and niece, they share a life together that exceeds easy incorporation into the ties of family.

Indeed, it would be hard to know what familial terms best represent them—mother-daughter, husband-wife, companion-sister. For Bradley, fifteen years Cooper's senior, takes on the care of her niece practically from infancy, later attending university with her. As adults the two share a household and find a circle of friends among homosexual couples; and they write together what was, even at the time, widely regarded as "Sapphic" poetry. Like many of their contemporaries, moreover, they adopt masculine names for their private as well as professional identities, affectionately referring to themselves as "Michael" and "Field" or "Michael" and "Henry."[1] Their biographer, however,

[1] Radclyffe Hall, for example, went by the name John, while Violet Martin (the "Martin Ross" of Somerville and Ross) used "Martin" as a personal name in her private relationships.

like other chroniclers of women's writing teams, goes to great lengths to naturalize these proceedings, insisting that "Michael's" devotion to her partner is anything but deviant: "On the contrary, it was the expression of her mother-instinct, the outflow of the natural feminine impulse to cherish and protect" (*Michael Field* 75). But if Sturgeon presents the choice of names as a male costume that reveals the "true woman" beneath, the story she tells of cross-writing and cross-identity admits of other, more unsettling readings—readings where the authors' writing relationship refuses "true sex" (as it refuses "true author") as an explanatory category.[2]

In the historical representation of women's collaborations, I argue, these refusals have remained persistently linked, facilitating our culture's continued resistance to the practice of double writing even as that practice comes increasingly under scrutiny. For by a kind of sleight of hand, women's collaborations have been haunted by what Terry Castle has called the "apparitional lesbian"—a phantom figure that both reveals and conceals lesbian possibilities. Indeed, throughout its history, the discourse that surrounds women's joint writing has inevitably turned on transgressive sexuality, introducing the specter of lesbianism at the site of women's textual productivity. Even for collaborative authors whose lives and writings less explicitly invite this type of inquiry, lesbianism has been ritually invoked if only so as to be dispensed with. The Brontës, for example, have not been exempt from speculation. And for Somerville and Ross, this has been the point of departure for virtually every biography.[3] In the case of M. Barnard Eldershaw, the rumors about the authors were so persistent that even a fellow writer with no particular liking for them felt compelled, as she put it, in the name of friendship and collaboration, to defend the coauthors against "aspersions of frustration and lesbianism."[4] As these examples suggest, women's collaborations cannot apparently be talked about without invoking lesbianism.

[2] For a similar gesture, see Geraldine Cummins's 1952 biography of Edith Somerville. Distinguishing Somerville's "real feminine charm" from her customary "male uniform (collar, tie and shirt)," Cummins testifies to Edith's "almost flirtatious passages" with men when she was in her seventies and eighties (*Dr E. Œ. Somerville* 8–9).

[3] See for example, Hilary Robinson's disclaimer, "Their friendship has been so much misunderstood that it is necessary to say that while their love and respect for each other could hardly have been greater, it never transgressed the bounds set by Christianity" (*Somerville and Ross: A Critical Appreciation* 19). Maurice Collis represents Somerville's same-sex identification as a key to understanding the partnership in *Somerville and Ross: A Biography*, while Gifford Lewis presents her study, *Somerville and Ross: The World of the Irish R.M.*, as a corrective to this and other imputations of lesbianism.

[4] The writer in question is Miles Franklin, the author of *My Brilliant Career* (quoted in Maryanne Dever, "'No Mine and Thine but Ours': Finding 'M. Barnard Eldershaw'" 71).

Here too, then, Sturgeon's formulations appear symptomatic, for even as she insists on her subject's "normality," Sturgeon invokes the love she dare not speak: "But of her devotion to Henry, its passion, its depth, its tenacity and tenderness, it is quite impossible to speak adequately" (*Michael Field* 44–45). And even as Sturgeon safely confines the writers' "Sapphic affinities" to "imaginary adventures in that region"— to fulfillment "on the spiritual plane" (74, 86)—her discourse opens up other possibilities. "[F]or it is safe to say," she writes, "that we owe the finest work of Michael Field to the fact that Henry did not marry her lover," did not marry the young man who courted her (86). It is safe to say, moreover, that the work of other writing partnerships similarly flourished because the women involved bypassed the conventional structures of marriage. It is perhaps, then, not entirely a joke when the Findlater sisters maintain, "*We* could only marry a Mormon" (Mackenzie 24).

In his study of the "erotics" of male literary collaboration, Wayne Koestenbaum has argued that "double authorship attacks not primarily our dogmas of literary property, but of sexual propriety" (8–9). But as the Brontës' story demonstrates, in the case of women the two are not so easily separable. Indeed, they come together in the practice of secret writing. Thus Katherine Bradley "corrects" her fellow writer Robert Browning for assuming that the "secret" of "Michael Field" is simply their dual authorship. "The revelation of that would indeed be utter ruin to us," she admits, but "the report of lady authorship" would be equally damaging. It "will dwarf and enfeeble our work at every turn," she explains. "Like the poet Gray we shall never 'speak out.' And we have many things to say that the world will not tolerate from a woman's lips" (*Works and Days: From the Journal of Michael Field* 6). Koestenbaum's project, then—to make the collaborative text speak its homosexuality—cannot simply be appropriated for the study of women's collaborative writing, when writing *as women* (let alone writing *between* women) appears to breach propriety. As Bradley's comments intimate, if *their* lips (i.e., the lips of women) are seen to speak together, they will cease to speak at all.[5]

Koestenbaum's model, then, of literary collaboration as "metaphorical sexual intercourse" (3) requires some adjustment when applied to

---

[5] Following Luce Irigaray and John Addington Symonds (who uses the term "speaking out" "to mean confessing homosexuality"), Wayne Koestenbaum invokes these terms as a code for homosexuality (*Double Talk* 174). But in its immediate context, Bradley's comment does not require such a particularized meaning; what cannot be said by women's lips, at this historical moment, includes *most* of what counts as literature, what Bradley refers to as "the tragic elements of life" (*Works and Days* 8).

the practices of women, and it is not just a question of reversing the gender terms. As Susan J. Leonardi and Rebecca A. Pope argue, "It doesn't transfer" (261)—even for late twentieth-century collaborators self-conscious about collaboration's erotic possibilities. It doesn't transfer, Leonardi and Pope suggest, in part because, as my own allusion to Irigaray suggests ("When Our Two Lips Speak Together"), the female body subscribes to a different economy of desire and pleasure. But it also doesn't transfer, as they point out, because they occupy a very different historical moment from the literary men who form the subject of Koestenbaum's study.[6]

But Koestenbaum's model doesn't transfer even to women authors who were the exact contemporaries of his male subjects, in part because, at that time, women came to authorship with such different histories of writing. In other words, at the historical moment Koestenbaum investigates (1885–1922), to claim an "erotics" for collaboration would mean something very different for men and for women; for before entering into collaborative writing arrangements, women could not be said to have enjoyed the full possession of an authorship imagined to be unmarked by the body. Nor could they be said, as authors, to have received general social and institutional acceptance. To insist that collaboration was an erotic process would thus not have the same subversive power for women as it might have for men. Indeed, the *literary* property of women's collaborations may be the feature we most need to recognize, precisely because it was not something women authors could take for granted.

Yet, as I argue in the next chapter, this "property" has proved difficult to recover, in part because women's collaborative authorship so frequently appears as a domestic arrangement. Keeping production in the family, these unions, in effect, keep women out of the marketplace even when the women profit there, making publication *appear* an insistently private matter—whatever its actual circumstances. When collaborators do resort to private publication, as Bradley and Cooper did after

---

[6] "Could we just reverse the gender terms," Susan J. Leonardi asks, to produce a new paradigm—"women who collaborate engage in a metaphorical sexual intercourse, and the text they balance between them is alternately a child of their sexual union, and a shared man" (Leonardi and Pope, "Screaming Divas: Collaboration as Feminist Practice" 260–61)—a proposition she clearly sees as absurd. Indeed, as Holly Laird points out, none of the women who contribute to her forum on collaboration accept Koestenbaum's model as applicable to themselves, nor, perhaps more surprisingly, do they "take eroticism or lesbianism as a central trope" (*"Forum: On Collaborations"* 2:15). Koestenbaum, it should be acknowledged, does not imagine his theory simply being transposed for women. But his suggestion that Susan Gubar's "Sapphistries" might serve as a model for an "entire other book" on "the history of female (and lesbian) collaboration" (13) has other limitations, as I will later discuss.

"Michael Field" was "outed" or as the Brontës did with the family circulation of their unpublished manuscripts, their writing appears doubly privatized. Not surprisingly, then, when such women describe their
professional partnerships, the private is never far behind. As Bradley
and Cooper suggest in *Works and Days*, the diary they write together under the name "Michael Field," the union of two *in work* depends on the
days they share. Their professional signature thus announces and protects both a private and public relationship. As Cooper puts it, "This
happy union of two in work and aspiration is sheltered and expressed
by 'Michael Field.'"

The "happy union," however, that "Michael Field" celebrates depends on a series of displacements: between public and private, life and
art, mind and body. It depends, that is, on the coupling that collaboration underlines, the "join" that the joint diary performs and illuminates.
"She has lived with me, taught me, encouraged me and joined me to her
poetic life," Cooper writes (*Works and Days* 4). Like other women collaborators, Cooper describes a relationship where traditional nurturing
bleeds into total fusion, where the union of minds in creative work calls
up a vision of the joining of bodies. For Cooper and Bradley, this figure
reaches its apotheosis when, at the end of their lives they seal their relationship by passing each other's poems between their lips: "It is par-
adise between us" (324). This idyllic transport, however, merely takes to
the limit the metaphor of marriage women collaborators habitually invoke to describe their writing relationships. For example, comparing
her domestic partnership to that of the Brownings, Bradley notes that
"those two poets, man and wife, wrote alone; each wrote, but did not
bless or quicken one another at their work; *we are closer married*" (16).

Viewed as a marriage, these writing relationships take on the quality
of something sacrosanct. Thus Bradley warns Havelock Ellis against trying to separate the two hands that make up Michael Field's writing: "As
to our work, let no man think he can put asunder what God has joined"
(qtd. in Sturgeon, *Michael Field* 47). And Somerville, declaring her collaboration with Ross to be a "a sacred thing," recoils from the public's
insatiable desire to unlock their secret: "how abhorrent is to me all the
senseless curiosity as to 'which hand held the pen'" (qtd. in Robinson
47). Like Marjorie Barnard, moreover, who compares her own collaborative writing to "a bedroom secret" (qtd. in Dever 68)—a privacy that
cannot be violated—Somerville conducts a daily correspondence with
her partner through what they call "bed-sheets" or "bed-writing." As in
the example above, moreover, she repeatedly introduces a sexualized
language in the very act of disarming it. Berating the press for an unseemly voyeurism, a "prying greediness in raking up any scrap of per-

sonal detail," she thus invites the question of what it is she is screening: Is it sex or is it writing?[7]

For why should the details of a mode of professional production be so insistently classed as "personal," and hence untouchable? Why should the mysteries of joint writing demand such vigilant screening? Why, indeed, must collaboration be classed as secret writing? The secrets of single authorship—no less mysterious, Somerville would claim—arouse in her no comparable outburst. Somerville's response, then, would seem to suggest that something in the fact of a collaboration unleashes more general anxieties about authorship, and more particularly, authorship for women.

These familiar representations of women's collaborations, then, operate in contradictory ways, both inviting public scrutiny and foreclosing it. If the language of marriage opens these relationships to a lesbian reading, the family structures they invoke mask this possibility. And the collaborations themselves further this containment; for the threat of transgressive sexuality called up by these unions can be displaced from the actual companionate relationship between women to the coupling performed in *their writing*. Such collaborations thus highlight the writing side of these unions while producing a form of writing not recognized publicly—a form of writing that, by definition, resists the structures of the visible. They thus simultaneously eroticize writing and domesticate it.

As such, these unions might be seen to reinforce contemporary prejudices that cast women's authorship as a species of curiosity—women's double writing being, as it were, only more of the same.[8] Unlike the male collaborations Koestenbaum studies, women's partnerships, when brought to visibility, do little, at first glance, to dislodge our conventional assumptions about literary and cultural authority. Indeed, where collaborations between men might challenge received understandings of the construction of masculinity, women's collaborations can be understood to reinforce—even perfect—the appropriate codes of femininity: selflessness, sympathy, nurturance, domesticity. Where male collaborations, moreover, can be read, as Koestenbaum suggests, as a historically specific response to the new cultural recognition (and regulation) of male homosexuality, an understanding of women's collaborations comes up against the instability of the category "lesbian" at this

[7] Barnard's account of her collaborative writing is similarly double—and even more suggestive: "It comforts me to empty my little vial into her fountain and see it lifted" (qtd. in Dever 69).

[8] As Koestenbaum demonstrates, male collaborations have not escaped representation as "curiosities," but this has not been the only definition available to them.

historical moment.[9] For as the work of Lillian Faderman and Carroll Smith-Rosenberg suggests, a culturally prescribed tradition of affectionate friendships can both shelter and express the "happy union" of women who write to, for, and with each other—even those like Michael Field who unashamedly refer to each other as "poet-lovers" (*Works and Days* 323).[10]

It should come as no surprise, then, that the stories told about women's turn-of-the-century literary collaborations prove insistently double, producing dual authorship as simultaneously harmless (a species of literary curiosity) and transgressive (a site of sexual and textual aberrancy), simultaneously the place where the "other woman" is materialized and where she is exorcised through prescriptive gender codings. Literary collaboration, popularly held to be a mistake, "for the reason that two men cannot combine so as to be one," remains for women a more open question—perhaps because for women, taught to deny the boundaries of their own identities, such combination need not be viewed as threatening.[11]

Indeed, for women writing together in the late nineteenth and early twentieth centuries, combining "as one" would seem to be the trope they most insistently appeal to in describing their joint creations.[12] "We worked it up together," Marjorie Barnard explains, "and our thoughts and ideas became inextricably blended into a whole. There was no mine

[9] Here, too, the historical specificity of Koestenbaum's project (1885–1922) is relevant: these are the years immediately following the Labouchère Amendment (1885) that criminalized acts of "gross indecency" between men. The act, significantly, did not include comparable acts performed by women. In 1921 Parliament considered, but chose not to amend the act in this direction, allowing many to believe that as late as the 1920s, there was still a widespread refusal to acknowledge the existence of lesbianism.

[10] Against this background of a wide range of acceptable same-sex relationships for women, Mary Sturgeon can claim, "Critics notwithstanding, it was not so audacious as it seemed for two Victorian ladies to plunge into the task of rendering Sapphic ecstasy" (*Michael Field* 89). Citing "the harmony that existed between the poets and their theme, Sappho," Sturgeon anticipates Gubar's argument in "Sapphistries" (incorporated into Gilbert and Gubar, *No Man's Land* 2). The fact that the concept of "romantic friendship" protected a wide range of same-sex relations should not, of course, foreclose the possibility that many of these relations were also sexual.

[11] The attack on collaboration is James Barrie's (qtd. in Koestenbaum 160), but it finds a close echo in Walter Besant: "If two men work together . . . the two men must be rolled into one" (*Autobiography* 188). By contrast, feminist theories of women's writing have often stressed the permeability of boundaries: between author, text, characters, and readers. Not all feminists, however, see this as something to celebrate. Recognizing the way such models have been used misogynistically and homophobically to regulate women's closeness with other women, Rebecca Pope expresses wariness of accepting the model "when the collaboration is two women, especially two lesbians" (Leonardi and Pope 268).

[12] While Holly Laird reads this "insistence on their oneness" as an internalization of "the dangers of multiple authorship" ("Contradictory Legacies" 117), my argument is, in some sense, the exact opposite: that it is the assertion of "oneness" (whatever its reality)

and thine but ours" ("Gentle Art" 126). Katherine Bradley concedes no more than an occasional "stray line" to the independent halves of the Michael Field team: "for the others, the work is perfect mosaic" (Sturgeon, *Michael Field* 47).[13] Edith Somerville proves even more uncompromising, asserting the absoluteness of a singular, double identity: "It is *impossible* to apportion general responsibility in our writings but even to have said '*hardly*' a 'paragraph, a phrase etc.' was written single-handed by either of us would have been an exaggeration" (qtd. in Robinson 47).

If, then, as Walter Besant suggests (himself a long-time collaborator), male collaborations inevitably falter because of the artist's desire "to enjoy the reputation of his own good work" (*Autobiography* 188), women collaborators would seem to betray no such self-interest, no such need to be recognized individually.[14] Indeed, Violet Martin's assertion, upheld by her partner as the closest thing to a solution to the mystery of how two people can write together, subjects collaboration to an entirely different economy of pleasure: "writing together is, to me at least, one of the greatest pleasures I have. To write with you doubles the triumph and the enjoyment having first halved the trouble and anxiety" (qtd. in E. Œ. Somerville and Martin Ross, "Two of a Trade" 182). When faced with too much *individual* recognition for her collaborative productions, Martin can, then, write to her partner, "*Why* aren't you here to take your share?" (Gifford Lewis, ed., *The Selected Letters of Somerville and Ross* 215).[15]

In fact, the accounts of women's collaborations read "as one," con-

---

that most threatens the idea of individual authorship. As I argue later in this chapter, when multiplicity can be acknowledged, as in the apportioning of authorial responsibilities, collaborations appear more tolerable.

[13] This statement, which appears in a letter to Havelock Ellis, continues, "we cross and interlace like a company of dancing summer flies; if one begins a character, his companion seizes and possesses it; if one conceives a scene or situation, the other corrects, completes, or murderously cuts away." Koestenbaum emphasizes the articulation of conflict ("a murderous contest for possession") in this passage (53); Yopie Prins ("Sappho Doubled" 180) and Holly Laird ("Contradictory Legacies" 118) also stress its invocation of difference and multiplicity. But what seems striking to me is the way representations like Bradley's erase conflict and competition, even as they admit it—treating it light-heartedly, as here, or parenthetically.

[14] Only Marjorie Barnard expresses some such anxiety. Deciding to give up her library position to pursue writing as a full-time occupation, she worries that her ability as a writer has not been adequately tested by independent production; thus she tells a friend, "you've seen nothing that I've written alone and there's no particular reason to think that any of the virtues of our joint work are my contribution" (qtd. in Dever 69).

[15] Something of the same sentiment requires Somerville to accord her partner her due share in posthumous publications (publications ostensibly effected via automatic writing). Explaining what seems to her "the most natural thing in the world," that "Martin's

structing an uncanny generic identity among women's collaborative efforts—efforts marked by "conversational" composition, dialogic interchange, felicitous sympathy, harmonious union, and, above all else, seamless production. For what the authors proclaim about themselves, their readers regularly restate: the impossibility of distinguishing one woman's writing from the other's. Thus of Michael Field, Mary Sturgeon explains: "But it is not possible, in the plays on which the two worked, to point to this line or that speech, and say 'It is the work of Michael' or 'It is the work of Henry.' You cannot do it, because the poets themselves could not have done it" (*Michael Field* 62–63). Maurice Collis writes of Somerville and Ross: "The collaboration, however, is so close that it is impossible to distinguish for certain the two hands. The miracle of a joint style is achieved" (*Somerville and Ross: A Biography* 103). And of Mary and Jane Findlater, Eileen Mackenzie observes: "It was in effect the writing of one person" (133).

Wayne Koestenbaum has argued that "a collaborative text exhibits (shamefully) symptoms of double authorship, despite the men's desire to make the work seem the product of one mind" (9). Women's collaborative writing, however, would seem to produce the reverse effect— a text so seamless as to defy the reader's most diligent efforts at discrimination. For if what Sturgeon claims of Michael Field proves true more generally—that "one may search diligently, and search in vain, for any sign in the work both wrought that this is the creation of two minds and not of one" (*Michael Field* 62)—then, for women, the marks of a dual operation can become the proof of a transcendent singularity. This collaborative model posits an inviolable space for women's shared writing remote from both masculine rivalry ("There's no 'your idea' and 'my idea,' it's completely shared"[16]) and such base material concerns as "which hand held the pen." Indeed, even where the writers are known to compose the initial portions of their texts individually, working in separate rooms and "seldom exchanging a word" with each other, as was the case with Michael Field, in the joint productions that emerge, the results appear identical: "the hand of one was indistinguishable from that of the other" (Kunitz 222).

---

mind, blended with mine, no less now than in the past, had aided, and made suggestions, taking, as ever, full share—and sometimes, I daresay, more than full share—in the task in hand," Somerville notes, "I recur to this point . . . only to clear myself to my own conscience either of taking more than my share, or, which would be equally serious, of cowardice" (*Wheel-Tracks* 273–75). Sturgeon notes a similar selflessness in Bradley's attitude toward Cooper after Cooper's death (*Michael Field* 45).

[16] Marjorie Barnard, "Marjorie Barnard *talking with* Zoe Fairbairns" 40.

If, then, as one Somerville and Ross critic suggests, collaboration marks the "revolution" that turns "two people into one writer" (Powell 7), the very success of such a union poses a critical problem, calling collaboration itself into question and thus threatening, doubly, to erase women's writing. For as this reference to Michael Field suggests, the problem of credibility puts women's dual authorship in an impossible position where it can only be believed at the price of its integrity as *double* inscription: "the diverse elements of these two minds were fused in a union so complete that the reader cannot credit a dual authorship" (Sturgeon, *Michael Field* 80–81). The productions of such a union, as standard reference works confirm, "can only be regarded as if they were by a single author." [17] Indeed, to maintain the sign of two, collaboration (as practiced by women) must be discursively reconstructed so as to undo its primary operation; the fact of a collaboration thus inevitably tends to generate a discourse that, in effect, works a reverse vanishing act, turning "one writer" back into two people—and more particularly, back into two women.

To return to Koestenbaum, then, what women's collaborative texts (shamefully) exhibit may be the *critic's* need to discriminate—to detect the *single* hand in the text and attach it to a pen and to the individual body that wields it. For in a paradox that speaks to the continued unease provoked by women's collaborative writing, what is most readily acknowledged about the practice (its seamlessness) turns out to be what is most forcefully resisted. The result is a narrative of prurient interest that confronts its uncertainties through a conflation of sexual and textual metaphors. In fact, the eroticization of the writing process would seem to be one of literary collaborations' most consistent legacies. For the metaphors of closeness, intimacy, intertwining, and reciprocity that govern double-handed writing appeal to the visual imagination, exposing the sexual underpinnings of all creative activity and authorizing speculations less immediately accessible to single-handed production. When the collaborations under consideration, however, are those between women, their representations mark a doubly problematic intersection: between codes of domesticity and the performance of female sexuality; between heterosexual conformity and lesbian difference (or differences). The need to know which author wrote which

---

[17] *Everyman's Dictionary of Literary Biography* 70. See also *The Dictionary of Irish Literature* entry for Somerville and Ross: "the collaboration was so perfect . . . . [T]he works seemed to derive from a single personality" (620), and the *Everyman* edition of M. Barnard Eldershaw's *Green Memory*, whose dust jacket proclaims, "A novel of Australian life so strongly unified in structure and feeling it seems incredible that it should be a work of collaboration."

thus frequently masks another set of questions: "Did they or didn't they? Were they or weren't they?"[18] As a response to the disturbing open-endedness of collaboration, then, the resistance to it is linked to homophobia even when not explicitly homophobic.

The discourse surrounding women's literary collaborations thus almost always appears as a discourse of voyeurism. Even the most sympathetic readers betray a fascination with the "mechanics" of collaboration, with the nuts and bolts of "how they did it." And, however much these readers applaud the writing's seamlessness, they labor to uncover the traces of individual handwritings and stylistic signatures—as if to insist that each writer stamp the work with her own personality. But as the instance of handwriting demonstrates, such bodily markings tend to be unreliable; in fact, collaborators notoriously come to write like each other, often displaying handwritings that are virtually indistinguishable. Moreover, even where individual authors can be identified, such empirical findings cannot do more than validate a moment of accidental transcription, which may or may not indicate authorial origin.

Yet if textual evidence fails to yield up the secrets of the collaboration, this has not forestalled the production of a discourse of knowingness. Sturgeon, for example, confidently claims, "One can even identify the various elements (when one knows) as more characteristic of one poet or the other" (*Michael Field* 62), although her basis for such knowledge remains vague and subjective. Collis proffers distinctions even more impressionistic; while repeatedly insisting that "to disentangle [Somerville and Ross's] individual contributions is not feasible" (65), he blithely points to certain passages that have "the feel of Martin" (103). Indeed, critical responses to the fact of a collaboration suggest that the practice can be tolerated only if demystified—i.e., only if rendered representable. Hence the relentless trotting out of a requisite set of distinguishing features: hierarchical orderings (Edith was the "senior partner," Martin was the true artist); temperamental and aesthetic discriminations ("[Jane's] nature, both in life and art, leant in the direction of the tragic . . . Mary's bent was towards comedy of manners" [Mackenzie 129]), and predictable divisions of labor ("Michael was the initiator . . . to Henry belonged especially the gift of form" [Sturgeon, *Michael Field* 62]).

Such reliance on a vocabulary of visible distinction speaks to the power of conventional notions of literary authority: of individual own-

---

[18] Dever critiques the heterosexist assumptions in such relentless and misguided questioning, arguing that "they lock the critic into a voyeuristic search for the kind of evidence seldom required to 'prove' the assumed heterosexuality of other writers" (71).

ership of literary property. It speaks as well to what Martha Vicinus has called the "insistence on visibility" (7) characteristic of both homophobic and lesbian-identified responses to the uncertainty of women's historical same-sex relationships—the figure through which the uncertainties of women's collaborative writing have so often been mediated. Not surprisingly, male collaborations yield similar hierarchies and divisions of labor, but such visible demarcations generally work to reclaim male collaborations for the mainstream. In the case of women, however, these "normalizing" procedures naturalize women's marginality to the enterprises of writing and publishing. For if seamless collaboration is what cannot be visualized, what is visualized in its place belongs to conservative histories of representation: the spectacle of woman. Indeed, faced with the challenge of a difference that is not readable in the writing, accounts of women's collaborations invariably turn to the distinctions of the body—or rather, bodies. And typically they invoke a version of the apparitional lesbian—the mannish woman—whose figure allows them to separate one partner from the other. For as Sir William Rothenstein's introduction to *Works and Days* intimates, to believe in the Michael Field collaboration one must first see the collaborators, and see them as distinguishable: "I see them in my mind's eye, Michael stout, emphatic, splendid and adventurous in talk, rich in wit; Field wan and wistful, gentler in manner than Michael, but equally eminent in the quick give and take of ideas" (*Works and Days* ix). Invoking women's lives and bodies at the site of literary production, such representations suggest that what may be obscurely repellent about women's collaborations is that their parts are not visible.

Although collaboration has long been recognized as a foundational category for feminism, the historical practice of literary collaboration has not, until recently, generated much interest among feminist literary critics.[19] Admittedly, this neglect results in part from the problem of weighing the historical evidence: Was collaboration, as practiced by women, a sufficiently widespread and coherent practice to warrant attention? Or did it consist in no more than a series of isolated instances? As with

---

[19] Laird makes a similar argument (*"On Collaborations"* 1:236). For other discussions of the place of collaboration in the history of feminism, see Marianne Hirsch's retrospective commentary in *Conflicts in Feminism* (Hirsch and Keller, "Conclusion" 380); the Abel-Gardiner debate in *Signs* (1981), which consistently links female friendship, collaboration, and (feminist) critical practice; and Mary Field Belenky et al., *Women's Ways of Knowing: The Development of Self, Voice, and Mind*, who identify collaboration as a distinctive form of "women's ways of knowing." In *A Literature of Their Own: British Women Novelists from Brontë to Lessing* (1977), Elaine Showalter noted the emergence of "sympathetically attuned women writing in teams" (30) at the turn of the century, but subsequent critics did not pursue this story.

other subjects of historical recovery, the problem posed by women's collaborative authorship hinges on a certain definitional uncertainty: How do we determine what counts as collaborative? Beyond the most explicit and self-evident instances, can we recognize collaboration when we see it—or, perhaps more precisely, when we *cannot* see it?

But I also want to argue that the particular ways early feminism defined its own recovery project ensured that its attention would be focused elsewhere, in the requirements of producing a new literary canon. Implicitly or explicitly, such a project was bound to leave the category of "author" intact, even as it taught new ways to read women's literary productions. The values collaboration celebrates (and that were seized upon by an emerging critical practice) could thus be located *within* the text—in the thematic treatment of women's affiliations and friendships; in the formal performance of double-voicedness—and in the interaction *between* text and reader. Consequently, writing in 1981, Elizabeth Abel could maintain that "the clearest emphasis on a collaborative relationship that echoes the dynamics of female bonding occurs in reader-response criticism" ("[E]merging Identities: The Dynamics of Female Friendship in Contemporary Fiction by Women" 434).

With increased knowledge about women's authorial relationships, both in producing literature and producing feminist criticism, we might now shift this emphasis to the practice of collaborative authorship. And within this framework, women's turn-of-the-century literary praxis assumes new interest, providing a kind of limit case for the theory it anticipates.[20] For even if the authors in question hardly saw themselves as transforming the nature of authorship, it would be possible to extrapolate from their collaborative practice the basis for a new aesthetic; grounded in the intimacy of private affection and informed throughout by shared authority, not to mention a communal production strategy, such an aesthetic would have everything to do with what feminist criticism has claimed to value.

The conversational method, moreover, attested to by so many female collaborators, whereby a book was literally talked and argued into existence, invites speculation into women's differential relationship to private and public, to speech and writing.[21] As Edith Somerville explains,

[20] Taking a different approach to the subject, Holly Laird provocatively links Michael Field's poetic practice to the project of feminist recovery, noting its emphasis on "archival creativity" in its reclaiming of distant historical subjects ("Contradictory Legacies" 112). Laird's excellent study shares many interests with mine, including an emphasis on the contradictory legacy of figures like Michael Field for modern feminist inquiry.

[21] This emphasis on "conversation" continues to define women's present day collaborations. As Laird notes, "I am struck by the fact that all the collaborative writers who have taken part in this forum recur to one phenomenon: that of conversation" ("On Collaborations" 1 : 12).

to "those who may be interested in an unimportant detail," her collaborative work was done "conversationally":

> One or the other—not infrequently both, simultaneously—would state a proposition. This would be argued, combated perhaps, approved, or modified; it would then be written down by the (wholly fortuitous) holder of the pen, would be scratched out, scribbled in again; before it found itself finally transferred into decorous MS. it would probably have suffered many things, but it would, at all events, have had the advantage of being well aired. (Somerville and Ross, *Irish Memories* 136)[22]

Positing a form of women's writing that privileges the interactive features of orality ("in a nutshell, they talked their stories," Somerville's nephew explains),[23] collaboration could even be seen to open up the possibility for a model of literary production explicitly feminist in orientation. For it projects a paradigm that might upset the decorum of masculine prototypes: of the single writer, diligently composing at his desk in a room of *his* own—the private, professional space of his study. In fact, as Edith Somerville suggests, the "writing" could take place anywhere: "There, prone on the yellow sand, we lay and talked and wrote, bit by bit" (qtd. in Robinson 43).

From this perspective, collaborative writing by women, as it articulates itself in the turn-of-the-century British literary arena, could be seen as the precursor of a self-consciously feminist critical practice that emerged in the academy in the 1970s. For the dramatic appearance of dual authorship in feminist criticism and theory at the very moment feminism began to establish itself academically was no simple accident. As Gilbert and Gubar claim in the introduction to *The Madwoman in the Attic*, it is, at least implicitly, an intervention that facilitates—and is in some sense inseparable from—the project of transforming the terms of literary study: "Redefining what has so far been male-defined literary history in the same way that women writers have revised 'patriarchal poetics,' we have found that the process of collaboration has given us the essential support we needed to complete such an ambitious project" (xiii). Moreover, among the stories Gilbert and Gubar tell of their own joint writing effort are ones fully consonant with the prototypes of their

---

[22] Similarly, Marjorie Barnard explains, "we talked . . . . We discussed every aspect until we came to agreement" ("Gentle Art" 126). For Somerville and Ross, even the letters they wrote to each other—their "bed-sheets"—were conceived as a vehicle for conversation. As Lewis points out, both women commonly referred to their letters as "talking" (*Selected Letters of Somerville and Ross* xix). As I discuss in Chapter 4, this was also the case for their automatic writing.

[23] Sir Patrick Coghill, "Opening Address," 6.

collaborative predecessors. Thus in a 1986 *Ms.* magazine interview, they describe their work on "the sequel to *Madwoman*."

GILBERT: [T]here are something like five enormous chapters in the opening sections, and we've been writing every word together.
INTERVIEWER: You mean one of you sits at the typewriter and the other leans over her shoulder?
GILBERT: We each have a notebook, and we both write the same words in the notebook. We sit there with our notebooks, and we—
GUBAR: And we talk.

("Gilbert and Gubar" 60)

The remarkable uniformity in the narratives told about women's turn-of-the-century collaborative writing might, then, hold a particular interest for feminist critics. Indeed, in the case of Gilbert and Gubar, it might shed light on their "invention" of a practice in whose history they participate. This is not, however, to suggest some general trans-historic truth about women who write together; rather, to read these historically distanced practices against each other is to investigate the cultural needs, at specific historical moments, that produced collabora-tion as this particular spectacle and to question the cultural needs that fuel current feminist interest in (and resistance to) the subject. For as the very different deployment of collaboration in other theoretical ex-amples might suggest, women's collaborative writing does not function as a monolithic entity, a universally understood and available feminist strategy. Accordingly, Gilbert and Gubar have been quick to disavow any strategic or political intention, representing their decision to col-laborate in much the way, as the next chapter will illustrate, turn-of-the-century authors did: as something they stumbled upon. "[O]ur col-laboration wasn't the result of a conscious political decision," Gilbert explains. "It was something exciting and fascinating that happened to us" ("An Interview" 37).

While admitting that the success of their collaboration has "some-thing to do with what is now called 'feminist process,'" Gilbert and Gu-bar define that process personally, inverting feminism's early rallying cry of "The personal is political." Their work, Gilbert suggests, grows instead out of "the notion that the political (or the poetical) is the per-sonal." "I'd say we *felt* our ideas, at that point," she goes on, "with a pas-sion that could only lead to friendship" ("An Interview" 38). On these terms, they can similarly maintain that they "feel" that their books are "fully collaborative," even when they draft individual chapters single-handedly (*No Man's Land* 2:xvii) .

But as Catherine Clément and Hélène Cixous dramatically demonstrate in their very different joint writing, both the terms "feminist process" and "fully collaborative" can be understood—and performed—differently. As their experience illustrates, moreover, collaboration *can* originate in an intentional political process, as an extension of political activism.[24] Thus in *The Newly Born Woman*, in the place of Gilbert and Gubar's rhetoric of dialogue and consensus, Clément and Cixous assert productive and unresolvable difference—a confrontational "dual discourse" of ideological embattlement and utopian possibilities. And where Gilbert and Gubar markedly divide their responsibilities, attributing individual authorship (in prefatory remarks) to the parts of a text that stand as a seamless whole, Clément and Cixous divide the printed page, producing a text whose evident sutures disrupt the reading process and call into question authorship itself.[25]

These differences, explained in part by the philosophical positions we once labeled "Anglo-American" and "French," unsettle the fundamental terms of collaborative difference: the understanding of singularity and doubleness. And they diverge, among other things, at the place where women's intimate friendships engage lesbian sexuality, where passion *can* lead to something other than friendship. It is perhaps no accident, then, that in a recent forum on collaboration, the assertion of collaboration *as* feminist practice—the insistence that collaboration be seen as "a political act with political consequences"—was voiced most distinctly by collaborators who represented themselves as openly lesbian.[26] These competing understandings of the collaborative project might help to explain why, as Holly Laird suggests, feminist collaboration has remained undertheorized; and they might help to explain why feminists jointly engaged in the project of literary recovery have not in fact seized upon their historical doubles: literary women who wrote together. For collaborative practices are embedded in specific personal and historical circumstances, raising the question of what exactly one might be taking on in claiming ideological kinship. Moreover, the double writing of women in Great Britain at the turn of the century, to the extent that it forms something of a cohesive unit, is not the only

---

[24] See "Interview with Hélène Cixous."

[25] As the range of stylistic voices that Laird showcases demonstrate (from the unified voice of conventional academic criticism to the aggressively performative or "experimental" split subject), present-day collaborators continue to exploit the different models of articulation collaboration facilitates. See "On Collaborations."

[26] Leonardi and Pope, for example, subtitle their essay, "Collaboration as Feminist Practice." As they suggest, moreover, collaboration *can* function as a form of lesbian seduction. Carey Kaplan and Ellen Cronan Rose, in "Strange Bedfellows: Feminist Collaboration," also claim collaboration as a feminist political act they name "lesbian," although they acknowledge that they are not lovers.

available model for collaborative precursors. Following a trajectory mapped in feminist criticism, this writing practice might be profitably read against its "French" counterpart: the double writing of the expatriate lesbian community located in Paris at the start of the twentieth century.

Within feminist literary studies, this latter group has received a significant share of critical attention, notably through such important works of recovery as Shari Benstock's *Women of the Left Bank*. Gilbert and Gubar also find a place for these writers in *No Man's Land*, their remapping of the literary history of modernism. Indeed, in the no man's land of lesbian poetics, collaboration receives from Gilbert and Gubar its fullest expression. But the "collaboration" they here associate with a lesbian aesthetic remains as ghostly as the one *Madwoman* adumbrated: the woman writer's collaboration with her own dark double. For as Gilbert and Gubar now define it, collaboration operates "spiritually," as the (single) author's relation to an empowering predecessor. The model for all lesbian collaboration thus becomes collaboration with Sappho.

Such a model, however, has obvious limitations once other understandings of collaboration are activated; thus even where the paradigm would seem most apt, as in Michael Field's *Long Ago*—a literal extension of Sappho's lyrics—the precise nature of the collaboration remains slippery.[27] Although Michael Field invokes her "collaborator" in the preface to the volume—"I have turned to the one woman who has dared to speak unfalteringly of the fearful mastery of love"—that "one woman," as Christine White points out, may be "either Sappho, a lover or a writing partner," an ambiguity White finds productive for rethinking "the presentation of love between women on the basis of the available cultural models" (201).

On the basis of the available cultural models, however, Gilbert and Gubar's constructions seem unnecessarily confining. Indeed, as Anne Herrmann has argued, the location of lesbian writing in *No Man's Land*—and, more precisely, its construction as "double talk"—leaves the lesbian writer outside Gilbert and Gubar's recuperative literary history, confined to a set of categories that continue to marginalize her: loneliness, collusion, pain, and isolation (511). If the avowedly lesbian relationships of these Parisian women put into relief the reticences that construct British women's "friendships," they also put into relief the different ways "talk" is conceptualized; for the talk that defines British women's partnership productions is almost invariably represented as utopian. *No Man's Land's* alternate representation thus suggests that talk

[27] For an excellent discussion of collaboration and lesbian poetics in *Long Ago*, see Prins, "Sappho Doubled: Michael Field."

becomes duplicitous—i.e., becomes double talk—precisely at the moment it might be read as sexual conversation. Figured through collaboration, the question thus remains, On what terms can lesbian authorship (and experience) be accommodated into mainstream feminist criticism?

Treating Gilbert and Gubar as symptomatic of "the nervous state of feminist criticism in a postfeminist age," Maureen Corrigan argues that the terms for such accommodation are simply not available, especially for authors who wish to address an audience wider than the academy. Taking the authors' dedication to *No Man's Land*, then, as her point of departure for a review in *The Village Voice*, Corrigan explains, "Gilbert and Gubar, feminist criticism's most famous duo, have always used such opportunities to announce, 'We're *not* lesbians'" (53). And to underline this point, the *Voice* includes a photograph whose caption reads, "Just good friends: Gilbert and Gubar contemplate modernism." But Corrigan's attack, as much as Gilbert and Gubar's defensive self-presentations, suggests the prurient interest women's collaborations continue to generate. For if, as Corrigan suggests, the "'we love men' dedications" signal that "Gilbert and Gubar don't want their colleagues to confuse them with the deviant literary company they keep" (53), this anxiety of identification has a specific location in a particular act of deviancy: the act of writing together. Indeed, the celebrity status Gilbert and Gubar currently enjoy, as the numerous articles and interviews testify, would seem to have everything to do with the company they keep—the company they keep with each other. It is not surprising, then, that Gilbert and Gubar should carefully circumscribe their writing relationship.

What is striking, though, is the extent to which, in doing so, they reproduce tropes employed by their turn-of-the-century predecessors. Indeed Gilbert and Gubar seem at pains to domesticate—even trivialize—their undertaking, relegating it to the conventionally feminized sphere of the "psychologically useful": a support service, a form of nurturing, a kind of cheerleading, an act of comforting. Unlike the lesbian writers, as *No Man's Land* represents them, whose "fantastic" collaborations cannot conceal the loneliness, pain, and treachery of their separate existences, Gilbert and Gubar, in their "real" collaboration foreground companionship and pleasure that is distinctly unthreatening—"just having fun," as Gilbert puts it.[28]

Yet given the institutional stature accorded to the Gilbert and Gubar insignia, such disarming self-representations would seem to border on

---

[28] This phrase appears in "A Conversation with Sandra M. Gilbert" (109); for the other collaborative tropes mentioned above, see "A Conversation" (96 and 109) and "An Interview" (38).

the duplicitous, suggesting as they do a complicitous relation between the practice of feminist collaboration and the performance of a culturally determined femininity.[29] As such, they might help explain why for all their talk of collaboration, Gilbert and Gubar do not seem to recognize collaboration as a category of *writing*. For when they do not insistently and narrowly personalize their collaboration, they come close to universalizing it out of existence, intuiting a place where all (women's) writing is some kind of collaboration with (women) readers and, more important, female literary predecessors. It is perhaps no accident that in the one place Gilbert and Gubar devote sustained attention to writing they designate as collaborative (in their chapter on lesbian double talk) those collaborations are explicitly marked as *metaphorical*; for "[w]hether lesbian authors wrote 'as' an ancient precursor associated with lesbian love or 'for' a lesbian lover," these choices leave no space for writing "with" the other (*No Man's Land* 2:222). Indeed, it could be argued, to borrow from Terry Castle, that Gilbert and Gubar invoke "the apparitional collaborator" at the site of lesbian literary production.[30] And much as Castle suggests that the apparitional lesbian often served a blocking function, diverting the gaze from the "reality" of lesbianism, for Gilbert and Gubar, the fantasy collaborator stands in for her material embodiment, enabling them *not* to see "real" collaborators even when they are right in front of them.

Gilbert and Gubar, in fact, have little to say about collaborations that are not metaphoric. The work of Michael Field, for example, receives but a glancing reference. And in the case of Renée Vivien and Natalie Barney, key figures in the Parisian lesbian artistic community, only their solo work commands Gilbert and Gubar's attention. Yet as Karla Jay has documented, both collaborated with other women in works not unconnected to their lesbian poetic identities.[31] These collaborative engagements, however, receive no notice in Gilbert and Gubar's treatment. Nor do the more material collaborations that Shari Benstock documents: the

---

[29] Janice Doane and Devon Hodges specifically address these issues in their account of their collaboration as feminist critics: "While our collaboration, both in practice and in content, explicitly works to provide a subversive alternative to patriarchal norms, it is also being produced within a patriarchal culture in ways that we want to explore" ("Writing from the Trenches: Women's Work and Collaborative Writing" 53).

[30] From this perspective, Amy Lowell's tribute to Somerville and Ross is also interesting, for she invokes the ghost of these real collaborators (whose personal relationship avoided sexual commitment) at the site of her own poetic practice—a "metaphorical" collaboration with her flesh-and-blood lover. To the "two unknown ladies," she thus writes, "I open up the queerest possibility,/ Namely: the visitation of a ghost."

[31] Jay discusses Barney's collaboration with Romaine Brooks, with her mother, and with Liane de Pougy (*The Amazon and the Page: Natalie Clifford Barney and Renée Vivien* 32, 91). She also discusses Vivien's alleged collaboration with the Baroness de Zuylen de Nyevelt in work published under the name Paule Riversdale (17–18).

collaborative efforts of women such as Nancy Cunard and Sylvia Beach, who supported the artists of the Left Bank as advisers, patrons, publishers, printers, and booksellers. Finally, when the question of *literal* collaboration becomes unavoidable, as in their discussion of Gertrude Stein's *The Autobiography of Alice B. Toklas*, Gilbert and Gubar decode the text's collaborative markings to uncover the single author beneath— only *their* single author turns out to be Toklas.

Collaborative writing, then, to follow Anne Herrmann's lead, remains, like lesbian writing, outside Gilbert and Gubar's literary history. In Terry Castle's terms, one might say it has been "ghosted." And *as writing*, it remains outside Gilbert and Gubar's construction of their own feminist authority. "To the extent that we are attacked by ultraconservatives as well as radicals who don't think we're 'feminist enough,'" Gubar explains, "collaboration really is a solace because it's easier to laugh with someone else. And you can reassure yourself that at least you think what you're doing is important and what you believe in"; "collaboration is a very special solace," Gilbert agrees; "It's like having someone else around to hold your hand while you leap into the abyss" ("An Interview" 38). But seen in a historical perspective, the joining of hands collaboration represents may be less a solace for than the locus of this impossible middle position.

Much of the difficulty in placing women's collaborative writing within a feminist perspective derives, I am arguing, from the problematic nature of the particular categories it activates—women's friendships, lesbian identity, double-voiced writing, female agency—categories themselves the subject of continuing, often contentious, feminist debate and discussion. Looking at the silences within much early feminism, for example, some recent critics have critiqued its celebration of women's friendship. "[F]riendship is typically constructed by the same ideas that construct the couple: seamless harmony," Mary Childers writes; and, as bell hooks explains, this is a construction that cannot readily confront or accommodate difference (Childers and hooks 79).

The insistence, then, on both the seamlessness of the writing and the "perfect, absolute equality" of the friendship in leading narratives of women's collaborations can be seen to lock these unions into the problematics of the idealized couple.[32] As such, it can also be seen to lock them out of a space for confronting lesbian difference. For the model of

---

[32] Lillian Faderman uses these terms ("perfect, absolute equality") to describe the relationships between Somerville and Ross and between Bradley and Cooper (*Surpassing the Love of Men: Romantic Friendship and Love between Women from the Renaissance to the Present* 213). Although Whitney Chadwick and Isabelle de Courtivron in *Significant Others* work with a less idealized image of the couple, their insistence on a sexual as well as artistic union could exclude all of the writing partners I have been considering here.

the idealized couple suggests either a relationship no different from a heterosexual one or, more commonly, the "sexless" union hypothesized by Faderman and others in the concept of romantic friendship. But if such a construct cannot sufficiently explain the life and work of these literary partnerships, neither can an identity-politics approach to lesbian studies that insists on visible proof of the sexual nature of the relationships.[33] Indeed, none of these partnerships can be proved to be lesbian in the term's most restrictive meaning. These unions thus remain resistant to even the most readily available interpretive structures contemporary feminism has generated. If they constitute what might be called "'lesbian' co-authorship," they are, as Laird suggests of Michael Field, "particularly unusual instances" of it ("Contradictory Legacies" 112). Contemporary critics, then, seeking in these partnerships prototypes for a distinctly lesbian writing practice, have not always been satisfied by what they have found there.

Faced with this dilemma, Christine White, in a recent study of Michael Field, turns to the collaboration itself—to "the development of the poetic persona Michael Field" (208)—to attempt to articulate an alternative position. But collaboration does not so much resolve the dilemma as replicate the paradox that constructs it. For, ironically, much of what White critiques in the concept of romantic friendship—its celebration of such "conventional attributes of femininity" as "passivity, gentleness, domesticity, creativity and supportiveness" (206)—applies to collaborative writing with at least equal vigor, at least to collaborative writing as Katherine Bradley, Edith Cooper, and other women of this period practice it. Part of the problem, then, of claiming women's literary collaborations for a feminist agenda lies in the ways they have functioned historically to enforce, as much as subvert, conventional gender hierarchies. The difficulty lies as well, as I will argue in the next section, in the way collaboration underscores the fractures within feminism: at once the hallmark of its promise and the site of its unraveling.

In recent years, the solidarity that once made collaboration appear a fitting emblem for feminist criticism has itself come under scrutiny, as mainstream feminism has attempted to come to terms with the voices

[33] For an overview of these problems within lesbian studies, see Martha Vicinus, ed., *Lesbian Subjects: A Feminist Studies Reader*. See also Lisa Moore, "Something More Tender Than Friendship: Romantic Friendship in Early Nineteenth-Century England," for a more sexualized reading of these relationships. In her study of Michael Field's lesbian poetics, Christine White, in "'Poets and Lovers Evermore': Interpreting Female Love in the Poetry and Journals of Michael Field," critiques Faderman (and by extension, much contemporary lesbian studies) for promoting a view of "lesbianism" or "women's romantic friendships" that insists on its desexualization.

of other women—women who, in Helena Michie's terms, are "not one of the family."[34] These voices, urging the specific claims of different races, classes, sexualities, and ethnicities, have challenged the common usages of the category "woman," raising the question of *which* women come together in the practices of feminism—and the practices of literature. While collaboration has reemerged as a powerful site for differentiating writing by women, the terms of the practice have undergone significant transformation.

This new awareness of the possibilities of collaboration has coincided with feminism's study of its own history and literature. Locating a shift in feminist debate from a focus on theoretical differences to an emphasis on institutional histories—a shift she traces to "around 1981"—Jane Gallop, for example, has turned her exacting attention to feminist critical anthologies. And she chooses them, she suggests, precisely because of their collaborative structure, because they "may be the best place to hear that collective subject" (*Around 1981* 8)—the historical agent of feminism. Updating Gallop, Holly Laird argues that, "[a]round 1991" literary scholars began to take up "the question of collaboration in feminist scholarship and women's literature" ("On Collaborations" 1:235).

Yet feminism's increasing self-consciousness about its collaborative bases continues to be vexed by the gap between theory and practice, vexed by the contradictions historical collaborators embody. Indeed, the tropes that recur with such persistence throughout the reception history of literary collaborations enjoy a strange afterlife in the latest articulations of the subject—perhaps nowhere more so than in the compulsion to produce the shadow figure of "the other woman." If the otherness of the other woman has taken on more complex and varied trappings, she functions nonetheless in much the same way as earlier manifestations of the apparitional lesbian. Much of the current discourse on collaboration, then, continues to depend on displacements of the sort that have insistently read collaboration and lesbianism through each other; and even as it points to the blind spots in earlier discussions, this new discourse stages its own resistance to collaboration in the very process of talking about it.

Taking Gallop's work, then, as symptomatic of this discourse, I want to investigate the scene of writing she calls collaborative. I begin with

[34] See "Not One of the Family: The Repression of the Other Woman in Feminist Theory," where Helena Michie performs symptomatic readings of three works of feminist theory, including Jane Gallop's "Annie Leclerc." My reading shares with Michie's an interest in how texts like Gallop's "simultaneously are and are not about the other woman, how they make textual space for her entrance onto the scene of feminist criticism and close it off" (19).

"Annie Leclerc Writing a Letter, with Vermeer," an essay that appears to work through a kind of collaborative layering. First appearing in 1985, Gallop's essay turns the plight of "the other woman" into something of a slogan: "We must know the women of another class," Gallop writes, "whose labor we rely on so that we can write"; "let us not forget the other woman" ("Annie Leclerc" 146, 154). Using Leclerc's "La lettre d'amour" to stage a critical intervention, Gallop grafts another lesbian love letter onto the letter Leclerc is writing. But the connection to the "other woman" Gallop applauds in Leclerc's writing remains in the realm of the imaginary, distinct from any material practice. In fact, Leclerc's "real" flesh-and-blood partner (the ostensible addressee of her letter) has been pushed out of sight by an "apparitional" lesbian: the serving woman in a Vermeer painting.

In Gallop's hands, then, Leclerc's lesbian love letter becomes "a meditation on, an explication of" Vermeer's "Lady Writing a Letter and her Maidservant" (144). But if Gallop figures Leclerc as collaborating "with Vermeer," Gallop's own writing "with Leclerc" replicates an earlier critical gesture that finds the analogue for feminist collaboration in reader-response criticism. For so closely does Gallop track her subject that what she calls "reading" enacts a form of ghostwriting. Reading Leclerc (as Leclerc writes a love letter), Gallop writes *to* and *with* her, replicating Leclerc's intervention in the closed circuit of desire that separates woman from woman.

The result is a radical "revision" of Vermeer's painting, with the maid who stands behind and apart from the writing woman now imagined as source and addressee of the lady's letter. This gesture, however, has its limits, for as Gallop argues, the act of writing figured in the picture highlights the rift the letter mediates: *between* women who write and those who (silently) serve them (mistress and maid); *within* the woman writer, who experiences writing as self-division. As Gallop illustrates, moreover, in relocating the difference between women within the privileged woman (whose left hand plays "woman-servant" to her right hand's "woman-mistress"), Leclerc risks writing the other woman out of the picture. Indeed, as Gallop notes in a kind of afterword, the cover to the volume where Leclerc's essay appears does this literally, reproducing Vermeer's painting with the maidservant deleted. Gallop's essay thus becomes "a meditation on, an explication of" the price we pay for our investment in "the single woman writing," the "woman alone at her writing table" (154)—the informing image of so much feminist criticism.

As a contribution to the discourse of collaboration as practiced by women, "Annie Leclerc" holds interest for a number of reasons—not least of them the way it links the performance of collaboration to the question of "the other woman": the lesbian woman in Leclerc's address; the woman of another class or race brought forward in Gallop's intervention. As such it reminds us of what may be suppressed or repressed in the "seamlessness" celebrated by pairs of writing women; in fact, if we turn to the writing partners discussed earlier in this chapter, it becomes clear that it is those women's very *sameness* (reinforced by ties of family) that makes possible the fiction of an untroubled unity in their collaborative engagements.

What Michael Field, for example, says of her circle of friends circumscribes even more closely the circle of two that constitutes her writing union: "We enjoy our allusive, literary English humour, fantastic, full of tolerance and banter. We are glad no American, Jew or Alien is among us" (*Works and Days* 267). As Edith Somerville explains, such similarities of class and upbringing make collaboration feasible: "For my part, it seems to me only natural that given similar conditions of life and general out-look on the world, they should evoke a similar point of view" ("Two of a Trade" 182). And as Martin Ross intimates (anticipating Leclerc and Gallop in her invocation of hands divided from each other), collaboration might heal the rift not only between but within women; for in her representation, successful collaboration does not so much enact as erase difference: "The reason few people can [write together], is because they have separate minds upon most subjects and fight their own hands all the time" ("Two of a Trade" 182). But in this formulation, only those who share a common inheritance can escape division. As important, then, as the question women's literary collaborations pose as to "how two women do it" is the affirmation they underwrite of the shared class status that makes literary writing—singly or doubly—appear "only natural."

Against this vision of collaboration as the natural extension of a singular identity (one mind, two bodies), Gallop offers the fantasy of an exchange across class (and by extension race) that has traditionally split along these axes: the power of the one woman to play mind to the other woman's body. Gallop's essay anticipates a shift in her own critical thinking away from "things French" to a new set of questions (marked here in terms borrowed from Gayatri Spivak)—questions with particular urgency for feminism: "not merely 'who am I?' But 'who is the other woman?'" ("Annie Leclerc" 154).[35] This shift, as Gallop later explains,

[35] See Michie for a provocative discussion of Gallop's use—and reuse—of this Spivak quotation, which, she argues, produces the effect of Gallop quoting herself ("Not One of the Family" 25); "The question, 'who is the Other woman,'" Michie argues, thus "transforms itself . . . into the questionable statement 'The Other Woman is myself'" (27).

participates in a growing self-consciousness among a number of academic feminists as to the exclusions written into their ruling definitions and public practices of collectivity ("The Coloration of Academic Feminism," in *Around 1981*). Yet Gallop's call for "greater future understanding" of the "rifts in an imaginary feminine and feminist plenitude" ("Annie Leclerc" 153) does not involve a "dialogue" with the "other woman"; like Leclerc's "transference" onto Vermeer's maid—or for that matter, her letter to her lover—the collaboration remains apparitional. In fact, insofar as Gallop's text can be called "collaborative," it is Leclerc's text that provides the "other" voice for Gallop's interior monologue.

Gallop's later account of her commitment to putting "color" into the text of feminist criticism recasts the other woman as a "real life" personage—the African-American scholar Deborah McDowell. As with the earlier instance of transference in "Annie Leclerc," this one also depends, in Gallop's words, on a "non-encounter." Asked on whom she "transfers" now that she has done with Lacan, Gallop recalls, "My first thought was to say 'no one.' And then one of the things I thought of was a non-encounter with Deborah McDowell" ("Criticizing Feminist Criticism" 363).[36] "For McDowell, whom I do not know," Gallop goes on to explain, "read black feminist critic. I realize that the set of feelings that I used to have about French men I now have about African-American women. Those are the people I feel inadequate in relation to and try to please in my writing" (363–64).

Gallop's engagement with race as an issue of urgency coincides with her re-reading of American feminist literary history—with her entering into dialogue with other women who share certain features of training, background, and institutional authority. Gallop's invocation of the other woman thus occurs in the context of a shared white middle-class identity and of a feminist history that affirms that the personal is political. When Gallop installs "the other woman" in her own psyche, she can affirm, then, that this turn is "not just idiosyncratic": "The way McDowell has come to occupy the place of Lacan in my psyche does seem to correspond to the way that emphasis on race has replaced for me something like French vs. American feminism" ("Criticizing Feminist Criticism" 364). Indeed, similar gestures of "inclusion" have begun to appear with such frequency that McDowell has recently critiqued the way (white) academic feminists have appropriated women of color to provide the "politics" for their "theory."

---

[36] In *Around 1981*, Gallop reinvokes the idea of a non-encounter, arguing that the reason race "is such a heated topic now" for white academic feminists (as opposed to the 1970s) is that it is now "also a debate about the institutional status of feminist criticism, an anxious non-encounter with the fact of our specific location as insiders" (6).

Insofar, then, as this critical turn can be seen as representative, it speaks to a new politics and a new poetics—as well as a new problematic—of collaboration in feminist critical practice in the academy. In *Conflicts in Feminism*, an anthology of feminist criticism, Marianne Hirsch and Evelyn Fox Keller jointly describe their mission: "Most importantly, we felt a certain urgency about identifying better strategies for practicing conflict, for restoring dialogue where it had broken down, and perhaps especially, for reviving the joys and pleasures of working together as feminists, for making productive our multiple and manifold differences" (3). In fact, almost every entry in the text engages to some degree in an effort to be "fully collaborative," even if only acknowledged as such in the footnotes. The vision of collaboration, however, as the volume represents it—both in terms of the embedded voices within single-authored contributions and the dialogues, conversations, and dual-authored pieces—highlights struggle, conflict, and difficulty along with "the joys and pleasures of working together"; where earlier feminist practice offered a utopian vision of collectivity, more recent work tends to emphasize—and often self-consciously stage—its difficulty.[37] To do otherwise, Gallop suggests, impedes the work of collectivity ("Criticizing Feminist Criticism" 367).

Against this articulation of collaboration as a feminist goal and problematic, the stories I have been tracking of women who wrote literature together—as much as a hundred years before these contemporary theorists—sound decidedly outdated, relying as they do on a rhetoric of perfect harmony and mutual assimilation. Indeed, one might question whether these literary partnerships really challenged the myth of the solitary author (the woman alone at her writing table) or reproduced it as an "individualism of two"—a union so complete as to make the partners, in effect, one author. Certainly, the particular ease and comfort in their union that the literary collaborators project (and that is consistently projected onto them) forecloses other understandings of the nonsolitary creative effort—what, for example, Hirsch and Keller have called "Conversations Across Differences." In fact, reading these earlier creative practices against the performance of recent theory, one might wonder what the two can say to each other. For their "non-encounter"

---

[37] Hirsch and Keller, for example, ultimately split their voices in the volume's conclusion, ending with "a final 'conversation'" that literally splits the page between them (380–85). This split, they argue, is necessary to give voice to the differences between women even as similarly positioned as they are: "Aware that we were acting out our own version of the practice of conflict in the practice of feminism, we came to see that no conclusion written under a single signature could do justice to the differences between the positions even we inhabit" (380).

raises questions about the commensurability between historically specific creative and critical practices as well as between feminine and feminist interactions—between the joys and pleasures of working together
and the concomitant gratification of working together *as feminists*.

In fact, while some turn-of-the-century collaborators identified with
such feminist causes as suffrage, a history of literary collaboration suggests no necessary connection between such affiliations and the decision to write jointly. Nor did these writing partners generally see their
writing as inherently progressive; for the most part, they appeared
content to be praised for their old-fashioned qualities and, at best,
"mildly feminist" themes. Marjorie Barnard, then, may be typical in insisting that she "never wrote politically" and that she never wrote "as a
woman."[38] Indeed, when asked how she sees herself as an author, she
shrinks from what she perceives as the subtext of the question: "Certainly not as a woman writer, if that's what you mean. I don't believe
there is such a thing" ("Marjorie Barnard" 41, 39).

Even where these writers more openly acknowledge their political
investments, they tend to represent their political beliefs and aesthetic
practices as no more than complementary. Moreover, if what Gifford
Lewis suggests of Somerville and Ross—that these literary women were
before their time in their commitment, as writers, to the professionalization of women— can be argued more generally, they saw this commitment in the fact of their authorship rather than in their method of
composition. Indeed, these collaborators did not necessarily see their
practice as specific to women. When Edith Cooper, for example, describes the "Michael Field" collaboration, she casts the practice in terms
of male precedent: "My Aunt and I work together after the fashion of
Beaumont and Fletcher" (*Works and Days* 3). And when subsequent
commentators seek analogues for it, they turn to things French—and
things male—for the closest approximation: "Yet there is hardly an English precedent for their career; and it is to France that one must look—
to the Goncourts or to Erckmann-Chatrian—to match the long collaboration, or to find similar examples of their artistic method" (Sturgeon,
Michael Field 239).

Yet if we take seriously the call to remember the other woman, these
literary partnerships are worth remembering—precisely because they
remind us of what changing feminist practices can and cannot assimi-

---

[38] This assertion contrasts with those of interviewers and critics who have stressed the
authors' political commitments. See, for example, Dever: "Both were also active in Left
cultural affairs in the 1930s and 1940s and played influential roles in politicizing the Fel-
lowship of Australian Writers (FAW)" (66). *Tomorrow and Tomorrow and Tomorrow* was, in
fact, censored because of its political content when it first appeared in 1947.

late. They are worth remembering, moreover, because the terms of their reception continue to haunt us, delimiting the way collaboration gets talked about in even the most sophisticated discussions. Indeed, the compulsion to repeat certain stories about collaboration in very differently motivated readings has prevented us from apprehending other stories about collaboration's historical and theoretical operation. If looking back on these partnerships today we can question whether they go far enough in challenging conventions of authorship and conventions of gender, this does not render them trivial. Indeed, simply by putting women's collaborations on the (writing) table, these practices disturb the solitary writer's comfortable occupancy of that position. If contemporary feminists have provoked this disturbance differently, collaboration, as historically practiced by women, provides them with theoretical access to the conversations foreclosed in the institutionalized histories of writing.

Among these conversations, as I argue in Chapter 4, are ones that take the fantasy of collaboration to its logical limits, rendering it, in the practice of automatic writing, the ultimate vehicle for Otherness: a means of conversing with the dead. But before turning to collaboration's outer reaches, I want to return in the next chapter to the literary partnerships this chapter has featured. For, I will argue, they have a story to tell too easily masked by a critical emphasis on collaboration's phantasmagoric and transgressive features: the story of literary collaboration as a prime, if vexed, avenue for women's professionalism.

3

Two of a Trade
Partners in Writing (1880–1930)

In June 1905 Violet Martin wrote to her cousin Edith Somerville, complaining of one of the fools she was forced to suffer. Having been asked to contribute to a volume memorializing her brother, the popular journalist and songwriter, "Ballyhooley Martin," Violet bristles when the book's sponsor sees her only as a woman: not an author in her own right but the sister of one.

> The gist of it all is the book is to be crown octavo—and as well as I could make out, my part is to be about 15000 words! He said "about twelve columns of *The Times*—but you write all you like, and we can select what is wanted"—I at once said that I was too busy to write stuff that might not be wanted, and he seemed quite surprised—I dont think he at all realises the position, or that I am a professional writer. (*Selected Letters of Somerville and Ross* 278)

By contrast, when Violet Martin writes to her cousin, she writes to someone who will recognize her professionalism—someone who occupies the same position that she does. For by 1905, Edith Somerville (E. Œ. Somerville) and Violet Martin ("Martin Ross") had, as Somerville and Ross, made quite a name for themselves in Irish fiction.[1] Yet as Martin's letter suggests, many men were still incapable of even imagining a woman writing professionally.

Given the force of such residual sentiments, it is perhaps not surprising that even as barriers appeared to be lifting for women, professional

---

[1] By this time, Violet Martin had also established herself as a journalist in single-handed productions. In this chapter, I have tried to use the name "Ross" to refer to the authorial persona and "Martin" for the historical personage. Such naming is especially confusing since Violet Martin also used "Martin" as a personal name; when Somerville, for example, uses this name for her partner, it is almost always as a given name.

authorship remained for many an elusive objective. Yet for a number of women who began their literary careers at the turn of the century, they could imagine this end if they imagined themselves writing together—supported by another who shared their aspirations and ambitions.[2] For a number of women, moreover, the joint labor they conceived (and practiced) was more than figurative: they made themselves authors by *writing* together. These writing unions, appearing at a historical moment when both the profession of authorship and the expectations of gender were undergoing significant transformation, offer unusual insight into the means by which women like Violet Martin could learn to say, "I am a professional writer."

Like the Brontës before them—and like other contemporary women—Somerville and Ross did not set out to write professionally when they took up the idea of collaborating in fiction. Like other collaborators (the Brontës included), they began to write as a kind of game, and they practiced their writing in secret. But what began in the spirit of friendship and adventure—the cementing of a bond between two newfound cousins—quickly grew into a serious undertaking whose success defied all expectations, earning for the authors both critical acclaim and an immense readership. It earned them the right, moreover, to proclaim themselves in all seriousness "Two of a Trade"—the half-ironic title under which Somerville would later celebrate their union. Somerville and Ross, in fact, accomplished what might be the ultimate professional achievement: brand-name recognition. For their name became (and continues to be) the signature for a distinctive literary product: "the Ireland of Somerville and Ross," "the world of the Irish R. M." (the Irish "Resident Magistrate" popularized in their stories). With sixteen books appearing between 1889 and 1915, and, after Ross's death in 1915, another fourteen books appearing under their dual name, "Somerville and Ross," it might be said, assumed in its own time the status of a minor culture industry.

As exponents of a particular type of Irish literature, moreover, Somerville and Ross have continued to flourish as a literary commodity, the subject of more than half a dozen monographs and dozens of critical essays. Their titles remain in print and continue to be reissued, and their

---

[2] Faderman argues precisely this point, contending that at the turn of the century same-sex companionate relationships provided would-be professional women with the support they needed to pursue their ambitions. Her chapter, "Love and 'Women Who Live by Their Brains,'" which treats Somerville and Ross as lead examples, borrows its title from Somerville: "The outstanding fact, as it seems to me, among women who live by their brains, is friendship" (qtd. in Lillian Faderman, *Surpassing the Love of Men: Romantic Friendship and Love between Women from the Renaissance to the Present* 205–6).

place in Irish literature seems secure, even as it remains politically contentious, associated with the now outmoded (if not discredited) values
of the Anglo-Irish Ascendancy. Virtually every history of Irish literature
gives Somerville and Ross at least passing notice, and standard references continue to credit them with producing one of the best novels to
come out of Ireland and the best series of comic stories: *The Real Charlotte* (1894), *Some Experiences of an Irish R. M.* (1899), *Further Experiences
of an Irish R. M.* (1908), *In Mr. Knox's Country* (1915). Yet apart from their
place in a literary tradition generally treated as distinct from the major
developments in English fiction, Somerville and Ross have had virtually no abiding literary reputation, entering the history of (women's)
authorship otherwise—through the back door of women's romantic
friendships.

Somerville and Ross, indeed, are hardly household names today for
any class of readers; and their collaboration has provoked little of the
widespread interest that accrues to literary favorites such as the Brontës.
Nor have the partnerships of their contemporaries, less ambitious and
less well known than theirs, invited speculation. Yet these partnerships
tell stories equally illuminating—and far more typical than the Brontë
saga—of the paths women followed toward literary professionalism.
Historically, moreover, these partnerships were not insignificant. Just
before Somerville and Ross's authorial debut with *An Irish Cousin* (1889),
the Gerard sisters created something of a minor stir with their unusual novels—novels that introduced English readers to scenes of Austrian military life, as well as to the various peoples and places of eastern Europe. Published under the name "E. D. Gerard," the novels were
the joint work of Madame de Laszowska (née Emily Gerard), a Scots
woman educated on the Continent and married to an Austrian noble-
man (then an army officer stationed in Galicia), and her younger sister
Dorothea, whose care Emily had undertaken after their mother's death
in 1870. From 1879, when their first novel, *Reata*, was published serially
in *Blackwood's*, to 1886, when the partnership dissolved upon Dorothea's
marriage (also to an Austrian army officer), the Gerard sisters published
three jointly written novels, with a fourth published in 1891 that was at
least begun collaboratively.[3]

If the partnership was brief and the output limited, it was enough
to earn the Gerards a name as novelists with a brilliant future. More
important, perhaps, the collaboration's success was such as to launch

---

[3] *Reata* was published as a novel in 1880, with a revised edition in 1881. Their other collaborative fiction includes *Beggar My Neighbour* (1882), *The Waters of Hercules* (1885), and
A Sensitive Plant (1891)—this last, initiated and drafted before the dissolution of their
partnership.

the sisters' individual careers as professional writers, suggesting the way many collaborations must have functioned as stepping-stones for women. Writing separately under their maiden names, Emily and Dorothea Gerard continued to practice their distinctive brand of authorship through the 1880s, 1890s, and into the first decade of the twentieth century. Dorothea, for example, went on to publish at least fifteen additional novels, while Emily, whose greatest literary success was probably her travelogue of Transylvania, *The Land Beyond the Forest* (1888), pursued a more diverse professional profile, reviewing German literature for the *Times* and publishing occasional essays on new German literature; she also wrote six additional novels and two collections of short stories (originally published in *Blackwood's* and *Longmans*).

Mary and Jane Findlater, another pair of sisters from Scotland, with writing careers spanning the years 1895–1923, reveal a story with an opposite trajectory: they became collaborators *after* establishing themselves as single authors. Before writing *Crossriggs* (1908), their first collaborative novel, they had each published six novels separately—novels that earned them admiring notice, both publicly and privately. Moreover, before perfecting their collaboration in the three novels they jointly authored between 1908 and 1923, they had practiced collaboration on more than one occasion: in a collection of stories they published in 1901 and in the round-robin collaboration in which they participated with two other friends in the early 1900s—a collaboration that yielded two light, easily forgettable works of fiction.[4] Henry and William James were long-time friends and admirers, and Virginia Woolf was known to have expressed her appreciation for their novels; in Britain they moved among established literary circles that included May Sinclair, Walter de la Mare, and Rudyard Kipling.

In choosing to write serious fiction together, Mary and Jane Findlater were, in some sense, enacting their devotion; they had committed themselves to writing from the time they were children, and their authorship was perhaps the most important thing they had to share with each other. But their collaboration was also the culmination of their professional practice—their ultimate achievement as novelists. For by general consensus, they produced as two something better than either could

---

[4] Of their collaborative works, *Crossriggs* (1908) has generally been considered the most significant; it was reissued in 1985 as a Virago Modern Classic. Their other collaborative novels are *Penny Monypenny* (1911) and *Beneath the Visiting Moon* (1923). Unlike their novels, their collections of stories and essays name single authors for the contributions. In *The Affair at the Inn* (1904) and *Robinetta* (1911)—written with Kate Douglas Wiggin and Allan McAulay (Charlotte Stewart)—each author assumes distinct responsibility for particular chapters, told through the perspective of a character assigned to her.

write individually. And they did not abandon collaboration until, in the 1920s, they abandoned novel writing altogether—having seen themselves fade from celebrated authors enjoying a respectful press, wide readership, and warm literary friendships to authors who seemed out of step with their time, relics of an earlier era.

Writing at a slightly later date, the Australian writers Marjorie Barnard and Flora Eldershaw ("M. Barnard Eldershaw") published their first collaborative novel, *A House Is Built* in 1928. Ranked among the leading Australian writers of the interwar period, they eventually wrote, as collaborators, five novels, three historical studies, and a volume of literary criticism (most published in the 1930s). As friends who met at the University of Sydney, Barnard and Eldershaw (neither of whom ever married) reflect a somewhat different pattern of professional development from the earlier family collaborations—a collaboration more in line, perhaps, with the expanding professionalism available to women. Barnard, for example, although she initially lived at home to look after her parents, chose not to marry because she viewed marriage as incompatible with her dedication to writing; like other women of the period, however, she did not find her relations with women similarly inhibiting, living much of her later life with a female companion ("Marjorie Barnard" 38–39). Eldershaw, even more visibly, exemplified the lifestyle of the new professional woman, maintaining a flat in Sydney where she and Barnard could meet with other people in the literary world as well as talk literature with each other. Like other aspiring authors, Barnard and Eldershaw each had other careers which provided their primary income: Barnard was a librarian, Eldershaw a schoolmistress. And like others for whom authorship was treated as a hobby, they had, at first, to squeeze their writing into time they could wrest from other responsibilities. Eventually, Barnard gave up her job to become a full-time author, and Eldershaw's job took her to Canberra and Melbourne, putting new pressures on the collaboration. But one could argue that the partners' ability to strike out on their own would not have been possible without the sustenance the collaboration initially provided.[5]

For audiences today, these instances of collaborative authorship might well seem doubly curious—remote in their subject matter and in their mode of composition. Yet in their time, all of these partnerships (and Somerville and Ross most especially) made a more than respectable showing in the literary arena—publishing with the best houses

[5] For an excellent discussion of the collaboration of M. Barnard Eldershaw, see Maryanne Dever, "'No Mine and Thine but Ours': Finding 'M. Barnard Eldershaw.'"

and receiving notice in the leading periodicals. Writing the final volume for the official house biography of John Blackwood's and Sons, John Blackwood's daughter even cites her father's cultivation of the Gerard sisters as a mark of his editorial perspicuity (Porter 358). Posterity, however, has sided with those who saw the work of these partnerships as decidedly minor—as work that even the partners' most devoted admirers might admit was never quite "of the first order" (Mackenzie 129).

As such, this work has largely disappeared from notice, preserved only through the labor of dedicated women who openly enrolled themselves in the ranks of enthusiasts. For example, Helen Black, the memorialist of the Gerard sisters, made a career out of writing thumbnail sketches of "Notable Women Authors of the Day," and Geraldine Cummins, Mary Sturgeon, and Eileen Mackenzie each devoted herself more fully and exclusively to a single figure: Edith Somerville, Michael Field, and the Findlater sisters, respectively. More concerned with the author's "story" than with questions of literary merit, these women wrote frankly admiring accounts of their subjects—accounts that frequently border on idolatry. Motivated, moreover, by deep personal investments, they tended to be overly protective of their subjects, quick to erase any sign of transgression in either the lives or the writings of these literary partnerships. However much, then, they stress their subjects' professional aspirations and literary achievements, they reinforce the idea of collaboration as an amateur operation—a suitable diversion for properly genteel women. Indeed, these early biographers color the collaborations with their own qualifications; for such unashamed adulation has rendered their accounts, whatever the authors' scholarly credentials, distinctly unscholarly, subject to dismissal as amateur testimonials to amateur writers.

These writing partnerships, however, have other stories to tell about women and professionalism at the turn of the century—stories not necessarily dependent on securing their aesthetic value. As writers not quite of the first order, these literary partners were, in fact, almost the same (their collaborations aside) as most other professional authors; and they were certainly more like most serious women writers than were the handful of exceptional cases dubbed "women of genius." Indeed, these writing partners might be said to epitomize what might be called, after George Eliot, the *serious* lady novelists, writers whose untold stories make up a crucial part in the history of authorship. These writers can be distinguished, then, from the women writers of an earlier generation—from both the "silly" lady novelists Eliot castigated and from Eliot herself. And it is precisely in this middle space that they staked their claims as literary professionals.

Unlike the Brontës, whose collaborative writing sustained a strictly private existence, challenging the very terms of professional recognition, these latter-day collaborators embraced the literary marketplace and its attendant conventions, and they exploited their collaborations to regulate ambition and erase all markers of their authorial difference. They cultivated, in other words, the modest and workmanlike achievements contemporary critics recognized as their hallmark: careful craftsmanship, extensive knowledge of technique, mastery of the art of entertainment. If, as Raymond Mortimer says of the Findlaters, these were writers who were in touch with their own generation—writers who, unlike their modernist contemporaries, could speak to "[t]he man in the street and the woman in the suburban drawing-room" (146)—later generations preferred the more difficult pleasures of Woolf, Joyce, and Lawrence.

Practicing authorship as a "trade," then, these writing unions participated in a new professionalization of the author that has since been rendered suspect by modernism's counter ideologies.[6] Even at the time, however, these new configurations had a decided doubleness, for the very vehicles that supported authorship's new professional status— e.g., the Society of Authors (1884), the advent of the literary agent— could be seen to sponsor rampant "amateurism," a charge to which these partnerships were especially vulnerable. For on the one hand, partnership writing could be seen to personalize, even trivialize, authorship, and on the other, to overprofessionalize it. Either way, the work of these partnerships could be distinguished from a more refined type of "professional" writing associated with the high art novel—the form that ultimately eclipsed them.

These partnerships, then, might prompt further questions about the very borders they historically demarcated. Could fiction produced in collaboration ever be considered of the first rank? Does collaboration compromise cherished notions of "originality" and "uniqueness," of the artist's individual imprint—categories prestige authorship invokes as its trademark? Is collaboration compromised by its implication in professionalism? Is it a hopelessly amateur undertaking? Can collaboration ever be taken seriously, or is it doomed to repeat its history as curiosity?

[6] For discussions of the professionalization of authorship, see Richard D. Altick, "The Sociology of Authorship: The Social Origins, Education, and Occupations of 1,100 British Writers, 1800–1935"; Victor Bonham-Carter, *Authors by Profession*; Nigel Cross, *The Common Writer: Life in Nineteenth-Century Grub Street*; N. N. Feltes, *Literary Capital and the Late Victorian Novel*; James Hepburn, *The Author's Empty Purse and the Rise of the Literary Agent*; J. W. Saunders, *The Profession of English Letters*; Gaye Tuchman (with Nina Fortin) , *Edging Women Out: Victorian Novelists, Publishers, and Social Change*.

At the turn of the century, when women's partnerships began to emerge, such questions would inevitably have had a different valence. For professional authorship was by no means a stable or singular entity, despite a protracted struggle in its name over the course of the nineteenth century. In fact, even as authors attempted to consolidate a new professional identity, authorship continued to oscillate between the drudgery of Grub Street (trade) and the leisured activity of the person of privilege (hobby), demarcating a borderline existence at once above and below professional consideration. For literary partnerships like those considered here—partnerships that highlighted authorship as both work *and* play, both arduous business and personal self-fulfillment—this precarious position was all the more evident. Women's participation in these unions thus illuminates one of the indirect ways women entered authorship's new professional configurations. Indeed, borrowing from Gaye Tuchman, one might conclude, it illustrates the way women "edged themselves out" even as they edged themselves into literary authorship's new institutions.[7]

Like Trollope, who never ceased to regard himself as a "gentleman who wrote books" (vii) although his autobiography would expose the unrelenting professionalism of his daily writing habits, these neo-professional partnerships never appeared to be entirely professional. By virtue, if nothing else, of the peculiarity of their writing situation, the authors who subscribed to these unions couldn't help being regarded as "ladies who wrote novels."[8] Against competing understandings of what it means to write professionally—to earn money by one's trade, to entertain one's contemporaries, to maintain the standards of a craft, to uphold the dignity of letters—these partnerships also resurrected an older idea of authorship: writing as genteel hobby. What these instances, of course, also demonstrate is that a cultivated hobby meant something very different for men and for women at this historical moment. If for men, amateurism could be read as a mark of class status and intellectual autonomy, for women it did not generally carry the same positive connotations. Although these writing partnerships, then, put up for public scrutiny the question (still being decided) of what it means

---

[7] Gaye Tuchman, writing with Nina E. Fortin, has called this historical moment "the period of redefinition" (1880–1899)—the period when "men of letters, including critics, actively redefined the nature of a good novel and a great author," and in doing so, began to edge women out of a market they once dominated. From 1901–1917 ("the period of institutionalization"), they argue, "men's hold on the novel, particularly the high culture novel, coalesced" (*Edging Women Out* 7–8).

[8] Leon Edel, for example, glosses a reference to the Findlaters in Henry James's notebook as "two Scottish maiden ladies who wrote popular novels" (*The Complete Notebooks of Henry James* 284).

to write as a trade, they broached the question from its margins: How can authorship be practiced by two? How can a trade be practiced by women?

At first glance, the coterie writing of Katherine Bradley and Edith Cooper, tradesmen's daughters who privately published vast quantities of verse under the name "Michael Field," would seem to have little in common with the contemporaneous unions of women novelists. Unlike the novel, poetry was not a highly marketable commodity when Michael Field published (1875–1913), and the bulk of the work the poet produced—twenty-seven verse dramas on classical and historical subjects—was work unlikely to appeal to all but a small audience. Only one of these dramas, Michael Field's *A Question of Memory*, was ever performed and that in a single performance for the Independent Theatre Society, a group founded to present plays that would appeal to an intellectual audience unsatisfied by the conventional offerings of the commercial theater. But it proved a distinctly unpopular offering even in a theater devoted to the dissemination of the unpopular.[9] The eight volumes of lyrics have had a more lasting reputation, but in their time they were far from a commercial success or a recognized literary breakthrough. Unlike the novelistic collaborators who happily dirtied their hands in trade and courted a middle-brow readership, Bradley and Cooper retreated into aestheticism, cultivating a high-art reputation. Indeed, surrounding themselves with beautiful objects (their books included), they shut themselves off from the world of trade and all its sordid associations.

Nonetheless, I want to argue, the Michael Field collaboration tells a story no less implicated in the discourse of professionalism—although the professionalism Bradley and Cooper cultivated was of a somewhat different order. They refused to write for the masses, stubbornly pursuing antiquated genres; but in doing so, they maintained their own high standards of artistic integrity. And they maintained these standards, in part, because they had each other to sustain them in the absence of public approbation. Most of their aesthetic choices, in fact, seem to come back to some uncompromising notion of what they considered due to "art"—their own art, particularly. Their decision to publish their work privately, at their own expense, for example, was, above

---

[9] Among the more notable plays performed at the Independent Theatre Society were Ibsen's *Ghosts* and *The Wild Duck*, Zola's *Thérèse Raquin*, and Shaw's *Widowers' Houses*. For Michael Field's experience with the ITS, see Jan McDonald, "'Disillusioned Bards and Despised Bohemians': Michael Field's *A Question of Memory* at the Independent Theatre Society."

all else, a declaration of artistic autonomy: a means to retain control over their literary product.

This desire for control, moreover, was no trivial matter. The Woolfs formed the Hogarth Press in 1917 in part to provide precisely such a vehicle for Virginia, who expressed her appreciation in terms that surely resonate for other serious authors: "Anyhow its . . . the greatest mercy to be able to do what one likes—no editors, or publishers, and only people to read who more or less like that sort of thing" (qtd. in Willis 9–10). As Allan C. Dooley has argued, moreover, for Victorian authors who had neither fame nor commercial success to recommend them, the amount of control they could exercise over their printed texts was often severely limited. Literary works were routinely cut, rewritten, and even expanded, sometimes without the author's notification; under these conditions, the authors of what was, in effect, closet drama could have little hope of preferential treatment.[10]

Michael Field's ambitions, however, were even more far-reaching, for the authors sought control not only over the style and substance of their writing, but over the print format of the published volume—a type of control, Dooley has argued, historically available only to those who "compose, print, and publish by their own hands" (7). Indeed, as I argued in Chapter 1, this was the type of control the Brontës exercised in their "self-published" early writings. If the Michael Field collaboration, then, allowed the authors to stand, like the Brontës, outside the literary marketplace, it engaged them more seriously than their predecessors in the knowledge of a trade—the practice of bookmaking. For the production of the book as a beautiful object required from the Michael Field partners a certain technical proficiency—proficiency the Brontës needed only to simulate. As Sturgeon explains, "[G]reat was their care for format, decoration, binding, paper, and type: for colour, texture, quality, arrangement of letterpress, appearance of title-page, design of cover. In every detail there was rigorous discrimination" (*Michael Field* 46). In these concerns, moreover, Bradley and Cooper were not alone but part of recognizable artistic currents: the arts and crafts movement and fin-de-siècle aestheticism. Indeed, their commitment to fine printing was the complement of their literary aesthetics, and the presses with which they published had a distinct "artsy" reputation. Publishing in

---

[10] The fate of Michael Field's poetry suggests that the authors had good reason to worry. Acknowledging that "Great works, by Shakespeare and Milton even, need to be cut if we would view their fine structures clearly," T. Sturge Moore explains, "With lesser poets, often more than half must be lopped away. . . . Therefore I have not hesitated to remove lines and stanzas where I felt certain the whole could thus be made more complete" (*A Selection from the Poems of Michael Field* 12).

select circles, they thus found themselves in touch with others of like aesthetic sensibilities: Browning, Wilde, Yeats, and Meredith.

Despite the admiration of important literary contemporaries, however, "Michael Field" has not been treated kindly in literary history. While the poet's early works were favorably received, Michael Field's reputation plummeted, at least as the partners tell the story, after the public disclosure of their identity. And subsequent history has followed this lead, relegating Michael Field to the outland of minor poetry, recalling the authors only as a literary curiosity. Although Yeats included a selection of their poems in the *Oxford Book of Modern Verse* and T. Sturge Moore collected their poetry, later critics do not appear to have shared this admiration. As Holly Laird observes, "No more than three citations to their name appear prior to 1990 in MLA listings" ("Contradictory Legacies" 126).

Indeed, it would almost seem that literary history had conspired to represent them as the ultimate amateurs. Although they attended university together (when Bradley was thirty-two, Cooper sixteen)—at a time when this was far from common for women—standard reference works treat them as eager enthusiasts, noting, for example, how *"the girls* zestfully studied the classics and philosophy" (Kunitz 222, emphasis mine). Similarly, fastening on their predilection for verse drama with historical themes, others have faulted them for being unimaginative hacks, overdiligent in their research. Siegfried Sassoon, for example, suggests that "one might almost call [their work] counterfeit literature" (218). Like other collaborators, moreover, they have been taken to task for their unseemly productiveness, for turning themselves, as it were, into a type of writing machine.

Often entering literary history as footnotes to the lives of their more famous male counterparts, Michael Field has, moreover, been subject to a particularly misogynistic rendering.[11] In biographies of Meredith, for example, where the authors appear with striking frequency and little variation in representation, the authors are repeatedly pilloried for not knowing their place: for demanding recognition from a great man of letters. When, like Charlotte and Branwell Brontë, they seek to introduce

[11] Siegfried Sassoon, for example, applauds Logan Pearsall Smith's "delightfully feline account of 'these intrepid ladies'" (*Meredith*, 218), accusing them of being "proud, touchy, self-occupied, and excessively tiresome" (219): "two maiden ladies" who "knew nothing of the world beyond their small coterie of artistic and literary acquaintances" (218). Lionel Stevenson compulsively refers to them as the "two spinsters" (*The Ordeal of George Meredith: A Biography* 286), "the two poetic ladies" (286), "[t]he two captious ladies" (326), and, most tellingly, "the unconventional pair of she-poets" (302). For the treatment of Michael Field by male critics, see also Daniel J. Moriarty, "'Michael Field' (Edith Cooper and Katherine Bradley) and Their Male Critics."

themselves as authors to their literary idols, they are represented as "she-poets" and harpies, stalking their prey and refusing to take "no" for an answer, repeatedly interpreting polite brush-offs as signs of genuine interest.[12]

Even their own most admiring biographer, Mary Sturgeon, appears at pains to represent them as appropriately feminine—and hence not *too* professional. In a gesture echoed in virtually every account of women's collaborations, she celebrates—if not exaggerates—her subjects' lack of professional acumen.[13] She notes, for example, with apparent approval, Michael Field's idea of "advertisement" as to "print at the end of her books the bad as well as the good reviews" (*Michael Field* 163)—a quality that might align her with the young Charlotte Brontë, who submitted her first manuscript to prospective publishers in the return wrapper in which previous publishers had rejected it. When Sturgeon, moreover, catalogs the authors' considerable knowledge of book production, she represents it as a species of connoisseurship; and she frames it in a context appropriately feminine: "They desired their children to be lovely in body as well as in spirit" (45–46). Even when she gets down to the hard-core business end of things, Sturgeon represents the performance of these tasks as "proof of Michael's devotion" to her partner, a glimpse into "her warm human soul" (45), as if even the imputation of professionalism required a compensatory feminization. Indeed, while Sturgeon acknowledges that the authors "welcomed experience as few Victorian women dared," professionally, at least, she relegates them to the position of cloistered women: "two souls completely innocent" of the "traffic and ambition" of the world, living in seclusion and laboring, "with no hope of reward, at [their] daily toil in the service of poetry" (239, 163).

Although the situation of women novelists was necessarily different, these constructions of the Michael Field collaboration remain instructive. For even for novelists with more overtly professional pretensions,

---

[12] See, for example, Sassoon, *Meredith*, and David Williams, *George Meredith: His Life and Lost Love*.

[13] See, for example, Violet Powell's representation of Somerville and Ross as "hopelessly unprofessional in their dealings with publishers" (*The Irish Cousins* 30), and Hilary Mitchell's insistence in "Somerville and Ross: Amateur to Professional" that the authors became professionalized reluctantly and only as a matter of necessity. Even Gifford Lewis, a champion of Somerville and Ross's professionalism, betrays a certain uneasiness with the subject, arguing simultaneously that they rode to success on the coattails of Martin's brother (*Somerville and Ross: The World of the Irish R.M.* 76) and that "Martin Ross" was "quite a canny operator" (*Selected Letters of Somerville and Ross* 291)—perhaps too canny a one. Her portrait of "Martin" remains less than flattering: a "string-puller supreme," "business-like and mercenary," with "a sales representative's grasp of the more mundane outlets of the book trade" (*Somerville and Ross* 76–78).

the stamp of the amateur was never far from the surface. The Michael Field example thus underlines what women's novel-writing unions also demonstrate: the contradictions in women's historical position as authors. Indeed, for women writing together, even the most professional considerations could invoke the amateurism implicit in their enterprise. Thus when Violet Martin writes to her cousin/partner about an authorial signature for their first novel, she takes for granted the need for a professional name distinct from their private identities: "*You must think of a name for yourself.* Two New Writers is every day more odious to me—" (*Selected Letters of Sommerville and Ross* 61). But she does not appear to anticipate how the choice of a dual name will erase their names entirely, turning them into "Two Merry Maidens," "the observant and clever collaborateurs," "The Two Ladies."[14]

As Martin's letter makes clear, however, the problem is already implicit in the condition of women's solo authorship. For when she invites her partner to invent a name for herself, she offers choices ranging from the most professional of names (names that, significantly, mask or disguise gender)—"Currer Bell, George Eliot, or any of them"—to the most facetious: feminine and private names that circulate as jokes within the family. Taken seriously, what these remarks suggest are the limited historical precedents for women to think of themselves as professionals. As Richard Altick has argued, the category "professional" simply was not available to most women in the nineteenth century: "[F]emale writers were either strictly amateurs, who would never have dreamed of enrolling themselves in the census returns as professional authors, or women who, like Mrs Trollope and Mrs Oliphant, were forced by circumstances to support themselves and their relatives by the pen" (392).

Collaborative writing, at a first glance, would support both these exceptions to professionalism, projecting alternatively an amateur practice (something done for amusement) and an expedient materialism (two can write more efficiently than one). In fact, most of the women who formed these partnerships claimed they did so for the fun of it. But most of these women, once they tasted some success, were also in it for the money. Neither explanation, however, fully comprehends these partners' literary investments. Even the Findlaters, who were reputedly so poor that they had to write their first manuscripts on the back of grocers' paper and were in fact supporting themselves and their family by their pens, saw their writing as more than journeymen's labor. These

---

[14] "Two Merry Maidens" is the title of a review of *In the Vine Country* (rpt. in *Selected Letters of Somerville and Ross* 183); "observant and clever collaborateurs" appears in *The Lady's Pictorial* review of *The Real Charlotte* (19 May 1894); "the two Ladies" is E. V. Lucas's chosen epithet for the authors.

were women, in other words, who *did* dream of counting themselves as professional authors. Collaboration, I want to argue, facilitated this dream by, in effect, masking it. For under the guise of collaboration's evident amateurism, a number of women were able to slip into a professional position.

Indeed, if women's authorship exists on some type of professional continuum, collaborative writing defines an important zone of transition, as women writers suggest in the stories they tell about it. The Findlaters, for example, undertake their first collaboration with their friends Kate Douglas Wiggin and Charlotte Stewart, when they find themselves housebound during a weeklong pleasure trip; quite literally, a rainy-day activity, the collaboration begins at the instigation of "the irrepressible Kate," who, reassuring her comrades that "[i]t will be only for fun" (Wiggin 343), presents the project as imperative: "Now girls . . . we can't go out . . . We must collaborate over a book" (qtd. in Mackenzie 44). In her account of the Gerard sisters' conception of *Reata*, Helen Black creates a similar backdrop: "It was not until 1877, that, being consigned to the deadly monotony of a little Hungarian country town, where the landscape was a desert and the society *nil*, the idea of writing a novel as 'something to do' was suddenly and almost without premeditation born in upon them" (155). In fact, if we are to believe the story, the Gerard sisters take on "the gigantic task of a three-volume novel, at first merely by way of amusement, without thought of publication" (156). Similarly, Marjorie Barnard explains how "not very seriously, more for fun than in the hope of achievement," she and Flora Eldershaw "thought about a novel we would like to write"—a project that quickly came to absorb them ("Gentle Art" 127). Even the prolific Somerville and Ross collaboration was, as Somerville explains, "[b]egun in idleness and without conviction" (*Irish Memories* 132). Finding themselves "with book" at the end of these experiments, all of these partners somehow secure publishers, crossing a threshold that transforms their enterprise.

That these narratives of origins should sound so remarkably similar suggests that they served a consistent function for the women who produced them; it also suggests that, at least for women, the practice of collaboration—if only as a form of private entertainment—must have been considerably more pervasive than standard literary histories would acknowledge. It was, these stories suggest, the kind of thing girls did if they had literary sensibilities. Like the Brontë sisters, then, other young women apparently turned to those close at hand to pursue their literary ambitions. It was, in fact, not that unusual for a young woman to accumulate a history of collaborative experiences. Edith Somerville, before meeting Violet Martin, collaborated on plays with another cousin, Ethel Coghill—a collaboration broken off upon Ethel's marriage. Kate Douglas Wiggin, best known as the author of the children's book *Rebecca of Sunnybrook Farm*, admits that in addition to the Findlaters, she also collaborated with her "author-sister," although in the latter case, "only in educational fields and in the making of anthologies" (340). Indeed, devoting an entire chapter of her autobiography to "Collaborations: Translations," Wiggin installs collaboration as a regular feature of an author's development.

Other households tell similar stories. Before publishing her first works of fiction, Louisa May Alcott collaborated on plays with her sisters. The Rossetti children (Michael, Dante Gabriel, Christina, and Maria) collaborated on a collection of tales to be printed on the press their grandfather kept in his basement; they also collaborated on two family journals, to which they contributed poems and stories (Weintraub 10–11). Later, Michael's daughters, Helen and Olivia Rossetti (writing as "Isabel Meredith"), would publish a collaborative novel *A Girl among the Anarchists* (1903) based on their experience as adolescents working on an anarchist newspaper printed out of their household. Virginia Woolf, from the time she was nine, wrote stories and novellas for the family newsletter, *Hyde Park Gate News*.

Such activities, moreover, were not restricted to the homes of the rich and famous. The Macdonald sisters, daughters of a lower-middle-class itinerant Methodist preacher, all of whom went on to marry into famous families, grew up, not entirely unlike the Brontës, as part of a small self-sustaining artistic society.[15] Louisa Macdonald Baldwin, whose son would eventually become England's Prime Minister and who herself went on to a career as a minor literary figure (the author of poetry, novels, and children's stories), was "publishing" stories at home even before she "could write anything but laborious capital letters" (Baldwin 39). Like Dorothea Gerard, who began her literary career by dictating stories to her mother, Louisa dictated her stories to an older sister, Georgiana, who not only transcribed but illustrated the stories for her. Georgiana, who married the painter Edward Burne-Jones, later began a collaboration with Lizzie Siddal Rossetti on a book of fairy tales, but the project was never completed. Yet another sister, Alice Macdonald Kipling, published a book of poems in collaboration with her daughter. When still teenagers growing up in India, Alice's children, Rudyard and Alice ("Trixie") Kipling, published two collaboratively produced

[15] For discussions of the Macdonald sisters, see A. W. Baldwin, *The Macdonald Sisters*, and Ina Taylor, *Victorian Sisters: The Remarkable Macdonald Women and the Great Men They Inspired*.

books: a collection of tales (including contributions by their parents) and a collection of verse parodies. While Rudyard would go on to become a famous poet and novelist, "Trixie" pursued another type of authorship popular among women of her generation, practicing automatic writing as the acclaimed "Mrs. Holland."

When women turned to authorship, then, at the turn of the century, they had a history of preprofessional writing to draw on—a history of writing often located in the family. It seems reasonable to assume, moreover, that suppressed collaborations stand behind many instances of women's solitary authorship. We know, for example, that Geraldine Jewsbury completed a manuscript version of her first novel Zoe in collaboration with her friend Elizabeth Paulet—a manuscript she sent to Jane Carlyle for a "good, hard, professional, practical opinion" (Clarke 168); whether or not Carlyle actually had a hand in the composition, we know that she was closely involved in the novel's subsequent development—providing editorial and administrative services and working as a type of private literary adviser (172).[16] And we know that Jewsbury entertained hopes of entering into "a literary partnership" with her (181). Yet Zoe (1845), like all of Jewsbury's other novels, ultimately appears as a solitary production. Jewsbury, whose instincts for what the market would tolerate would make her a respected publisher's reader for Bentley's in the 1860s and 1870s, may well have intuited in her debut as a novelist the professional cover she required. Certainly, the fate of women's acknowledged collaborations suggests good reason for wariness. For no matter how successful the partnership, the participants were likely to be seen as no more than "inspired amateurs."[17]

If, then, as Hilary Mitchell has argued, the career of Somerville and Ross tracks the development of the writers from "amateur to professional," what seems most remarkable is that their collaboration survived the transition. Indeed, what is remarkable about all these partnerships is that they saw collaboration as something other than a one-time thing. They refused, in other words, to treat collaboration as either a gimmick or mere apprenticeship—models of collaboration the public found more acceptable. When William Dean Howells, for example, or-

[16] Susanne Howe suggests that the novel was originally begun in 1842 in collaboration with both Paulet and Carlyle, but that both coauthors "had tired of it" (Geraldine Jewsbury: Her Life and Errors 71). My discussion here, however, follows Norma Clarke, who emphasizes the detailed advice Carlyle offered for rewriting as well as her role as mediator in Jewsbury's dealings with her publishers—roles Carlyle experienced as akin to coauthorship.

[17] Paul Binding admits as much in his introduction to the 1986 reissue of Mary and Jane Findlater's Crossriggs, defending the partnership as "wholly serious" and "successful" and not what his readers might expect, the union of "two inspired amateurs" (vii).

ganized eleven other authors (including Henry James and Mary Wilkins
Freeman) to produce with him a serial novel for *Harper's*, the public ea-
gerly entered into the game of guessing which celebrity author wrote
which installment—a game sponsored alike by authors and publisher.[18]

But for women writers who did not apportion their work so neatly,
the persistent guessing games, as seen in the last chapter, could force
them to retreat from their own professionalism. Thus confronted by
Andrew Lang with the insinuation that her works could not be truly
collaborative—"I suppose you're the one who did the writing—," Violet Martin plays the part of the suitably feminine dilettante: "I said I
didn't know how we managed, but anyhow that I knew little of bookmaking as a science" (*Selected Letters of Somerville and Ross* 209).[19] If the
joke on Lang can be privately shared with her partner, the laugh is not
entirely at his expense. For confronted by a fundamental disbelief in
the idea that writing could be shared completely, there were only a limited number of moves these partners could make. Indeed, lacking a
public discourse that would lend them credibility, these partnerships
could never fully extricate themselves from their status as curiosities—
whether they indulged the public's interest or resisted it.

If the literary culture of the turn of the century demanded a single author (if only the single author of individual parts) for writing to be
deemed serious, what double writing inevitably achieved was to bring
the *work* of writing into visibility. The very terms that governed public
curiosity about these collaborations focused attention, in ways perhaps
unprecedented, on the material of writing: on the hands of the author,
the control of the pen, the possession of the page—not to mention the
mechanics of character and plot construction, the components of a stylistic signature, the art of producing dialogue, the process of revision.
Appearing at the very moment when popular writers' guides began to
codify these processes and procedures, literary collaborations could
thus be read as a kind of living handbook to the art of fiction. Marjorie
Barnard's description of the "method" of her collaboration, for example,
reads like the accounts, popularized in the new writers' manuals, of the

---

[18] *The Whole Family* was published in *Harper's* in twelve parts from December 1907 to
November 1908 and as a novel in 1908. For discussions of this collaboration, see Alfred
Bendixen, "It Was a Mess! How Henry James and Others Actually Wrote a Novel," and
Dale M. Bauer, "The Politics of Collaboration in *The Whole Family*."

[19] While male collaborators did not escape similar curiosity, they were less likely to
claim to do all their writing together, as a fuller account of the conversation with Lang indicates: "He said he didn't know how any two people could equally evolve characters
etc.—that he had tried, and it was always he or the other that did it all" (*Selected Letters of
Somerville and Ross* 209).

discussions any author might have with himself or herself before he or she begins writing: "[W]e talked about it to one another, discussed it at length, story, characters, background, treatment, in that order, getting the feel of it, coming to know it in depth, all this without putting pen to paper" ("Gentle Art" 126).[20]

When Edith Somerville, then, complains about the persistent questions regarding her collaboration—"Why don't they ask me how I write by myself? I could assure them that it is much harder than writing with Martin and much more of a 'mystery' to me how I do it" (qtd. in Mitchell 30)—she points to what very well may be a pointless distinction between double- and single-handed productions: "How does *anyone* write if it comes to that? (How do you make the words come one after the other, in fact?) How does any artist or maker do anything that is not actually manual?" (qtd. in Mitchell 29). Indeed, collaboration in novels may be the special case that illuminates novel-writing in general. For by authorizing the question of "how one does it," collaborative writing exposes writing as something constructed; and by invoking images of double-handedness, it marks writing, quite literally, as something crafted—made by hand(s), as the Brontë miniatures dramatically illustrate. Even as it invokes the concept of "mystery" to cover its own operation, collaboration can be seen, then, to demystify the romantic views of authorship—to demolish the myth of art that springs effortless from the author's brain, of authorship as a solitary labor of love or act of selfless devotion.

From this perspective, collaborative novel-writing can be seen as writing that insists on its status as professional—the product of joint labor, however much the division of that labor resists visible demarcation. In fact, if we turn to male authors who wrote collaboratively during this period—Walter Besant, Andrew Lang, Anthony Hope, Robert Louis Stevenson, Rider Haggard, and even Conrad and Ford (at least as far as their collaborative writings were concerned)—these are precisely the writers commonly seen to embody authorship's new professionalism both in the genres they favored and their patterns of production.[21] If these male collaborators staked out the territory of romance and adventure, their female counterparts perfected a type of writing of local

---

[20] Percy Russell's *The Literary Manual; or, A Complete Guide to Authorship* (1886), for example, includes chapters on such topics as "Novel Writing Reduced to an Art," "The Way to Success in Fiction," and "Constructing of Plots" (Alan L. Dooley, *Author and Printer in Victorian England* 14).

[21] Wayne Koestenbaum distinguishes these "mainstream" or "professional" collaborators from the "coterie" homosexual collaborators also writing at this period (*Double Talk: The Erotics of Male Collaboration* 143–77). For a discussion of the new breed of professional authors, see Cross.

color (tales and sketches of Irish, Scottish, and Austrian life). And as Besant argued in an 1892 essay "On Literary Collaboration," genres such as these were especially suitable for collaborative writing, dependent as they were on plot, atmosphere, and storytelling (204). While most of the male writers in this grouping subsequently repudiated collaboration, it remains significant that for them, as for the women (who experienced their partnerships less competitively), collaboration both facilitated and served the development of a professional reputation.

The nearly daily correspondence of Somerville and Ross (who did not regularly share a household for most of the years they wrote together) offers a privileged window onto the process of collaboration. And it reveals, among other things, how two women could professionalize each other.[22] Thus in roles that come to assume a ritualized quality, we find Ross inciting Somerville to exploit her family connections to procure reviews for their novels (*Selected Letters of Somerville and Ross* 142, 144), and we find Somerville schooling Ross in writing for the public (192). We find, moreover, extensive evidence of how the two negotiated with each other. Thus after completing some copyediting, Somerville writes to her partner to express her unbearable anxiety, urging her "for pity's sake" to "try and write by return of post to say if you like pages 71 and 72" (63). In fact, the letters are filled with materials singularly pragmatic: verbatim accounts of discussions with editors, agents, and publishers; minutely detailed editorial suggestions; calculated business speculations—all contained within a *personal* correspondence. These testimonies to a professional life of letters thus frequently slip imperceptibly into private matters, as in this excerpt from a letter of Ross's: "You will admit that I have done some work among the editors and made them toe the mark in style—I will send you tomorrow before I start for Ireland patterns for your dress . . ." (224). Like other contemporary accounts of women's writing, then, the Somerville and Ross correspondence reveals the fluidity of boundaries for the professional woman at this historical juncture.

Indeed, while the competing claims of living apart and writing together entailed for Somerville and Ross a particularly complicated balancing act, especially when it came to arranging working visits with each other, the difficulty of finding time and space for writing between familial obligations and a demanding social schedule was one experienced more generally by most women attempting to write at this period. The necessity of corresponding by post over crucial revisions to

---

[22] For other treatments of Somerville and Ross as *professional* writers, see Gifford Lewis, *Somerville and Ross: The World of the Irish R. M.*, and Hilary Mitchell, "Somerville and Ross: Amateur to Professional."

their writings posed particular logistic problems for collaborative writers. A single manuscript amassed ever-accruing commentary, sometimes, as with Somerville and Ross, including commentary from other members of their families. But even solitary writers had their host of hidden collaborators: friends and family members whose advice could be at times quite substantial. Accounts of collaboration allow us to see the types of negotiations, often not acknowledged so explicitly, that inform most acts of women's professional writing.

What these accounts also let us see is what gets glossed over when collaboration is subsumed under the rubric of romantic friendship. When Somerville, for example, writes to her friend and partner, "I wish you were here, or I was there—it would save much time and trouble" (*Selected Letters* 103), she expresses more than conventional sentiment; and Ross is even more blunt about their motives, "But the sooner you can come, without seeming unkind to your family, the better. I *must* make money—so must you—and the Welsh Aunt [the working title for their novel] is an awful business" (164). Indeed, for Edith Somerville and Martin Ross *and* their families, much of the value of their literary partnership rested in the fact that it brought in money. Although Somerville could declare, then, that in a social context, she and her cousin, "when immersed in literature" were "more trouble than [they were] worth" (169), when valued against the cost of upkeep of two once great country houses (now deteriorating in the twilight of the Anglo-Irish ascendancy), the "worth" of their partnership increased considerably. In fact, if as story has it, Somerville resorted to a pseudonym for their first novel because her mother "had not wanted the good family name to be used in 'trade'" (143), such qualms disappeared when the Somerville and Ross productions proved financially successful. Collaboration served Somerville and Ross, then, as it undoubtedly did other women, with a privileged venue to discuss such unseemly subjects as an author's financial compensation.

If we take Somerville and Ross as representative, collaboration assumes a new professional dimension: a site where women could acknowledge and protect their business interests, where they could, in effect, act like "men of business." It is perhaps no accident that Somerville and Ross were among the first women to join the Society of Authors—a group formed for precisely these reasons. And they were among the first authors to employ the services of a literary agent—in their case, J. B. Pinker, who also represented Conrad, James, Wells, and Bennett. Indeed, availing themselves of all of authorship's new institutional structures, Somerville and Ross test the limits for granting collaboration professional credibility.

What their experience suggests is that collaboration can be tolerated—even embraced—if it maintains the fiction of the proprietary author. It can be embraced, that is, when it becomes a trademark. While Somerville and Ross always insisted that their best work was *The Real Charlotte* (their major achievement as serious novelists)—a judgment confirmed by many recent critics—their reputation was made on their comic hunting stories: *Some Experiences of an Irish R. M.* (1900) and the two sequels that followed. And it was Pinker who encouraged them to make these stories their hallmark, appealing both to their mercenary interests and to their desire for literary distinction. Advising them that "from all points of view that is the work to do" (qtd. in Mitchell 33)— the work, indeed, he could best sell to his editors—he assures them that "this is *your own stuff* & no one else does anything like it—" (*Selected Letters* 243).

Significantly, Somerville and Ross's "own stuff," as Pinker helped shape it, was precisely the type of stuff—"Satire, fun, humour, pathos of a kind"—that partnership writing could be seen to excel at (Besant, "On Literary Collaboration" 203); by contrast, the serious fiction that the authors themselves favored might have stretched the public's indulgence of their dual authorship. And it was as two, Pinker seemed to understand, that they stood as a unique literary property. Contrary to Pinker's prediction, however, Somerville and Ross's "own stuff" quickly drew its imitators, forcing them, in one case at least, to appeal to the Society of Authors to defend their property interest against the infringements of a dual pretender: a pair of authors borrowing not only their central comic conceit but their trademark double signature.[23] Practicing authorship as two, then, and practicing it professionally, Somerville and Ross could be seen to uphold the single-author model of literary production even as they extended it.

Of course, this story of accommodation is not the only one women's partnerships illuminate. But for women, as for men, the extensive history of collaboration stands at odds with its nearly invisible and narrowly circumscribed legacy. Besant, for example, cites "Charles Dickens, Wilkie Collins, Charles Reade, Erckmann, Chartrian, Dumas, Rider Haggard, Andrew Lang, Rudyard Kipling" as prominent instances of collaboration in fiction, but he remains adamant that one cannot collaborate on *serious* literature—that it is not suitable for art that touches "the deeper things" ("On Literary Collaboration" 201, 203). Collaborations on nonfictional material, on the other hand, were regularly coun-

---

[23] For a discussion of this episode, see Mitchell, "Somerville and Ross" 34–35.

tenanced, even for women, as were collaborations on anthologies, trans-lations, and children's literature. Isabella MacDonald Alden ("Pansy"), for example, the best-selling American author of more than a hundred books, much of it children's and adolescent fiction, collaborated with other women on at least ten occasions.[24] Collaborations on plays also had a long history—one in which women regularly participated. But novels—especially ones with claims to literary merit—would appear to be another matter. And the pressures on the novel were especially evident at the time women collaborators started putting themselves before the public. In fact, the claims for the writer as "artist" (and, con-comitantly, autonomous individual) became increasingly vocal as authors—and novelists in particular—came increasingly to be recog-nized as practitioners of a trade, or members of a profession.[25]

Part of the interest, then, of these women's writing unions is the way they focus problems of professionalism. Besant, for example, despite his lobbying for the author's professional recognition, strictly separates "the artist" in each author from "the man of business," the latter emerg-ing only when the work is "finished and ready for production" (*Auto-biography* 227–28). His own experience aside, moreover, Besant insists that the "artist" is ultimately solitary. "[I]f I were asked for my opinion as to collaboration in fiction," he maintains, "it would be decidedly against it. . . . [A]fter all, an artist must necessarily stand alone" (188). Women collaborators, on the contrary, tend to refuse these distinctions, insisting they can both collaborate in literature and be recognized as writers of significance. However much they pandered to the public, then, they refused to see themselves as mere entertainers. And they re-fused to see their partnerships as distinct from the artistic part of them.

In saying as much, these professional women were, from one point of view, merely continuing a venerated tradition. J. A. Sutherland has argued that many of the great novels of the mid-nineteenth century which "appear to be the unaided product of creative genius" must be understood as the "outcome of collaboration, compromise or commis-sion"; these works, he suggests, "cannot be fully appreciated unless we see them as partnership productions" (6)—partnerships between au-thors and powerful publishers. By the latter part of the century, literary agents, publisher's readers, journal editors, literary critics, and review-

[24] Most of "Pansy's" fiction was published between 1865 and 1914. At the height of her career, around 1900, "Pansy's" books sold at the rate of 100,000 copies a year. See "Isabella MacDonald Alden."
[25] For a discussion of the "public debate about 'the art of fiction' carried out by Walter Besant, Henry James, and Robert Louis Stevenson in 1883–84" (Feltes 65)—a debate about "craft" versus "art" as the author's *metier*—see Feltes 65–102.

ers had become the new legislators of taste. And these modern "collaborators," many of whom were themselves novelists and poets, played
no small part in the production of fiction.[26] But although such silent
partnerships could pass unnoticed or be written off to the proper business of writing, the acknowledged partnerships of writers with each
other made collaboration too visible for most people's comfort—and
visible precisely in the private realm of creativity.

Indeed, the violence and persistence of the questions joint authorship
regularly generated as to "which hand held the pen" would suggest that
as authorship became increasingly professionalized, writing itself—the
act of putting pen to paper—came to be seen as a last preserve of artistic integrity. To refuse the authority of a single wielder of the pen—to
deny even the validity of the question—could be seen to deny the special claims of "the literary." Thus one fellow author informs Somerville
that while she "cannot pick out the fastenings of the two hands" in
Somerville and Ross's first collaborative novel, she thinks the next novel
"ought to be" by only "*one* of them" (*Irish Memories* 137). For if authorship were a profession, to collaborate *in writing* might be, in effect, to
professionalize the wrong part of the operation, as other professional
women clearly recognized.[27]

Yet if Somerville and Ross risk being seen as inappropriately professional, they themselves probably did more than any commentators to
deprofessionalize their image. In fact, in a curious feature of their self-
presentation, Somerville and Ross seem to admit to professional exper-
tise only in private statements—in personal letters to each other. In
public they insistently personalize their collaboration, striking a light
autobiographical note consistent with an amateurism marked as feminine. In *Irish Memories*, for example, Somerville suggests with characteristic flippancy that "the final impulse towards the career of letters

[26] Linda Fritschner, for example, notes that it was common for publishers' readers to
"go beyond the grammatical and technical to rework and rewrite manuscripts in their en-
tirety" ("Publishers' Readers, Publishers, and Their Authors" 64). Comparing "the 'hack'
readers as exemplified by Miss Jewsbury and the 'influential' readers as represented by
Edward Garnett" (47–48), she demonstrates both the wide range of authorial services
these readers provided (constituting a kind of minor coauthorship) and the gendered
ways these services were often distributed.

[27] Vera Brittain and Winifred Holtby, for example, working together in the interwar period, did not pretend to write with each other; as Jean Kennard notes, they wouldn't even
respond to each other's work until it was completed, for fear of stifling the other's "individual creative act" (*Vera Brittain and Winifred Holtby: A Working Relationship* 11). Violet
Paget, who, writing under the name "Vernon Lee," was a prolific author of literature and
literary criticism, never ventured to collaborate on her fictional undertakings, although,
with one of her lovers, Kit Anstruther-Thompson, she participated in a notorious collaboration on the psychology of aesthetics (see Phyllis F. Mannocchi, "Vernon Lee and Kit
Anstruther-Thompson: A Study of Love and Collaboration between Romantic Friends").

was given to us by a palmist." And when Somerville comes to write the partnership's retrospective, she colludes in the mystification of its professional components. In fact, although Somerville was twenty-eight and Ross twenty-four when they first became acquainted, Somerville represents the partnership as originating in "the Mutiny of two playmates." She breaks off the account, moreover, well before the publication of their first novel, and resumes with a discussion of the collaboration's continuation through automatic writing. "Two of a Trade" thus elides the crucial years of professional engagement when Somerville and Ross wrote and published together.

Written at the end of Somerville's life—in fact, the last essay she ever published—"Two of a Trade" reverses the trajectory of the Somerville and Ross career, overwriting the life of two professional authors into a story of perfect female friendship. As such, it reconstructs the collaboration along lines more in keeping with conventional assumptions about gender. But it also opens the collaboration to the type of prurient speculation that, as I argued in Chapter 2, regularly occurs when collaboration and intimate friendship are collapsed into each other. In Maurice Collis's authorized biography, for example, the famed collaboration turns on an unholy alliance of complementary needs and forces: for *his* Somerville is a sublimated lesbian seeking a woman who "would be all and all to her" and *his* Ross is "a literary genius in embryo" seeking "an outlet" for her creative potential (36, 37). If more crudely rendered than other representations, Collis's scenario plays upon familiar couplings; for in this particular nexus, collaboration, like lesbianism, is always a drama of arrested development. The story thus remains the same even when, as in Somerville's narrative, the perfect friendship is sexless. In Collis's story, moreover, as in other less extreme versions, Somerville and Ross are the ultimate novices: amateur writers and amateur lesbians.

Indeed, as Gifford Lewis suggests in a "corrective" to Collis, such imputations of lesbianism derive from a misogynistic refusal to accept women's professionalism.[28] As Lewis explains it, a belief in the authors' lack of proper sexual development licenses a reading of their incom-

---

[28] Lewis's counterargument, however, remains deeply homophobic. Hence her relentless scouring of the Somerville and Ross correspondence to "prove" there could be no basis for attributing lesbian sentiments to them—an argument that depends upon such dubious evidence as the insistence that references to each other as "lazy slut" or "You are the Queen of Pigs feet" are "not the language of a Sapphic sexual love" (*Somerville and Ross* 201). Even as she denies the lesbian possibility, however, Lewis insinuates that if there were any such feelings they belong to Martin, not to Somerville, making her argument a mere inversion of Collis's. Like Collis, moreover, Lewis seems unable to conceive a lesbian relationship as anything other than adolescent experimentalism.

plete or imperfect professional maturation. In her account, Lewis thus rewrites the partnership's symbolic history so that its turning point now occurs not when the cousins first meet each other, but when, years earlier, Somerville had "rejected marriage and turned herself into a self-supporting, single woman" (*Somerville and Ross* 32). Like Collis, then, Lewis undoes the partnership in the very act of "rescuing" it, insisting that for the union to work the partners must remain "single"—distinct and separable from each other.

Although Somerville and Ross would probably not have recognized themselves in these portrayals, their personalizing gestures play into the hands of the curiosity-seekers. For insisting that their collaboration is "what can never be explained" ("Two of a Trade" 186), they veil it in a mystery that provokes detection; what the authors, however, seem most reluctant to talk about are the *professional* dimensions of the collaboration. Their personal reflections thus collude with conventional prejudice to foster the impression of their professional amateurism. When Amy Lowell, in her poetic tribute "To Two Unknown Ladies," complains about the authors' lack of artistic commitment—"A book tossed off between two sets of tennis, / Or jotted down . . . / When the hounds could not run"—she merely echoes their own self-projections. And when she admits her reluctant admiration, Lowell casts it as a reproof to *real* professionals.

That Somerville and Ross should provoke such an ambivalent tribute from a woman writer committed to the professional life of letters should not be surprising.[29] For what their collaboration does is to make explicit what goes on behind the scenes in most women's "non-professional" writings: the collaborations never named as such that operate as the extension of family and friendship. Collaboration, for women, thus becomes a means to publicize and professionalize the private domain as well as to privatize the public dimensions of writing. Somerville and Ross, in fact, could be said to have literalized the idea of "family collaboration" and with it the professionalization of the family: turning to the family for the grounds of their own union; milking their families for their subject matter; deserting their families for their writing; using their family as trial readers; exploiting their family's social and professional connections (as in their letter-writing campaigns). But in rendering materially visible what underwrites women's fiction, these literary

[29] Lowell, who represented her own poetry as collaborative, the product of her loving relationship with Ada Russell, apparently contemplated putting a sign over her doorway, "Lowell & Russell, Makers of Fine Poems" (Sandra M. Gilbert and Susan Gubar, *No Man's Land* 2:237); Lowell's ambivalence, then, may also be a response to the tameness of the personal relationship Somerville and Ross were willing to acknowledge (see Chapter 2).

partnerships pose a problem for other women. For in literalizing collaboration's metaphorical possibilities, they both bring joint writing under scrutiny and delimit its operation, keeping writing, as it were, in the family. Collaboration, as such, thus stands as both the "special case" of women's writing and the exemplary instance of it.

At the end of her life, Somerville lamented her lack of literary authority and the lack of enduring fame for her partnership productions: "[I]t is an undoubted fact that when the writers of these later generations—since Trollope, and Rhoda Broughton, and Kipling—are enumerated, Somerville and Ross are never included" (qtd. in Cummins, *Dr E. Œ. Somerville* 192). Somerville attributes this fact to her immersion in the hunt and her isolation at Carbery, but the collaboration itself must surely have contributed to this marginalization. For the contradictory understandings of the Somerville and Ross partnership speak to the unstable place of collaboration in the configuration of authorship—and of female authorship, in particular. In fact, for Somerville and Ross, collaboration can be said to have both made their career and unmade it. For the collaboration was a source of nearly endless fascination—for the press and for the public. Indeed, so much was collaboration a condition of their literary existence that Somerville ultimately risked her professional reputation over it. Not only did Somerville insist, after Ross's death, in continuing to publish under their dual signature, but she insisted that, via automatic writing, she continued to "write with Martin."[30] Invoking metaphors of trade to explain this peculiar practice, Somerville contended that there was nothing peculiar about it: as the firm was still in business she felt justified in linking her name with Martin's (Powell 197).[31] And when, seventeen years after Ross's death, Somerville was awarded an honorary doctor of letters from Trinity College, Dublin, she refused to accept the honor unless Martin Ross were named co-recipient.

If these theatrical gestures opened the collaboration to ridicule, on another level, they simply made explicit what made women's literary collaborations so problematic: the uneasy alliances they forged between

[30] This was Somerville's term for Ross's automatic communications. When "Martin" first communicates with Somerville in a séance, it is to announce the need to maintain their *professional* relationship: "You and I have not finished our work" (qtd. in Collis 177).

[31] On one level at least, this was simply good business sense. As Simon Eliot, for example, points out, when Besant, after long years of partnership with Rice (cut off by Rice's illness), published his first solo novel, *All Sorts and Conditions of Men*, his publishers continued to advertise it (in pre-publication announcements) as a Besant-Rice production, only dropping Rice's name when they were reassured that the book would be successful ("'His Generation Read His Stories': Walter Besant, Chatto and Windus, and *All Sorts and Conditions of Men*" 27–30).

professionalism and idiosyncrasy, alliances for which the Brontës might be seen as paradigmatic. Beginning their career with the more reputable collaboration of painter and poet, Somerville and Ross quickly transformed their union into a writing partnership that openly defied the hierarchies readers attributed to them; indeed, the more successful they became on a professional level, the more they figured as eccentric, insisting in the face of relentless questions about their collaboration that there was nothing to tell about it. If Somerville's term, then, for her automatic writing—"writing with Martin"—reopened the whole question of what it meant for Somerville and Ross to write together, this was a question, Somerville implied, never previously answered to anyone's satisfaction.

In answering the question so definitively, however, Somerville made "spiritual collaboration" the partnership's new professional insignia, casting doubt on the partnership's earlier professionalism and ensuring its lasting reputation as a cultural curiosity. Indeed, if the death of a partner could be said to put a collaboration into perspective, Somerville's response highlighted the partnership's eccentric features: its refusal to acknowledge the authors' separate existences. Somerville's response to Ross's death took this position to an extreme, but it could be said to typify what made women's collaborations distinctive. For unlike their male counterparts, women's collaborations appear not to know limits: not to know where to draw the line, when to stop, and so on.

When Besant, then, at the end of a ten-year collaboration closed off by his partner's death, comments, "Now that Rice is dead it is impossible for me to lay hands upon any passage or page and to say 'This belongs to Rice—this is mine' (*Autobiography* 188–89), he locates the impossibility in the fact that his partner cannot now defend his property interests; but comparable claims by women suggested the inadequacy of the very categories of proprietary ownership. And where Besant argued for the necessary limits to any literary collaboration—a time after which the authors must claim an independent literary position—women collaborators seemed to recognize no such necessity; even death, Somerville suggested, provided no "natural" conclusion to a joint endeavor.[32] In fact, Somerville ultimately proved willing to admit only that their "technique of writing together has had to be changed, and, to a certain extent, modified" after her partner's death ("Two of a Trade" 185). Thus while newspapers could lament no longer seeing their names coupled

---

[32] By contrast, when Besant laments the death of his partner, he laments the fact that the partnership did not end sooner, granting Rice the chance to achieve what he has been granted: "an independent literary position" (*Autobiography* 189).

together, Somerville would not subscribe to this reading of things: "But our signature is dual, as it has ever been, and I recognize no reason why I should change it" ("Two of a Trade" 185). Taking collaboration to its literal and figurative limits, Somerville, in the end, took the practice beyond the bounds of credibility; but in doing so, she may have done no more than illuminate the borderline position of women's literary partnerships in the domain of professional respectability.

4

Writing at the Margins
Collaboration and the Discourse of Exoticism

When Mrs. Gaskell writes her *Life of Charlotte Brontë*, she implies that the special genius of the Brontë siblings cannot be properly understood without knowledge of the peculiar borderland they hailed from. Representing the landscape as wild, rough, and intractable and the customs of the people as commensurately coarse and brutish, Gaskell makes Haworth out to be a barbarous outpost of nineteenth-century England, an anachronistic reminder of a more primitive era. Indeed, for Gaskell the Yorkshire of the Brontës' childhood appears so distant from the culture of England proper as to belong to an entirely different planet.

Even though Juliet Barker contends that this picture is completely inaccurate (*The Brontës* 92), the mythology it has spawned has proved remarkably durable, turning the Brontës into, as it were, our favorite Martians: English literature's homegrown exotics. Such exoticism, I am arguing, plays a constitutive role in the collaborative project, for collaboration is, as the preceding chapters document, preeminently a borderline phenomenon, demarcating the boundaries of respectable authorship. But collaboration has historically also been a resource of the culturally marginalized, which explains in part its particular appeal for women living outside the English metropolis.[1] It seems no accident, then, that the writing partnerships I have been exploring should flourish at the outer reaches of British identity—in Scotland, Ireland, and Australia, and among expatriate communities in Europe. And it seems no accident that interest in these collaborations has fastened on their Otherness.

In fact, however cosmopolitan their experiences, partnership writers

---

[1] Discussing the American lesbian expatriate community in Paris, Sandra M. Gilbert and Susan Gubar make a similar point, arguing that collaboration is the perfect response to a profound sense of exile. See *No Man's Land* 2:222.

seem fated to be treated as the denizens of some remote backwater. Marjorie Barnard and Flora Eldershaw, for example, although educated at the University of Sydney and long-time residents of a thriving Australian metropolis, found a market only in London, where Australian literature, like Australia itself, was considered a curiosity.[2] The Findlater sisters, despite prolonged residence in England and despite their ties in Scotland to Edinburgh's elite society, remain the daughters of the remote Scottish parsonage of their birthplace, Scotland's answer to the Brontë sisters; despite the lack, moreover, of the usual local color markings, their works cannot be read as other than "Scottish."

Indeed, going back at least as far as the Brontës, partnership writing would appear to have made its name by trading on the exotic. In the case of the Brontës, this exoticism resides both in the remote foreign settings they choose for their stories and in the peculiar style and format of their literary product. But as I argue in Chapter 1, the very peculiarities of the Brontës' early writings mark the children's access to an exclusive English authorship; collaborating to produce the Other, they thus ensure their own insider status. With this in mind, we might return to one of the leading tropes of the collaborative project: the authority to write *as one*, assumed so unquestioningly by the writing partners who succeed the Brontës at the end of the century. For the sameness that upholds these unions covers a variety of stories, including ones about the Other these partnerships rely on.

Closer to home than the fantasy islands of the Brontës, the partnerships that begin to appear in the 1880s illuminate another history of colonial encounters—the history that produces the United Kingdom and its commonwealth satellites. In fact, to a large extent, it is as purveyors of local color—of, as it were, regional exoticism—that women's literary partnerships made their reputation. Even the Rossetti sisters ("Isabel Meredith") can be seen to work within this tradition, offering in their novel *A Girl among the Anarchists* "a journey into the space of the Other," the "working class anarchist haunts" of the back streets of London (x). In addition, then, to the dual authorship they publicly or privately announce, these unions require collaboration of another kind: with the speakers of "colorful" native dialects—with a "mother-tongue" that stamps these works as authentic, making them seem, as it were, "characteristically Scotch" or "Irish right through." If in these works, then, the hands of the authors prove indistinguishable from each other, the "writing" thus produced by "two ladies"—as literature in English, both literate and literary—remains distinct from the "voice" of the people written about.

<hr>

[2] See M. Barnard Eldershaw, "The Writer and Society" 222.

For Madame de Laszowska (née Emily Gerard) and her sister Dorothea, who lived in eastern Europe and moved from military station to
station after Emily's marriage to an Austrian army officer and member
of the Polish nobility, the gulf between "us" and "them" determines the
contours of their fiction. But the figures who made the Gerard sisters so
popular in England—the Austrian army officers, the Polish peasants,
the Jews, the members of the Polish aristocracy—delight precisely because they are Other. As Helen Black explains, they provided a dose
of "novelty" for the English reading public, who could share the sisters'
apprehension of habits and ideas "still refreshingly primitive" (161). Indeed, so "other" are these characters and settings that even the most
outlandish descriptions appear to bear the mark of authenticity. Thus
The Spectator writes of *Beggar My Neighbour*, E. D. Gerard's second novel,
"The author's effort to throw himself into Polish ways of thinking is
extraordinarily successful. One would think, but for the idiomatic
English, that it was the translation of a native novelist that one was
reading"—a description that might give one pause, especially when the
reviewer adds, "Not the least characteristic part is the description of
Jewish agents and money-lenders" (239–40). For what is characteristic
in these descriptions is their reproduction of familiar stereotypes: the
Jew's "orthodox hook" nose, "orthodox corkscrew curls," hooded eyes,
sallow skin, and hands resembling "claws"; indeed, the Jews are represented as having "wormed" their way into "the machinery of public life," where they have their hands on all the strings and are spread-
ing like "a network" over the entire countryside (*Beggar My Neighbour*
57–59).
    If the novels of E. D. Gerard, moreover, have been upheld for their
"local traits of scenery and manners"[3]—for the "graphic realism that
comes of intimate knowledge acquired in the country described" (Porter
356)—they have been equally praised for their imaginary landscapes.
Thus writing of *Reata*, one reviewer declares the scenes in Mexico to
be conveyed with "such vividly realistic picturesqueness" that "it was
hard to believe [the author] had never visited the country."[4] What seems
most to impress the critics is that the Gerard sisters appear "equally
at home" with all types and in all settings: whether describing German
watering-place society, the tropical scenery of a Mexican forest, scenes
of Austrian military life, a country house in Poland, a Prussian officer,
a Creole heiress, a Jewish money lender.
    If a quality of at-homeness characterizes their writing, it may be be-

---

[3] Review of *The Waters of Hercules* by E. D. Gerard. *The Spectator* 58 (1885): 1206.
[4] This reference occurs in a review of E. Gerard's *The Land Beyond the Forest* (330). *Satur-
day Review* 65 (March 17 1888): 330–331.

cause their engagement in fiction provided the expatriate sisters the dose of home that enabled them to secure their "Englishness" in an alien setting. Dorothea Gerard's later remarks—while residing in Galicia after her marriage to Captain Longard of the Austrian Lancers—might shed some light on the condition of cultural isolation that prompted the sisters' decision to write together: "'It is difficult to convey to you,' says Dorothea Gerard, 'or indeed to any civilised British mind, a correct idea of my present home. With the exception of my husband, I do not talk to a really educated person more than about six times a year'" (Black 159).[5] Indeed, as Black explains, so great was this isolation that Dorothea "confesses to feeling the danger of forgetting her mother-tongue, and in order to avoid the chance of such a catastrophe she reads as much English literature as opportunity will admit" (159). How much more, then, would writing English literature with a sister allow two transplanted women to exercise their mother tongue, and with it, the privileges of British civilization; for writing about what came closest to hand—"Jews and Polish peasants, very far back in cultivation" (160)—these chroniclers of the "the manners and customs of diverse nations" (159) could confirm not only the superiority of their powers of observation but of their culture and education.

The collaborative works of Edith Somerville and Violet Martin ("Martin Ross"), two daughters of the Irish gentry, performed a similar cultural negotiation, preserving the fiction of an Ireland divorced from contemporary social reality—whether "The Ireland of Somerville and Ross," familiar from the R.M. stories, "a land of reckless, improvident fox-hunters and their disreputable retainers" (Flanagan 55) or the Ireland of the Big House (the Irish country manor) of the Anglo-Irish aristocracy, the theme and setting of their major novels. But where Emily and Dorothea Gerard wrote self-consciously as outsiders in their adoptive country, Somerville and Ross occupied more ambivalent territory, caught between "two Irelands" and hence neither alien nor native in their home country. As their first collaborative project indicates—"a dictionary of the words and phrases peculiar to [their] family" (*Irish Memories* 65)—they recognized themselves as speakers of a language different from the "English" of both the residents of England and the Irish peasantry. But the nuances of this language also reflect the particular inflections of a common ancestry that linked the houses of Ross and Drishane (the Martin and Somerville estates, respectively) through the figure of Charles Kendal Bushe (Edith Somerville and Violet Martin's

---

[5] When she speaks to her husband, moreover, she speaks in German, since neither she nor her husband knew the other's language well enough to communicate in it.

great-grandfather); in other words, if Somerville and Ross could merge their voices as one, this was because they not only came from the same class, but were, in fact, blood relatives.[6]

Although Somerville later dismissed the dictionary as "a solemnly preposterous work" (*Irish Memories* 65), in many ways, it illuminates the principles of their collaboration. For like the dictionary, their works of collaborative fiction document and preserve—by, as it were, translating into English—the morals and manners of the Irish (and Anglo-Irish) people; like the dictionary, moreover, their works of fiction perform a service for a "language"—a way of life—passing out of existence, and hence in need of translation and transcription. Indeed, the success or failure of the Somerville and Ross corpus has been judged, by and large, on the question of dialect. For while the works of fiction depend upon a common "family" language of class and nation, they have attracted the most attention for their portrayal of "the living language" of the people—a language that the admirers of Somerville and Ross (and even some of their detractors) praise for its "astonishing fidelity" (Lyons 120).

But the use to which this dialect has been put remains a subject of fierce disputation. For the Findlater sisters, who eschewed broad dialect—writing fiction unmistakably Scotch, but "Scotch with a certain difference"[7]—and who wrote in a political climate less conspicuously volatile than the one that troubled Ireland, their "claim to be remembered whenever the history of the Scottish novel is brought up to date" (Mackenzie xii) would not appear particularly controversial. But for Somerville and Ross, as Stephen Gwynn notes, "when there is a question of Ireland's output in literature, these ladies are generally overlooked" (346). In fact, although Violet Martin was a cousin of Lady Augusta Gregory (who asked her to write a play for the Abbey Theatre), and although Somerville and Ross wrote at precisely the same time as the Irish Literary Revival, they are rarely seen as having anything in common with this nationalist literary movement[8]—a movement itself deeply grounded in a collaborative aesthetic, as witnessed in the folklore collections (like those produced by W. B. Yeats and Lady Gregory)

---

[6] Analyzing Somerville and Ross as the preeminent chroniclers of "the life and death of the Big House" (55), Thomas Flanagan invokes the two authors' separate homes only to insist on their imaginative union: "The houses seem joined by the imagination—the Big House of Ross-Drishane" (58); hence Flanagan's singular title: "The Big House of Ross-Drishane."

[7] Review of *Penny Monypenny*. *Punch* 141 (1911), 405.

[8] Conor Cruise O'Brien offers one of the few qualifications to this standard representation: "The world of Somerville and Ross may not be quite as remote from the world of the Literary Revival as we sometimes think" (*Writers and Politics* 110). See also John Cronin, "Dominant Themes in the Novels of Somerville and Ross."

and in the collaborative ethos of the Abbey Theatre. In fact, like their more famous contemporaries, Somerville and Ross "attended classes in the Irish language" and "foraged among the country people in search of phrases and habits of speech" (Cronin 10). Like the revivalists, moreover, they recorded what they heard "with all the tender precision of a folk-lorist" (Lyons 120). Throughout their writing career, Somerville and Ross regularly kept notebooks where they collected, on one side, the "things said by servants, country people and the like" and recorded, on the other, their novelistic transcriptions of this material (Collis 78). But they differed from their contemporaries in being *popular* writers— at once closer to "the people" and, by virtue of this fact, more suspect in their treatment of them. As Cronin puts it, "When Somerville and Ross saw an old woman going down the path," they saw a literary opportunity—a living, breathing, walking wordbook. The woman "might not have the walk of a queen," he admits, "but she was quite likely to have a remarkably vivid tongue in her head and a striking individuality" (10)—qualities the author-cousins were quick to seize on. Indeed, if they were folklorists, Lyons concedes, they were folklorists "with a highly developed sense of the ridiculous" (120). The down-to-earthness their admirers praise in Somerville and Ross's cultural excavations can thus be seen to open a space where "appreciation" fades into "appropriation," where literary collaboration can become a consorting with the (English) enemy.

Commenting on the dictionary of their own family language, Somerville once remarked, "It might possibly—in fact I think some selections would—entertain the public, but I can confidently say it will never be offered to it; Bowdler himself would quail at the difficulties it would present" (*Irish Memories* 65). Yet Somerville and Ross apparently experienced no comparable scruples about entertaining the public (and each other) with the "racy" and "colorful" language of the Irish peasantry. Although in an early letter, Martin admits to some doubt as to the propriety of the anecdote she offers for her cousin's perusal, once their writing career was launched they would rail at the censors of such lively material: "Let me before I forget it tell you what a woman said to Mama at Gouran—in talking of another woman having lost her husband—'Oh indeed ma'am—there she is—the crayture—and he having left her with one child and the invoice of another'—*Is* it very improper—I feel that it is, but am not sure" (*Selected Letters of Somerville and Ross* 10). The impropriety, of course, that might now claim our interest is not the questionable content to which Violet Martin alludes but its entire mode of presentation—the trafficking in "other women" recounted in the anecdote and reperformed in the letter; for like the Somerville and Ross fiction, what the letter transmits for personal profit and gratification is the "remarkably vivid tongue" and "striking individuality" of the unknown woman.

When Mary Childers and bell hooks, in a 1990 publication, attempt to perform "A Conversation about Race and Class," they invite their readers to listen for the silences that inevitably inform a "cross-race dialogue," to hear their struggle and disagreements as well as their conviction (60–61). When Somerville and Ross, however, discourse on "race" and class—on "Irishness"—in their fiction, their text appears as unbroken and uninterrupted, their disagreements resolved before they put words to paper; in fact, they write without apparent self-consciousness about their position to each other. But we may read the silences that mark their differences (not from each other but from their fictional subjects) precisely where the "other woman" speaks: an other who speaks "authentically"—with remarkable precision, fidelity, and accuracy—but without the authority of those who hold the pen. Indeed, if Somerville and Ross, as they repeatedly suggest, never know when to say "I" or "we"—a pronoun difficulty shared by their faithful admirers[9]—it is in part because the "we" they occupy so handily is exclusive as well as inclusive, defining a place where their individual differences pale before their common authority as members of the class of writing women. Of course, the kind of exchange across class, race, and nationality envisioned (and enacted) by contemporary feminist theorists would be unthinkable for women positioned as Somerville and Ross were within their historical circumstances and culture; such performances of difference, however, render visible the types of "conversations" foreclosed by the particular understanding of collaboration that rode Somerville and Ross to fame (and subsequent obscurity).

From this perspective, Somerville and Ross remain, as authors, border figures, standing in relation to "the hidden Ireland" in the same position they occupy toward their fictional universe: "on the threshold of a new world, that was yet our own old Province of Munster, peopled with unknown yet entirely familiar beings" (qtd. in Robinson 43). If Somerville and Ross, then, knew the "other Ireland," they knew it from the vantage of Ascendancy ladies, unlikely to question the discursive rules and political structures that govern and delimit cross-class interchange—rules that leave the Other simultaneously "unknown" yet "en-

---

[9] See, for example, C. L. Graves ("Indeed, one of the chief difficulties of writing about the cousins is that one never knows when to say 'she' or 'they,' for they were of one mind . . . It mattered not which hand held the pen" ["Martin Ross" 350]) and Stephen Gwynn ("Yet I think that in what may be said here, there should be no separation of persons" ["Lever's Successors" 354]).

tirely familiar"; in fact, it could be argued that their gender and class position ensured their power of surveillance, offering them privileged access to "the other woman," to "what a woman said to Mama . . . in talking of another woman."

The image of the speaking (female) body, circulated between women in an exchange of letters, represents with disarming explicitness the material base for the Somerville and Ross style of collaboration; it illuminates, indeed, the practice, as Somerville articulates it, whereby their characters were talked over—and into—existence: "Gradually we talked and argued into existence one after another of the little group of men and women. . . . One after the other of Major Sinclair Yeates' friends and neighbours came effortlessly to our call. It seemed as if we had always known them. I can truly say that in order to identify an actual representative of any of them, it would be necessary to tear each of them to pieces, and, collecting the fragments, resume them into a sort of human rag bag"(qtd. in Robinson 43).[10] If this practice reflects the general politics of Anglo-Irish writing (where the Irish people come effortlessly to the gentry's call), the collaboration simultaneously puts up for scrutiny the dismemberment that precedes this achievement of a unitary fictional perspective, what E. V. Lucas calls the writing's "all-of-a-pieceness" (9). For in effect, the collaboration dramatizes—plays, as it were, before our very eyes—what goes into (and out of) the class-bound text of contemporary Ireland, whether authored singly or doubly.

In Somerville's hands, the collaboration would ultimately play out a very different spectacle—one no less involved, however, in the power of "talk" to materialize a living presence. Indeed, the interest in spiritualism Somerville and Ross shared with their Irish literary contemporaries might be seen as the ultimate literalization of the revival movement. Somerville's account, above, of how the Irish R.M. stories originated could thus be seen to illuminate how she would later talk her dead partner back into existence, for it was as "talk" that she explained her automatic writing.[11] Even if we do not credit the reality of Ross's continuing existence, Ross's hand remained after her death for Somerville to draw on—most visibly in the letters, diaries, and notebooks where the cousins collected and recorded the "sayings and phrases of

[10] While Somerville and Ross also summon characters of their own class in this peremptory way, the politics of representation come most vividly—and problematically—into play where class difference is at stake.

[11] "And she *is* helping me. I am quite sure of it. By suggestion, not by direct writing. Yet I cannot be mistaken and when we are writing (the daily talk that I am now able to have with her), she has often confirmed my own feelings as to which bits she inspired and which originated with me and were touched up by her. Just as always was our practice" (qtd. in Mitchell 36).

the Irish around them" (Robinson 49). Collis, then, is perhaps being something less than entirely fanciful when he imagines, in this later work, hearing Ross's voice behind Somerville's classic "Irish" writing, behind the passages she pens "so rich with feeling for the old Irish scene and so subtly worded." If in moments like this, Collis suggests, "we seem to see the shade of Martin leaning over her and whispering the words in her ears, and do not find the visionary collaboration strange or unlikely, indeed find it certainly real" (224), his comments suggest that the collaboration is most real, whether visionary or otherwise, when it confirms the authors as the ultimate connoisseurs of "authentic" Irishness.

Although Somerville and Ross connoisseurs might declare that at times they can almost credit Edith Somerville's automatic writing—that, seen in the right light, they do not find such a visionary collaboration "strange or unlikely"—the same latitude was not generally granted other women who wrote in this fashion. Indeed, most of the middle-class women who engaged in such practices—and there were quite a number of them at the time Somerville conducted her own writing experiments—found that their visionary collaborations were more than the public was willing to stomach. So strange, in fact, did people find mediums' claims to be communicating with the world of the spirits that even the most prominent practitioners of this trade often felt compelled to keep their writing secret, except among a closed circle of sympathizers and believers.

Somerville's automatic writing was, however, by no means typical. Most mediums, for example, did not claim that their putative collaborators were people with whom, in this life, they had enjoyed a writing relationship. Most mediums, for that matter, did not communicate with spirits of their own conscious choosing. More typically, they performed their writing at the behest of another: a sitter who would, in effect, "hire" them to facilitate otherworldly communications. In such instances, there were, then, generally witnesses to the communication—the sitters themselves and sometimes psychical research investigators. At its extreme, a medium's work might be witnessed by large numbers of observers, all qualified in some way to comment on its authenticity; Geraldine Cummins, for example, who produced a series of automatic scripts based on "early Christian" materials, documents those who observed her writing: "three members of the medical profession, two Fellows of the Royal College of Physicians (Ireland), a Doctor of Law, a Doctor of Philosophy, three Doctors of Divinity, ten clergymen, a well-known historical scholar, the editor of a literary monthly, journalists, a sculptor, novelists, and representatives of English and American Societies for Psychical Research, including the late Dr. W. Franklin Prince" (*Unseen Adventures* 110).

As a joint venture, automatic writing, as practiced by its leading figures, was not entirely like the collaborative writing authors such as Somerville and Ross engaged in; one of its peculiarities was that the identity—indeed existence—of a good half of the team could not be empirically verified. The writing itself—not clearly literature and certainly not grammatically or stylistically conventional—was, furthermore, of a rather different order from the polished consumer products churned out by women's recognized "literary" unions; multivoiced, rambling, and with all its parts showing, the "scripts" of automatic writing were anything but seamless. But mediumship was, as I argue in the next chapter, a serious practice of authorship, sharing the ambiguity—professional, sexual, textual—of other forms of collaborative writing. Indeed, as I argue in the remainder of this chapter, it takes to the limit what it means to write from the margin.

While much of the sponsored activity of mediumship was centered in London, where the Society of Psychical Research had its headquarters, mediums themselves regularly maintained their special relationship to England's borderlands—past as well as present. Ireland, as W. B. Yeats reminds us, was a hotbed of spiritualist activity—and not incidentally. Yeats himself attributed this phenomenon to some direct link between Irish heritage and mediumistic capacities,[12] although in his own most famous experiments, he drew on the medium of an English wife to access his psychic susceptibilities (see Chapter 6). Hester Dowden, Geraldine Cummins, and Eileen Garrett, some of the most respected twentieth-century mediums, all claimed Irish nativity—both as a matter of biographical fact and as a spiritual foundation for their mediumship. Mrs. Piper, who was one of the SPR's most important subjects, was American, as were other prominent early twentieth-century mediums. Winifred Coombe Tenant, who performed important experiments for the SPR in the 1910s and 1920s under the name "Mrs. Willett"—and who, allegedly, later communicated from the afterlife with Geraldine Cummins—was Welsh. "Mrs. Holland," whose work, along with Mrs. Willett's, Mrs. Piper's, and Mrs. Verrall's (an English medium residing in Cambridge), was crucial to the "Cross-Correspondence Experiments" (where fragmentary parts of a single message were received by different mediums working independently of each other), was residing in India when she first began receiving automatic writing, allegedly from her own Scots ancestors. And Mrs. Leonard was famous

---

[12] See W. B. Yeats, "Swedenborg, Mediums, and the Desolate Places."

for the communications of her "Indian" control, purportedly the surviving spirit of her own great-great-grandmother.[13]

But mediums, whatever their birthplace or current residence, also occupied other less tangible borders—simply by being what they claimed to be. For to be a medium one had to become Other to oneself. And mediumistic writing often appears more a reflection of this internalized border than the writing of some exotic geographic homefront. The literature of mediumship is thus filled with allusions to the "double life" of its exponents—the everyday life of seemingly unexceptional middle-class women and the secret life pursued in their unseen adventures, when they gave themselves over to those who spoke through them.[14] For mediums who lived more of their ordinary life in the public spotlight—as was the case, for example, with Winifred Coombe Tenant ("Mrs. Willett"), a society lady, justice of the peace, and League of Nations delegate—the gap between their acknowledged and unacknowledged lives was all the more striking. "When my legal personality expressed itself from the Bench," "Mrs. Willett" writes in the scripts recorded by Geraldine Cummins, "it was quite different from what many would regard dubiously as an illegal personality, that aspect of myself that played out its part in my secret life—Mrs. T. making experiments with O. L. and G. B. on the quiet, or as I should call the character—Mrs. Willett" (Cummins, *Swan* 108).[15]

[13] The mediums mentioned here are the ones generally taken most seriously by their contemporaries; both skeptics and believers alike credited them with an unimpeachable integrity. Their careers sometimes overlapped, as in the Cross-Correspondence Experiments (see Renée Haynes, *The Society for Psychical Research, 1882–1982: A History*, and Alfred Douglas, *Extra-sensory Powers: A Century of Psychical Research*), and they have often been treated as a group in the available literature. As professional women, they also had spiritual—and sometimes material—connections to each other. Mrs. Willett, for example, felt encouraged to try her hand at automatic writing after reading an account of Mrs. Holland's mediumship; Hester Dowden initiated Cummins into mediumship, and they collaborated on several psychical research projects, even at one time sharing a household. Eileen Garrett's mediumship was predicted by Mrs. Leonard's control, "Feda." While all of these mediums at times produced standard automatic writing, Dowden often relied on the ouija board, spelling out messages that others recorded. Leonard and Garrett typically produced scripts by *speaking* messages—messages, like Dowden's, transcribed by designated observers. All of these practices, however, share similar structures and raise related questions about the mediation of authorship.

[14] In her repeated references to her "dual life," Garrett, for example, contrasts an outer world where she remains "docile to [her] husband's wishes" to an "inner world" of adventure and excitement (Eileen Garrett, *Many Voices: The Autobiography of a Medium* 34). In a similar gesture, Leonard titles her autobiography *My Life in Two Worlds*. And "Astor," the control spirit who introduces "Mrs. Willett" to Cummins, explains, "To put it crudely, she would and often did live in two worlds" (Geraldine Cummins, *Swan on a Black Sea: A Study in Automatic Writing: The Cummins–Willett Scripts* 9).

[15] Interestingly, "Mrs. Willett" distinguishes the public woman's commitment to the contemporary women's movement from the private woman's involvement in spiritualist activities. As justice of the peace for Glamorganshire, Wales, and as a League of Nations

Whether one takes these expressions to be the genuine words of the historical woman who produced automatic writing as "Mrs. Willett" or the projection of a fellow practitioner, the point is essentially identical. For whether practiced on the sly by married women such as Mrs. Tennant, or, more openly by single women such as Cummins—women who often lived with other women who shared their psychic interests— mediumship was generally perceived to be incompatible with the normal demands of home and family. Indeed, for several of its practitioners, mediumship was one of the few spaces they allowed themselves to express homosocial ties to other women. And for some, like Radclyffe Hall and Una Troubridge, not mediums themselves but sitters and investigators, their involvement with mediums was a place to pursue and cement an openly lesbian relationship.[16] Mediumship was generally perceived, moreover, as involving, if only metaphorically, some form of sexual transgression—even if its transgressions were most often cast in terms of heterosexual relations. "Mrs. Willett's" allusion to "my secret life," the title of the premier work of Victorian pornography, thus seems apt even if not intentional; for the practice of mediumship relies on the language of sexual adventure, and, more particularly, on an idiom of exotic practices and behaviors. When "Mrs. Willett," then, describes her "initiation" into the mysteries of mediumship, an initiation facilitated through the hands of a female intermediary, the pornographic cadences seem unmistakable: "She made me an eager explorer, as eager as was any participant in the ancient Greek mysteries. But I did not go in for any elaborate practices or preparations. How could I? I had various duties, a husband, a son, a household to look after. I was carrying a child in 1909" (*Swan* 76).

Much the same story emerges in the official record, the extensive study of Mrs. Willett's mediumship published in the *Proceedings* of the SPR in the 1930s. Based largely on transcripts of Mrs. Willett's earlier automatic writing, the SPR study documents the "experiments" to which Mrs. Willett was subjected, the "psychic education" framed es-

---

delegate, "Mrs. Willett" was the first woman to hold these positions. Where recent scholarship on mediumship has stressed its affinities with feminist practices and movements, "Mrs. Willett" here suggests that the two are in conflict, if not mutually exclusive.

[16] See, for example, Richard Ormrod, *Una Troubridge: The Friend of Radclyffe Hall* 113. There seems some evidence to suggest that mediumship held a special appeal for the lesbian community—as a sanctioned space to express an unorthodox relationship. Terry Castle introduces this idea in *The Apparitional Lesbian*. In their dealings with Mrs. Leonard (whom they investigated for the SPR), Hall and Troubridge received messages not only from "Feda" but from another spirit, "AVB," who claimed to be Hall's former lover, Lady Batten. In these messages, "Ladye" advises them on their relationship and bestows her blessing on them. H. D. and Bryher were heavily involved with mediums in the 1940s. See Helen Sword, "H. D.'s *Magic Ring*."

pecially for her by communicators from "the other side"—F. W. H. Myers and Edmund Gurney, influential figures, when alive, in establishing the SPR—and performed with the help of two living SPR investigators, Sir Oliver Lodge and Gerald Balfour, the "O.L" and "G.B." of Mrs. Willett's communication (Balfour, "A Study of the Psychological Aspects of Mrs. Willett's Mediumship" 51). Manipulating Mrs. Willett "at their pleasure" (288), the communicators announce their desire to produce in "Mrs. Willett" a "trance-medium of a new kind" (58)—one who "retains a consciousness of self during the whole process of automatic production" (45). They expect her, however, simply to lie back and not ask any questions. Indeed, concerned lest the strain of comprehending the messages she communicates damage the "instrument," the communicators solicit a medium who, if conscious, nonetheless does not know what she is doing, does not know for what ends her "instrument" is utilized. As "Mrs. Willett" puts it in her communications with Cummins: "I closed my eyes and then the communicator began to use my instrument, my organ, pulled out the stops, as it were, took control, and my lips spoke the message" (*Swan* 90).

It would seem difficult to distinguish, then, the type of systematic "psychic education" Mrs. Willett describes (in which the female subject is trained to perform to her mentors' particular specifications) from the sensual educations familiar from contemporary pornography. Indeed, there would appear to be no terms other than the sexual to describe the experience by which a female medium gives herself over to the disposal of men other than her husband, literally lends her body and brain to their "special experiments." In Mrs. Willett's case, moreover, the communicators are quite explicit. In a classic bit of male rivalry, for example, "Gurney" accuses his fellow communicator of, in effect, spending himself too quickly, of not knowing how to handle a woman: "Myers doesn't manage things as well as I do. He takes more out of her. He doesn't shield off from her sufficiently; he lets the whole blaze come out in his impatience" (Balfour, "Study," 130). And "Myers," in what can only be seen as the exchange of the medium between men—between (male) communicator and (male) investigator—entrusts his private "preserve" to one of the researchers: "I'm trusting this machine to you, Lodge. . . . You are not to let anyone else experiment with her but Mrs Verrall. I won't answer for it if you let anyone else meddle" (167). In this context, it is perhaps not surprising that when Mrs. Willett finally permits her husband Charles to witness one of these experimental sessions, she passes out at the sitting. "I felt so cheap, so drained after it," she confesses to Cummins. "But Charles was very kind and understanding about it" (*Swan* 23).

Compared to their contemporaries, then, who collaborated on fiction, women mediums collaborated in ways more evidently transgressive. But the special experiments on which mediumship depended often proved more academic than sexual; indeed, in many cases, the secret lives mediumship uncovered could best be described in terms of *intellectual* adventure. That such adventure should come clothed in erotic trappings—indeed, that it should require the elaborate machinery of mediumship—suggests the lengths many women were prepared to go to express (or disguise) their intellectual ambitions. It suggests as well the way particular forms of knowledge, out of reach to women in their ordinary existence, took on the erotic charge of something exotic and untouchable. Where novelists such as Somerville and Ross, E. D. Gerard, and the Findlater sisters recorded the things seen and heard around them in their daily existence, mediums such as Cummins, Dowden, and, on occasion, Willett specialized in dead languages and ancient settings. Working with Mrs. Verrall, for example, Mrs. Willett produced a series of scripts based on obscure classical references—scripts ostensibly communicated by Mrs. Verrall's late husband, a distinguished Cambridge professor of classics; earlier in her own career, Mrs. Verrall, herself a university lecturer in this subject, had produced copious automatic writing in Greek and Latin.[17] Other mediums, meanwhile, while generally confining themselves to the English language, betrayed a special affinity for the pre-Christian and early Christian periods. In what she called "a curious adventure of the mind," for example, Cummins produced in the *Scripts of Cleophas* eight volumes of material dealing with the Apostolic period of early Christian history—a body of writing taken up in more detail in the next chapter. Similarly, Hester Dowden facilitated the *Scripts of Philip*, a work purportedly dictated by a contemporary of Jesus, as well as documents ostensibly from St. Francis of Assisi and from associates of King Arthur. Shirley Carson Jenney, the "Shelley psychic," published a curious document called the "Christ Script," a compilation of early Christian teachings ostensibly dictated by Percy Bysshe Shelley in an earlier incarnation as "scribe to the Lord Christ" in the thirteenth century. And "Patience Worth," in the work she considered her "masterpiece," wrote, through the agency of

---

[17] Mrs. Willett's scripts, published by Balfour under the title "The Ear of Dionysus," were purportedly posthumous communications from Dr. A. W. Verrall and Professor S. H. Butcher; designed as an academic puzzle outside Mrs. Willett's powers of decipherment, the scripts were intended, through their display of specialized scholarship, to confirm the identities of the supposed communicators. It was not uncommon for mediums to produce occasional words, sentences, and even passages of writing in languages in which they had no knowledge or formal training, but extended automatic writing in unknown "foreign" languages was certainly the exception. As a university-educated woman and a lecturer in classics, Mrs. Verrall was better educated than most contemporary mediums.

the American medium Mrs. Curran, an epic novel of more than six hundred pages set in the time of Christ—a work consistently praised for its striking local color.[18]

In these cases, automatic writing offered the mediums access to privileged knowledge unmediated by the regular channels of authority, by the demands, for example, of an Oxford or Cambridge education. Dowden, for instance, though the daughter of a famous scholar, had, according to her biographer, "no particular knowledge of Greek history, nor had she read anything, as far as she was aware, concerning the Great Library at Alexandria" (Bentley 81) before producing, through the work of her primary control "Johannes" (who claimed to be a Greek who studied at the Great Library around the year 200 B.C.), new articulations of Neoplatonic philosophy.[19] In fact, although Dowden claims that at the time she first began to receive Johannes's messages she had not read any Plotinus, the communications spark her interest, leading her to Dr. Inge's *Gifford Lectures* on the subject (Bentley 89). As a conduit of knowledge, however, Johannes offers Dowden the immediacy of experience: firsthand accounts of someone who attended the famous lectures on Plato at the Library of Alexandria.

In recording these experiences, then, mediums would seem to act much like local color writers, bringing to life customs and occurrences distant to their readers. But the events that mediums describe are completely foreign to them in their ordinary existence, even though they describe them with vividness and detail, and as if they were present. Thus Balfour writes of one striking episode in Mrs. Willett's mediumship: "[S]he describes in considerable detail, and almost as if it were a contemporaneous experience of her own, the scene immortalised in the *Symposium* of Plato" ("Study" 223). Like Cummins, for whom the Cleophas scripts appeared "as if a cinema moving-picture of history had been passing before [her] inner vision" (*Unseen Adventures* 75), Mrs. Willett confirms the experience's immediacy, a sense that the incidents are being "enacted before her very eyes": "There was such inter-

[18] Walter Franklin Prince cites numerous responses on this order: "[S]he shows the most wonderful command of local color and of the customs and humors of the past, so that one is tempted to say that she must have seen the events and characters that she describes"; "There is local color totally unlike that of the encyclopedia-crammed author of the usual novel of the Holy Land" (*The Case of Patience Worth: A Critical Study of Certain Unusual Phenomena* 56, 57). "Patience Worth" was, allegedly, the surviving spirit of a seventeenth-century English woman. "Patience Worth's" other historical fiction included *Telka: An Idyl of Medieval England* and *Hope Trueblood*, a novel set in the nineteenth century.
[19] Dowden's biographer identifies Johannes as the surviving spirit of the Athenian philosopher Carnaedes (216 B.C.–129 B.C.), the founder of the New Academia and Principal of the Third Academy at Athens (Bentley 82–83). "Johannes's" earthly life would, then, have preceded Plotinus's by about three hundred years.

course of the human mind going on in that room, and I know it so well I almost fancy I must have been there, though it happened a long time ago" (Balfour, "Study" 223).

As these examples suggest, these communications were in many cases a distinct source of pleasure—pleasure often represented through the tropes of a classical education. Representing the *Symposium* scene, for example, as "a picture that I love and often see," Mrs. Willett makes clear that its particular attractiveness is to belong to a select company of men, an exclusive intellectual community: "Marble pillars everywhere—a most heavenly scene. A company of men—small company, discussing everything in heaven and earth" (69–70). As her own elaboration of this scene indicates, mediumship opened to women a once forbidden place that they could now define as their territory. In what Balfour calls "the sequel" to this scene, Mrs. Willett explains, "[M]y picture that I like to look at" becomes "my room where I choose to walk" (71)—a shift that emphasizes not only the medium's increased agency but the spatial dimension involved in time traveling. In this scenario, the medium's presumed access to the past resituates her in the present, making her, in effect, a part of a masculine coterie: a group of men, making up the psychical research community, committed quite literally to the discussion of "everything in heaven and earth." For Mrs. Willett, then, who was written off by the very Cambridge men who investigated her mediumship as "intelligent but no scholar," her automatic productions installed her in their orbit.

Mrs. Willett's productions, as her investigators were quick to acknowledge, regularly displayed familiarity with materials "outside the scope of any knowledge with which she [could] reasonably be credited" (Balfour, "Ear" 218). "Mrs. Willett is in no sense a 'learned' lady," Balfour writes in one of his reports to the SPR. "She has a taste for poetry, and a good knowledge of certain English poets; but with classical subjects she is as little familiar as the average of educated women" (227). Yet in the scripts investigated by the SPR, her knowledge of English poets appears formidable, straining the resources of her investigators to identify the allusions that pepper her outpourings. And although at times her professed knowledge of the classics appears below even Balfour's expectation—"The word *Symposium*," he admits, "seemed to convey no meaning to her" ("Study" 72)—the classical references displayed in other scripts exceed what one would expect from a specialist. As Balfour explains of some of the more abstruse allusions, "The number even of professed classical scholars able to supply the required knowledge without consulting books of reference is, I venture to think, an extremely limited one" ("Ear" 235). Indeed, he suggests, one particularly complex set of allusions can only be traced to a single book so technical in character "[o]ne would certainly be surprised to come across it anywhere outside a scholar's library." "Merely to open [this book]," Balfour maintains, "would repel anybody but an expert" (234).

But if automatic writing could turn ordinary women into "experts," it did so largely without their knowing it—indeed, often without their conscious participation. Thus the "Mrs. Willett" of the Cummins–Willett scripts describes the way her communicators haunted her unconscious mind, "preparing it, training it for the inception of scholarly words not in [her] conscious memory." Confiding in her fellow medium, Geraldine Cummins, she notes, "It might be likened to training a retriever to sit and to fetch game when their masters are out shooting" (*Swan* 80). In fact, when shown some of the "trance-productions" she authored, Mrs. Willett, in a telling analogy, assures her investigators that they were "'so much Greek' to her, and leave her utterly bewildered and *bored*" (Balfour, "Study" 300–301)—an assessment the men who studied her were only too quick to believe in. When faced, for example, with some display of sophisticated philosophical thought or remarkable erudition in the script writing, Balfour repeatedly falls back on the same formula: "the normal Mrs Willett is unable to throw any light upon this question" (305).

If mediumship, however, raises the question of how an "author" produces writing perceived as other than her own—as outside her ordinary powers and inclinations—the question is not confined to scholarship. Commenting on the *Scripts of Cleophas*, for example, Cummins admits that it was "contrary to all my tastes and inclinations to produce narrative dealing with religious history of the first century" (*Unseen Adventures* 106). More particularly, she expresses dislike for St. Paul because of his reactionary attitudes toward women, acknowledging that she was "compelled against [her] will and prejudices to write of him." "I am not proud of the Cleophas Series," she writes in her autobiography, "as I feel such writings are not of me, are foreign in character to my Celtic, racial self" (111). Indeed, as a fiction writer, Cummins confines herself to Irish scenes and settings, aspiring to the kind of success that Somerville and Ross so notably achieved and that Cummins herself would later celebrate in her biography of Somerville. Advancing the conventional theory of authorship that writers write best when they write what they know, Cummins wonders "how I, an Irishwoman, with no known Jewish ancestors, could have written these books." And she projects this question onto her Jewish "informant," Mrs. Clive Behran. For Behran, Cummins tells us, a "highly cultivated member of the Jewish race," marvels that Cummins could write these texts "without hereditary knowledge or feeling for the inner self of the Jewish nation" (110, 111). Such a question might be posed to automatic writing more generally.

Indeed, when Cummins acknowledges that when an author writes of his own race, he "knows, as no foreigner, their particular idea-idiom," that the "inner mentality, the character of his people, are in his very bones" (*Unseen Adventure* 110), she speaks to an experience that mediumship facilitates: the capacity to know the experience of an other in, as it were, one's very bones, to feel, in Mrs. Willett's words, "somebody's heart beating inside" you (Balfour, "Study" 182). Transforming the foreign into the native, mediumship thus releases and records the voice of the Other. Even when, as in the Cummins–Willett case, medium and communicator share certain experiences and characteristics (they write, after all, woman to woman and medium to medium), the communicators must still "write . . . through a stranger" (Cummins, *Swan* 58). As both parties to the exchange acknowledge, the scripts must be written over and through the differences between women: differences of class, "race," experience, and temperament.[20]

Like the collaborative novelists discussed in the first part of this chapter, mediums depend for their authority on their ability to translate; more radically, moreover, than their fiction writing counterparts, they depend for their authenticity on the testimony of what for want of a better word might be called "native informants," figures of the unknown who act as familiars. Mediumship thus extends and formalizes the implication of collaborative writing in the domestication of the foreign. Indeed, it openly performs its trafficking in the exotic. This feature of mediumship is perhaps nowhere more evident than in its reliance on so-called control spirits—the colorful otherworldly beings who serve, as it were, as the medium's "medium," orchestrating and facilitating the dialogue between medium and communicator. In the practice of controls, mediumship found the ultimate vehicle for articulating the otherness of automatic writing.

Historically, Mrs. Willett's mediumship was unusual in that it lacked "controls"; there was, as Balfour notes, an absence of "anything corre-

[20] Cummins describes the differences between herself and Mrs. Willett as essentially racial—the English being to her as a foreign nation; as an Englishwoman, Mrs. Willett, she suggests, is as alien to her as the Jews of the first century. Her production of this contemporary script thus appears to her no less incredible than her production of the ancient one. "Mrs. Willett" tends to represent the differences as experiential: the difference between a guilt-stricken mother and a childless spinster. For commentators on the scripts, the differences in the women's class and social positions appear most evident.

sponding to the *Phinuit*, or the *Rector*, of Mrs Piper, to Mrs Thompson's *Nelly*, or to the *Feda* of Mrs Leonard" (Balfour, "Study" 60). Nor were there any of the strange-sounding guide figures—Thomas of Dorlowicz, Ameritus, Apple, Aymor, Fish—who appear with such frequency in the Yeatses' automatic productions. In fact, at the time she produced the bulk of her script writing, almost every medium of Mrs. Willett's caliber had a repertoire of control spirits, without whose assistance no writing would have seemed possible. Cummins, for example, had her "Astor" and Dowden her "Johannes"; even the scripts Cummins receives in the 1950s—scripts ostensibly communicated by "Mrs. Willett"—are facilitated by Astor, although his role appears to diminish as the communications continue. Mrs. Willett's case, however, was different. In direct contrast to those instances where a control "supplants the spirit of the medium," using the medium's "physical organism" to "express its own ideas or to transmit messages from other spirits," Mrs. Willett never goes into the type of trance where she loses her sense of personal identity (Balfour, "Study" 164). As Balfour explains, "It is Mrs Willett herself, *in propria persona*, who is in touch with the communicator" (60).

But if the trick of the Willett mediumship is that the medium retains consciousness of self, she does "lose all consciousness of her actual surroundings," entering "a world of her own in which her communicators appear to her as palpable and life-like human beings, of whose features and dress she can take note, whose touch she can perceive, and in whose presence she feels 'at home,' as in a company of friends" (Balfour, "Study" 86). Indeed, she tells Mrs. Verrall, "[I]t gives me no more sense of oddness to be talking to these invisible people than it does to be talking to my son for instance" ("Study" 52–53)—a practice not entirely at odds with the way authors sometimes refer to their fictional creations. In classic trance mediumship, however, the "spirit of the medium quits the body," its place taken by an "invading personality" ("Study" 172, 45). The medium, as Charles Richet notes of Mrs. Piper, is possessed by another: "Her voice is changed; she is no longer Mrs Piper, but another personage, Dr Phinuit, who speaks in a loud, masculine voice in a mingling of negro patois, French, and American dialect" (qtd. in Sage 9).

The "controls," so strangely absent in Mrs. Willett's mediumship, were, in fact, the subject of considerable discussion and debate in the early twentieth century. The central question was whether these spirits, like other spiritual communicators, represented dissociated elements of the medium's own personality or truly external presences (the surviving spirits of the dead they purported to be). There was also some question as to the exact origin and function of the controls: Did they serve as interpreters and amanuenses or, as Dowden and other mediums more frequently maintained, did they merely "arrange the séance and decide who among those who wish to speak from the other side shall communicate" (Hester Travers Smith, *Voices from the Void* 14). Mrs. Leonard, for example, refers to her control Feda, as a "kind of spiritual Mistress of Ceremonies" (30), and Feda was in many ways typical; for as Dowden explains, controls generally give themselves "quaint names" and claim to have lived "in distant countries many hundreds of years ago" (*Voices from the Void* 14). Feda gives this practice a more personal application, identifying herself as the surviving spirit of Mrs. Leonard's great-great-grandmother—a fourteen-year-old Hindu girl who married an Englishman in India and died about 1800 after giving birth to a son on the eve of her planned departure for England. As Dowden recognized, these upstart controls threatened to compromise the profession. Writing in the *North American Review* in 1923, for example, she complains of "a continual epidemic of 'little nigger controls' among spirit guides of professional mediums" (689). While Dowden refers here to the "physical" or "materialization" mediums, among "mental" mediums like herself, these "vulgar" controls were replaced by spirit guides that proved no less exotic: ancient Arabs, Asians, Egyptians, and Greeks, often with scholarly pretensions.[21]

Cummins's primary control, Astor, for example, purports to be an ancient Greek, while her "Christian control" (responsible for the Cleophas scripts) calls himself Silenio or Silentium, suggesting Mediterranean lineage. Eileen Garrett's spirit repertoire included Uvani, a "'control' personality of Oriental origin" and Abdul Latif, an "alleged Persian control who claimed to be an astronomer and physician at the court of Saladin in the twelfth century" (Eileen Garrett, *Many Voices* 47, 92). Hester Dowden's controls included, in addition to Johannes, Eyen, a control with a proclivity for fiction writing and the initiator of Dowden's automatic writing who "says he was an Egyptian priest who served in the temple of Isis in the reign of Ramses II" (Bentley 29), As-

---

[21] For discussion of nineteenth-century materialization mediums, see Alex Owen, *The Darkened Room: Women, Power and Spiritualism in Late Victorian England*. These mediums regularly materialized beings who crossed lines of race, class, and gender, frequently appearing as "Red Indians," Negroes, lower-class men, Hindus, and Arabs. The shift to a more verbally based practice corresponds to a class shift in mediumship to the middle and upper middle classes—a shift correspondent with new emphasis in mediumistic "texts" on education and literacy.

tor, a control Dowden shared with Cummins, and Sharma, a female control of Hindu origins (Bentley 32).[22]

These cultural Others had been the stuff of the mediums of the late nineteenth century, who at the height of their powers claimed to materialize these spirits outside their bodies. With the advent of "mental" mediumship, however, these performances became more subtle; in effect, they went underground, replacing the inarticulate sounds and broad theatrical gestures of earlier séance performances with a drama that played itself out as a function of language transmission. Such refined transmissions, however, posed certain additional difficulties. For, on the analogy of dictation, words and concepts unknown to the medium (and the presence of such words increased in proportion to the specialization and sophistication of the communications) require more effort to "get through," often needing to be spelled out letter by letter. And where these messages were filtered through a control, the letters themselves (if not part of the control's native alphabet) often had to be transmitted pictorially.

Even without the presence of a "foreign" control, the process could be formidable. As "Mrs. Willett" explains, where the communications contain unfamiliar proper names—Latin and Greek phrases, technical terms, etc.—"the word or words unknown . . . come in the form of sound images to the medium's inner hearing." "She is like a reporter for a newspaper," she goes on. "It is extremely difficult for a reporter to take down words in a foreign language unknown to him. It is even more so for a medium" (Cummins, *Swan* 80). Drawing on her own professional experience working with translators or interpreters, she notes how often they "miss the idiom . . . damage the essential sense, the shape of the speaker's remarks in another language" (*Swan* 36)—a problem endemic to mediumship. The experience Mrs. Willett confesses—"I can see the thoughts . . . but it is so difficult to get the words"; "I can hear the words, but I can't make my lips say them"; "*Oh!* I see it a hundred ways, but I can't get it out" ("Study" 128, 134, 137)—is not unfa-

[22] Not only did mediums harbor multiple controls, they sustained hierarchical relations among them—relations based on quality and intelligence and not infrequently marked by "racial" and "class" distinctions. Dowden's first control, for example, Peter Rooney, was considered "vulgar" and did not produce any writing, while Johannes, with his superior pedigree and intellect, "dwarfs the personalities" of all the rest. Mrs. Piper's controls expressed the full range from the vulgar to the superior, her earliest controls being Chlorine, a "red Indian girl" and Phinuit, a French doctor with a tendency to rather "vulgar phrases" and only scanty knowledge of either French or medicine (M. Sage, *Mrs Piper and the Society for Psychical Research* 31). With the takeover of Mrs. Piper by the "Imperator Group" (led by "Rector"), Mrs. Piper's writings, by all reports, "acquired a coherence, clearness and exactness unknown before" (Sage 124).

miliar in the annals of mediumship. By all accounts, the communication process requires a certain amount of ingenuity, since as "Mrs. Willett" explains, words and sentences not in the medium's "memory centre" must be "registered so as to create familiarity with them in her subliminal or submerged mind" (*Swan* 80).

Indeed, both the official and unofficial studies of mediumship, regularly record the elaborate mechanisms and expedients through which the necessary familiarity is created; the process often resembles a modern game of charades, with its reliance on syllable-by-syllable spellings, use of homophones, or free associations.[23] Where a "control" operates as intermediary, the difficulties of communication multiply, the "translation" the medium performs having also to be performed by the control (often a native speaker of a language other than English), who, like the medium, generally receives messages in the form of images and symbols. These problems, moreover, are compounded at the level of transcription, with messages generally appearing without punctuation or paragraphing and with letters, words, and phrases often run into each other. Words and syllables are sometimes misplaced and spelling is often idiosyncratic, and it is not unusual for all or part of a message to appear in mirror or backwards writing.

What seems most striking in these instances—and most relevant to women's writing practices more generally—is the inability of the medium to access private or privileged knowledge without such elaborate mediating mechanisms, and in particular, without the intervention of a being whose Otherness is unmistakable. On the one hand, this Otherness stood as proof of the communication's authenticity, the argument being that it was too strange to have come from the medium, even from her unconscious. Garrett, for example, who generally inclined toward the theory that controls were secondary selves of the medium,[24] professed bewilderment at the ethnic makeup of her own control spirits;

[23] As Gerald Balfour reports, "Often there is a fairly long period of—don't get that word—it contains a *g* and an *s* and a *t* and an *a*." In other instances, the communicator has recourse "to the visual representation of a word" ("A Study of the Psychological Aspects of Mrs. Willett's Mediumship, and of the Statements of the Communicators concerning the Process" 122). On still other occasions, as "Myers" explains, the desired word must be slipped in through a pun or "wrapped" in a quotation: "I got the WORD in by choosing a quotation in which it occurs and which was known to the normal intelligence of my machine" ("Study" 124).

[24] In *My Life as a Search for the Meaning of Mediumship*, Eileen Garrett rejects "the idea that a *control* personality could have any genuine existence" (133). In *Eileen Garrett Returns*, the purported afterlife communications of the medium, "Eileen Garrett" reverses her position, arguing that she now knows that "none of the controls were part of my personality. They are what they said they were—individual human beings, each with a distinct personality and history" (Robert L. Leichtman, *Eileen Garrett Returns* 20).

describing the appearance of Uvani, she notes, "I also wondered if this Oriental might not be a figment of my imagination; I could hardly believe that I had 'made him up,' as I had no particular interest in Orientals" (*My Life* 131).

At the same time that these cultural Others could be seen to authenticate the communications, they were also a source of introducing error into the transmissions (they often spoke ungrammatical, broken, or anachronistic English). Feda, for example, except when she purported to be reporting a message verbatim (in which case, her English was deemed "almost correct"), spoke in a markedly idiosyncratic English, a language "peculiarly her own," marked by infantile phraseology, chronic mispronunciations, irregular syntax and usage, a shaky knowledge of the English alphabet, and a tendency to speak of herself in the third person ("Feda says . . ."). As investigators reported, moreover, "For some reason unknown she seldom fails to substitute an L for an R" (qtd. in Susy Smith, *The Mediumship of Mrs. Leonard* 49)—a trait that would seem to mark her generically as "Asian." Not surprisingly, then, Radclyffe Hall and Una Troubridge, who investigated Mrs. Leonard's mediumship for the SPR, admit to a difficulty in transcribing Feda's "broken English": "it would have taken too long to think out suitable spelling for her idiosyncrasies" (qtd. in S. Smith 32–33). Compared to an English-speaking control, moreover, her linguistic performance could be frustratingly laborious. As Troubridge explains, "[I]t is invariably quicker to call a book a book than to describe it in the Feda manner. . . . [T]he A.V.B. personal control [purporting to be the spirit of the Englishwoman, Lady Batten], in the course of an hour's work will easily outstrip a two hours' Feda control in the number of evidential points volunteered" (qtd. in S. Smith 59).

While the official investigators of Mrs. Leonard's mediumship refrained from any definitive identification of Feda's nationality, her case prompted, at least within SPR forums, an extended public discussion on the subject of her "Indianness." The famous "Word Association Tests," for example, attempted to assess, using scientific methods, the exact nature and extent of the "Oriental flavor" (S. Smith 52) in her thought and speech patterns. Yet as the substance of these experiments suggests, the Otherness that controls such as Feda demonstrated rarely deviated from the most conventionalized and stereotypical representations. To the word "make," for example, Feda responded "curry" and "sari"—a response, one would presume, of little evidential value. The lively commentary, however, that Feda's test results provoked suggests the limited frame for imagining alterity within which these studies were conducted, leaving "Feda" to stand as a kind of poster child for early twentieth-century constructions of the Other. Feda's authenticity, of course, was not uncontested: Bishop F. J. Western, for example, a British missionary residing in India, questioned "the Oriental flavor of Feda's association words" and E. R. Dodds argued that Feda's responses were "not distinguishable in quality from faked results."[25] But others, more frequent in number, applauded the responses for the "Oriental atmosphere" they conveyed and for their lively "picturesqueness," leading more than one observer to conclude, "Feda's response words might have been those of a Hindu girl of long ago" (qtd. in S. Smith 183–85).

Such representations, despite their flimsy claims to authenticity, often overlapped with "official" perspectives. Feda, for example, notwithstanding her distinctive intonations, mouths the typical British critiques of native oppression of women—critiques harnessed to a crude expression of contemporary feminism. To the word "Drive," for example, Feda offers the surprising response, "Purdah"—a word choice explained as follows: "When you are in purdah you wants to go for a drive and you can't" (S. Smith 186). To the word "Dead," she replies "Pyre," echoing the British outrage at what was perceived as the ubiquitous practice of sati or widow-sacrifice: "We should not be put on it now. It was stupid. Some of the widows that was put on the pyre was nicer than the man who died. But they didn't want to go—some of them didn't" (187). Far from demonstrating immersion in another culture, these personifications merely confirm contemporary Western prejudices.

Yet the question remains why, in a case such as Mrs. Leonard's, where her psychic work largely entailed personal communications from the dead (most of whom had no particular connection to India or other foreign settings), these communications should require this specious show of Otherness. Leonard herself observes that controls were generally chosen for their "peculiar suitability for the task of messenger or transmitter" (Leonard 221): their ability to link the mind of a communicator (the sender of the message) to the mind of a sitter (the ostensible recipient of the message). The prevalence of allegedly "foreign" controls in the ranks of the most prominent and respected mediums suggests that such suitability depended on Otherness. That this is the case reinforces the idea that mediumship is located outside the cultural mainstream, but the conventional way in which Otherness is repre-

[25] These critiques were themselves often grounded on dubious ideas of authenticity. Bishop Western's suggestion, for example, that Indians "thought of curry more as a relish then as a meal," and that their response "would more likely have been 'rice'" (qtd. in S. Smith 183) does little to advance the discussion.

sented places it within the dominant contemporary discourses of Empire and Orientalism.

From this perspective, Mrs. Leonard's case may be seen as exemplary, playing out in almost allegorical fashion, the racial politics inherent in common configurations of mediumship: in the imagination of an Other inhabiting the medium's mind and body. Mrs. Leonard even goes so far as to project mediumship as, in effect, "the white woman's burden": a higher calling that entails distinct responsibilities—to the self and to a "lesser" order of being. In a striking episode, recounted in her autobiography in a chapter called "My Brown Self," Mrs. Leonard fleshes out this allegory. In what she represents as an out-of-body experience, Leonard describes her sensations upon entering a room where she observes "the figure of a woman, apparently asleep," a woman whose image she finds unrelentingly depressing: "[E]verything about her was brown. Her dress, hair, and even her skin, were of a dull muddy brown. As I stood there, I felt an overwhelming pity for her." Bending over her "as one would over a child," with the intent of offering counsel and encouragement, Leonard is shocked to discover that the figure is herself: "It was a terrible shock, and I stood paralysed, not knowing what to do or say. 'Oh, you poor ugly thing,' was the only thought in my mind." Informed by a voice that "the 'brown woman,' as I have always called her in my mind, was my lower self," Mrs. Leonard is rebuked for failing to maintain the spiritual and ethical superiority her position confers on her. Acknowledging that "the privilege of communicating brings a great spiritual and moral responsibility to us, which we cannot and must not shirk," she resolves to "bring [her] spiritual development into line"—to, as it were, "take [her] lower self in hand." Fittingly, then, with this resolve, the "brown woman" noticeably whitens: "I thought I saw a slight lightening or clearing up of the muddy depressing shade, and gradually she melted before my eyes" (Leonard, *My Life* 124–26).

More starkly than in most other accounts, this episode illuminates the fantasies mediumship plays upon—the "unconscious or racial memories," Eileen Garrett suggests, that mediumship may activate (Garrett, *My Life* 223). In the case of Mrs. Leonard, it is difficult not to read this autobiographical narrative in terms of Feda, the "brown woman" who so dramatically shares her body and whose training and development Leonard assumes as her mediumistic responsibility. Indeed, if mediums regularly resisted the whole idea of being "controlled," Mrs. Leonard suggests the possibility of a more particular discomfort: a dislike of the idea of being controlled by some racial Other, by a being one deems inferior. Thus, while Leonard acknowledges that her mediumship involves an "association with higher entities" (124), she resists the idea that Feda, her primary channel to the unknown, should occupy this position. As Troubridge reports, "She resents actively the suggestion that has been made to her by certain spiritualistic sitters, to the effect that Feda is her higher self, justifiably pointing out that her normal self does not share many of Feda's childish weaknesses and limitations" (qtd. in S. Smith 47).

Even, then, as she works her mediumship through Feda's intervention, Leonard constructs a narrative that ensures her supremacy— a narrative in which the white woman's burden is the brown woman's domestication. Her own spiritual elevation is thus achieved by assuming responsibility for Feda's education.[26] "It is Mrs Leonard's own opinion," Susy Smith writes, "that Feda grew and developed as a person from the beginning of her activities as a control," that "flighty though her personality was, Feda showed character and determination as she worked hard to become serious and dependable in performance of the obligations she had undertaken" (53). Indeed, in the many extant representations of Mrs. Leonard's mediumship, a Feda described as lovable, childlike, and ignorant of accepted values is "improved" through Mrs. Leonard's civilizing influence; like her presumed historical predecessor (Mrs. Leonard's great-great-grandmother), the present incarnation of Feda must find salvation through the embrace of Englishness— this time in the person of Mrs. Leonard. In fact, if Mrs. Leonard's mediumship represents Feda's work as a control as the determinant of her "spiritual progress," that progress is marked, significantly, by Feda's growing facility with the English language—the loss of her accent and other linguistic idiosyncrasies.[27] If, then, one reads Mrs. Leonard's mediumship as a narrative of progress, it is one in which the "brown woman" ultimately vanishes; for a Feda whose intonations are noticeably lightened is ultimately replaced by a proper English "personal" control capable of assuming a voice more like Mrs. Leonard's.

But if Feda, with her genealogical ties to Britain's imperial history, makes the connection to empire explicit, she is not alone in signaling

---

[26] Garrett goes so far as to argue that in the development of mediumistic powers, the training of the medium is not nearly as important as "adequate training and development of the control" (*My Life* 186).

[27] Enlarging upon her duties as an honest and conscientious control, Feda is reported as saying (in Feda speak), "This work is Feda's ploglession, if Feda told lies, Feda wouldn't plogless." This "progress" is confirmed by several investigators: "She rather grew up in the language" one investigator observes, while another comments on "a gradual loss of accent" (qtd. in S. Smith, *The Mediumship of Mrs. Leonard* 50, 52). Feda herself, moreover, distinguished herself from other dark-skinned people, noting, "we aren't colored people, we are only brown" (qtd. in S. Smith 187).

this aspect of mediumship. The accounts of Hester Dowden's mediumship record an appeal from an Indian communicator, "Bhanji," for her to spread her work to India. When Dowden suggests there must be Indian mediums who can perform this task, her communicator responds with the standard imperialist rhetoric: you can't get good help in India because Indians are too lazy and no one there is willing to put in the long training and so on. Yet even the most cursory glance at the operation of mediumship suggests that the transfer of knowledge across cultural boundaries is not unidirectional.[28] If controls must be properly trained and developed, it is precisely because they provide access to privileged knowledge the medium needs in order to practice her profession—knowledge she can ultimately retrieve only if she gives herself over to the care and wisdom of the controls. Mediumship thus operates through a fantasy of reverse possession—possession *by* the Other. Even in a case such as Mrs. Leonard's, which appears to conform so neatly to the dominant power structures, the colonial paradigm her mediumship invokes includes a space for the colonized to talk back to (and through) the colonizing medium. In other words, the control might be seen to speak independently—apart from the medium who acts as the control's instrument. According to Troubridge, for example, Feda viewed Mrs. Leonard much the way Mrs. Leonard viewed her— as an object of her patronage: "Feda, on her part, has not a high opinion of Mrs Leonard. . . . She frequently, indeed, expresses open scorn of Mrs. Leonard's opinions, likes and dislikes, and speaks of her as of a not very satisfactory and distinctly inferior instrument, who must be protected and humored" (qtd. in S. Smith 47).

If the imagination of the control as a "lower self" taps colonial anxieties regarding miscegenation,[29] mediumship simultaneously facilitates a reverse fantasy of the control as a "higher self," the conduit of esoteric knowledge and spiritual enlightenment. As the example of Mrs. Leonard suggests, these contradictory fantasies were often played out in the same person. The representation of the control's superiority

[28] It could be argued that the very structure of mediumship (as well as the content of certain messages) depended on filtered-down Eastern teachings regarding the afterlife, spiritual enlightenment, and human personality. Madame Blavatsky comes immediately to mind, but she was not the only medium to colonize Eastern philosophy. In the particular colonialist fantasy mediumship facilitated, however, the "indigenous" knowledge mediumship retrieved required not only an "Eastern" control but a Western intermediary in the person of the medium.

[29] Garrett's first response to being introduced to her control was to express fear that the control would "spy on [her] most intimate and private behaviour" (*My Life* 131); the problem of cohabitation posed by a control's occupation of a medium's body was ultimately recast, as I have been arguing, as a problem of speech and writing: a problem of language purity.

is especially prevalent in mediumship's more scholarly manifestations. When Eileen Garrett introduces her second control, the Persian doctor, Abdul Latif, for example, she notes that her work opens itself to "certain entirely different levels of understanding": the usual flow of "spiritualist messages" that attempt to prove survival in an afterlife are replaced with advanced meditations on Eastern "healing, philosophy and religion" (*My Life* 165). In Dowden's case, Johannes performs a similar function, imparting "more lofty and spiritual tones" to her automatic productions. With Dowden, however, as with Cummins, mediumship provided access to the religious and philosophical foundations of Western civilization—access facilitated through a relay of intermediaries marked as belonging to different cultures.

If these intermediaries stood as idealized Others, such idealizations were, of course, no less a part of the discourse of Orientalism than the negative stereotypes mediumship frequently materialized. Both suggest the extent to which the racial Other could be readily drawn on to mark the crossing of significant cultural boundaries. The association of mediumistic work with sexual possession suggests that one boundary invoked was that of transgressive sexuality—a boundary not infrequently linked to the manifestation of the Other. I want to argue, however, that these Others also participate in a particular history of boundary markings connected to the representation of new worlds and knowledges. They figure, for example, in the narratives of exploration so avidly read about in the late nineteenth century (and upon which popular representations of mediumship were so often modeled) and in the burgeoning of Orientalist scholarship during the nineteenth century; as Anne McClintock has argued, moreover, such nineteenth-century emanations can themselves be traced back to the border figures (women, monsters, Others) that graced Europe's earliest efforts in cartography. From this perspective, the "controls" serve the same function as their historical predecessors: marking the boundaries of worlds they announce as "new" or "Other." With the growth of empire, however (and the disappearance of the world's "blank spaces"), psychical research turned its energies inward, mapping its own "imaginary" territory, which was understood in terms of temporal rather than spatial "colonization." Perfecting what McClintock has called the "invention of anachronistic space" (*Imperial Leather* 40), psychical research quite literally projected anterior time into the space of the present. For as the controls suggest, the belief in another world coterminous with the present depends on a necessary anachronism.

If the exotic and anachronistic control figures, however, signal an entry into unknown worlds and the opening up of new forms of knowledge, they borrow their trappings from available colonial paradigms. The particular knowledge that the controls "let through" is not in itself new or distinctive; indeed, the verification of mediumistic communications requires that the knowledge they display be shown to conform to recognized authority. Mediumship, then, as an intellectual undertaking functions largely in a reproductive capacity: it replicates knowledge that can be verified and tested. Its contribution to available scholarship thus lies not in something new it can tell us about early Christian theology, for example, or life in ancient Egypt, but rather in the questions it raises about the way such knowledge is received and transmitted.

If, as I have been arguing, then, the "controls" function as border figures to announce new worlds of knowledge, the knowledge they inaugurate is emphatically *not* knowledge of their supposed place of origins; nor, I should add, is it "authentic" knowledge of the afterlife. If nothing else, the conventionality of these figures renders them suspect, stereotypic as they are. But it is this conventionality, I want to argue, that defines their function, allowing them to serve as *generic* markers of Otherness; as such they signal not some specific field of knowledge (for which the control might be seen as an authentic native informant) but, rather, the act of knowledge-making. What is new, then, about mediumship—and what aligns it with contemporaneous discursive practices (many of which have fared better historically)—is its emphasis on process, on the mode of knowledge production in which it participates. Like psychoanalysis, for example, whose development coincides with that of psychical research, the study of mediumship provides a mechanism for mapping the mind, for analyzing the structures of both individual and collective memory. Like psychoanalysis, moreover, it reveals the mind (or psyche) to be an elaborately coded, multiply mediated, and hierarchically structured entity.

As a sustained discourse on the way "information" is processed— the way knowledge is received, transmitted, and recorded—psychical research, then, tracked the same territory as other social sciences. Illuminating what Balfour once called a "difficulty of margin," it defined as its special study the space the medium negotiates between competing requirements (e.g., the need to receive versus the need to transmit elaborately coded messages).[30] In this it can be seen to illuminate what often went unnoticed in more "respectable" forms of cultural expression and scholarly practice: the mechanisms on which these practices relied to

---

[30] Balfour suggests that in the need to balance the medium's ability to receive and transmit messages, all mediumship entails "a difficulty of margin"; "To lose control is to lose the power to record" ("Study" 133, 131).

control and manage the margin. What today seems so crude about mediumistic representations—their clunky machinery and vulgar parade of exotics—may thus reflect no more than our recoil from mediumship's insistent literalization: its *undisguised* performance of the act of mediation. This performance, moreover, had important consequences, enabling mediumship to stake its claims in the practices of cultured literacy—literally, in the act of writing. Yet its uncompromising literalization may also account for the readiness with which mediumship has been marginalized as a cultural practice and for its virtual absence from the history of authorship in which it so clearly participated.

As a new form of writing (and speaking), mediumship both acted out and acted upon the mechanisms that produce and transmit writing, simultaneously locating authorship outside the body (in some discarnate being, aided by an attendant spirit, a kind of exotic master of ceremonies) and inside the body of the medium, who becomes, in effect, a kind of writing machine (or, in a word frequently used by mediums, an "instrument"). The consequent merging of voices and bodies produced a relationship (between medium and communicator, and medium and control) described, in the words of "Mrs. Willett" as "nearer than near": "It seemed as if somebody else was me, as if a stranger was occupying my body, as if another's mind was in me" (Cummins, *Swan* 105). When the strangers in question characteristically crossed boundaries of gender, race, class, and nationality (not to mention the crossing out and over of centuries), they suggest, among other things, the space mediumship provided to both enact and regulate cultural fantasies—including fantasies of miscegenation.

What seems most striking about mediumship, however, as a practice with particular attractions for women is the way its fantasies consistently return to the problem of intellectual and cultural authority—in particular, to the fantasy of unrestricted access to the institutions of authorship and higher learning. Indeed, more self-consciously than other contemporary practices, mediumship put women on display as agents in the making and transmitting of culture, but it did so in a way that allowed for the simultaneous avowal and disavowal of their agency. Mediumship problematized even as it represented women's agency, displacing women's authority (including her authority to mediate) onto a host of other mediators.

That mediumship should require its own mediating structures—its elaborate layers of interpreters and intermediaries—suggests the way it mimicked the structures of the very institutions it stood outside. But if mediumship's promise of unmediated access to the seats of knowledge proved anything but unmediated, its alternative mediations were not without their cultural efficacy; for the practices of mediumship challenged, however fitfully, the authority of the university (and allied institutions) to be the sole arbiter of the production, distribution, and reception of knowledge. If, then, mediumship (along with psychical research as its investigative machinery) ultimately lost its bid for cultural authority, it nonetheless opened a space for viewing cultural practices at work; indeed, it rendered visible the historically contingent structures of mediation in which it took part. Redefining what it might mean to write from the margins, mediumship invoked the Other to speak, in effect, from the *inside*. Ironically enough, then, what would seem to mark automatic writing as most Other could be said to most align it with the mainstream. Like other alternative writing practices, automatic writing, in fact, called into question, even as it displayed, its own eccentricity. As such, it offers a compelling commentary on the history of authorship we have inherited as well as on a practice of writing that history has left behind.

5

The Scribe and the Lady
Automatic Writing and the Trials of Authorship

In perhaps one of the strangest cases to make its mark on the history of copyright in Great Britain, the court of Chancery ruled in July 1926 in favor of Miss Geraldine Dorothy Cummins—the same Cummins whose exploits as a medium and as the first biographer of Edith Somerville have already been discussed to some extent in earlier chapters. Cummins, a journalist, fiction writer (of plays, short stories, and novels), and practicing medium, sought to restrain Frederick Bligh Bond (a fellow sitter at her séances) from producing or reproducing a text titled *The Chronicle of Cleophas*, a work allegedly composed by Cummins via automatic writing and subsequently punctuated and transcribed by the defendant.[1] While Cummins insisted that Bond had no legitimate claim to authorship—his role being, at best, that of an assistant—Bond argued that Cummins was, in this case, no more an author than he was, the work having been "dictated" to her by the surviving spirit of a Christian scribe who lived in the first century. Cummins herself acknowledged as much, noting that "she played no conscious part in the writing" and readily admitting that "the scribe of Cleophas directed her hand" at every stage of the inscription (*London Times*, 22 July 1926, 5).

In determining the owner of the copyright in this unusual instance, the court entertained the idea of collaborative authorship only to dismiss it, noting, somewhat facetiously, that the "authors would . . . appear to be the scribe and the lady" (*London Times*, 23 July 1926, 5). In the case of the lady, the judge maintained, her claims were unassailable, it having been "abundantly proved" that she "was the writer of every

---

[1] The text in question, the first in a series of books Cummins produced on early Christian subjects, was eventually published by Cummins under the title *The Scripts of Cleophas* (1928). The entire series was generally referred to by the title of the first volume.

word"; literally, hers was the hand that held the pen that produced all the writing. As her counsel affirmed, "There was no suggestion that it was dictated [by any living person] or was a copy of any existing book or work" (*London Times*, 22 July 1926, 5). From a legal perspective, then, Bond's claims to be counted an author need not be taken seriously. In the case of "the scribe," the court, not surprisingly, was equally dismissive. For since, as the judge explained, he had no jurisdiction in the afterlife, he could make no determination concerning the scribe's authorial responsibility. Consequently, "he was obliged, having regard to the Copyright Act of 1911, to confine the copyright to the plaintiff" (*London Times*, 23 July 1926, 5).

In upholding the principle of "a medium's copyright,"[2] the case of *Cummins v. Bond* underscores a feature of automatic writing virtually ignored in most contemporary and modern discussions: its status as *literary* production. Indeed, Cummins's attorneys premised their case on the claim that the *Chronicle* constituted "an original literary work" and hence was deserving of legal protection. As such, the case could be seen to comment on a theory and practice of authorship extending well beyond the immediate circumstances of this one peculiar literary creation. To what degree, it asked, does any claim to authorship require the "author's" conscious participation? Is literary property a corporeal or incorporeal entity? Is it a product of cerebral inspiration (the state of the author's mind) or of manual labor (the work of the author's hands)? What work counts as intellectual labor? Are all authors, in effect, mediums—the instruments through which discarnate voices achieve materialization? More so, then, than the more conventional instances of literary collaboration this book has already treated, this case brought under scrutiny the peculiar nature of literary property as defined through copyright legislation; and it brought to the surface the fundamental assumptions about authorial agency, as seen in earlier chapters, that collaborative authorship implicitly challenges.[3]

In determining the authorial rights of a medium, however, the court

[2] "A Medium's Copyright," a title clearly meant to be facetious, heads the account of the trial in the *New York Times* (23 August 1926).

[3] For the history and theory of copyright, see Mark Rose, *Authors and Owners: The Invention of Copyright*; John Feather, *A History of British Publishing*; Chris R. Vanden Bossche, "The Value of Literature: Representations of Print Culture in the Copyright Debate of 1837–1842"; Martha Woodmansee, "The Genius and the Copyright: Economic and Legal Conditions of the Emergence of the 'Author'"; David Saunders, *Authorship and Copyright*; and essays in *The Construction of Authorship: Textual Appropriation in Law and Literature*, edited by Martha Woodmansee and Peter Jaszi. As a limit case for the practice of copyright, the rights of a medium expose the fault lines in the codification of proprietary authorship, reopening central questions in copyright history.

glossed over the tensions in a relationship that, historically, had been anything but easy; arguing, in effect, that automatic writing was no different from any other form of authorship, the court adopted a position unlikely to please either practicing "automatists" or defenders of traditional literature.[4] For if authorship constituted the space where "literature" and "spiritualism" met, this identification, as Daniel Cottom has argued, was one vigorously denied by both parties throughout the nineteenth century.[5] So powerful, indeed, were these dividing lines that as late as 1951 Cummins could still present a belief in the *likeness* of creative artist and medium as a "heresy."[6] Yet it was precisely this heresy that the court endorsed when, in finding for Cummins, it absorbed her writing practice into established models of authorship.

In doing so, the court could be seen to affirm a woman's right to professional recognition (and remuneration), for on the surface, at least, Bond's claims looked like a classic case of male appropriation of female labor. Moreover, the court's sanction of Cummins's "heresy" most immediately affected women, providing legitimation for their work as both authors and mediums (where they continued to outnumber men as active practitioners). For if, as the court acknowledged, it was not unknown for eminent men of letters to sometimes write (or claim to write) without conscious agency—as in the case of Coleridge's "Kubla Khan," for example—for women of letters (a class the court never specifically addressed) this was a normative way to represent their creativity—for some the only way to put themselves forward as authors.[7] In fact, the way Cummins describes her automatic writing sounds a lot like the

---

[4] The term "automatist" was used in British psychical research circles as the technical name for mediums who produced automatic writing; the term "medium," however, was the preferred term among spiritualists (those who believed in survival in an afterlife) and was the term most commonly used by the public to include all practitioners of "psychic" phenomena.

[5] For a full discussion of this subject, see David Cottom, *Abyss of Reason: Cultural Movements, Revelations, and Betrayals* 78–107. See also "Modernist Mediumship," and "Necrobibliography: Books in the Spirit World," by Helen Sword, who has been exploring the intersections of early twentieth-century mediumship and literary modernism. Working independently, Sword and I have been drawn to some of the same cases and to certain overlapping questions.

[6] "I know that I am uttering a heresy when I say that I consider that the work of fine mediums with skilled investigators is more in the nature of art than science. An artist's finest pictures are the result partly of things outside himself " (Geraldine Cummins, *Unseen Adventures: An Autobiography Covering Thirty-four Years of Work in Psychical Research* 132).

[7] Cummins frequently cited Blake in this context (see, for example, *Unseen Adventures* 74). According to Woodmansee, it was common practice for writers "to employ the convention of ascribing the creative energy of a poem to an external force through the Renaissance and into the eighteenth century" ("Genius" 427n). From the nineteenth century on, however, with the alliance of ideas of proprietary authorship and original genius, this claim became increasingly the preserve of women.

way other more established women writers describe the creative process: "I remain passively alert until I become conscious of a kind of inner hearing and sometimes inner sight. I hear word for word a description or narrative as my hand writes it down. I am not usually aware of the last part of a sentence when my hand is writing the first words of it. I feel like a secretary automatically recording words from dictation" (*Unseen Adventures* 53–54).

As Cummins's subsequent career makes clear, however, her victory was not without its ironies, for despite the collapsing of terms her case effected, the sticky terms "author" and "medium" (with their very different histories and institutional structures) could not be made to jell without cost to their possessor—in Cummins's case, a kind of psychic disenfranchisement. As a medium who wanted her work to be taken seriously, Cummins had to disown the qualities of an author. In fact, when the Cleophas materials are finally published, Cummins appears on the title page not as author but as "recorder," and the anonymous editors who introduce the work insist that much of what the scripts contain "appears quite inexplicable on the supposition of human authorship" (*The Scripts of Cleophas* xiv). In other words, if the works of automatic writing bear certain affinities to other works of creative inspiration, at a certain point, to be what they claim, they must resist such incorporation. And in Cummins's case, her practice as an author established the limits of her creativity. Ironically, however, the more Cummins distinguishes her automatic writing from her conscious literary efforts—as a conscious writer, for example, she claims she can only create convincing Irish characters and Irish country scenes—the more she aligns her unconscious writings with works of literary genius. When she writes best—i.e., "automatically"—the process takes her outside herself, permitting her to write authoritatively of things beyond her own experience, education, and provincial upbringing. Writing as a medium, with a speed and fluency unavailable to her as an author of literature, she thus best approximates an ideal of literary authorship.[8] Indeed, Cummins's mediumship could be said to have transformed a run-of-the-mill author into an author of exceptional abilities.

As a medium, however, such an achievement is paradoxical. For if authorship affords her wide professional recognition for her psychical research, it does so by glossing over the very different understandings of authorship mediumship articulates. Yet it was as the "author" of more than a dozen volumes of automatic writing and the chronicler of more

---

[8] Though not generally a rapid writer, Cummins wrote with remarkable speed when she produced automatic writing, usually averaging over 1600 words per hour. Such feats were common among successful mediums.

than thirty years of experimental work in psychical research that Cummins achieved a leading place in the annals of parapsychology. And it was as the medium who facilitated the *Scripts of Cleophas* (eventually running to eight volumes, containing more than a million words) that she most visibly came before the world in the character of professional author.

In restraining Bond from publishing "scripts" produced through Cummins's automatic writing, the court cleared the way for Cummins's subsequent (and much acclaimed) publication of these materials in the *Scripts of Cleophas* (1928, 1930, 1933, 1937, 1939, 1944, 1950). Although the decision depended on a restrictive definition of authorship (authorship resides in the hand that writes), the effect of the ruling was to extend the name of "author" to a class of writers working outside established literary institutions: mediums who produce automatic writing. In doing so, however, the court ignored those features of automatic writing that did not fit its governing ideas of authorship; fixing authorship as singular, for example, it ignored the profoundly collaborative structures on which mediumship rested—structures that extend well beyond the most evident: the presumed collaboration between the dead and the living.

Yet in extending copyright to a medium, the court acknowledged, if only implicitly, a model of authorship in conflict with the proprietary model its ruling was designed to protect;[9] indeed, in introducing and dismissing "the scribe" as a partner to the text (unlike "the lady," the scribe had no legal standing), the court, in effect, authorized the lady *as scribe*, simultaneously opening and foreclosing this alternative configuration of authorship. If we read the *Cummins v. Bond* case, then, for what its decision could not incorporate, it opens to analysis a history of authorship left unexamined by its explicit endorsement of the conventional authorial function—a history embodied in the practice of mediumship.

Certainly, around the time of the Cummins copyright case, authors and mediums were seen to have a certain affinity for each other. Mediums often frequented salons where they mixed with writers, artists, and

[9] If taken at face value, automatic writing would threaten some of the fundamental components of the modern copyright system: the establishment of the "author's life" as the baseline measure for determining authorial protection (the 1911 law granted copyright for an author's life plus fifty years); the criterion of "originality" that distinguishes protectable writing from mere "copying." It also complicates and confuses, if not undermines, the distinction between mental and physical labor, the distinction that makes writing an author's intellectual property.

intellectual thinkers drawn to spiritualism and other occult studies; Cummins's mediumship, for example, like Hester Dowden's, brought her into contact with some of Ireland's leading literary figures: AE (George W. Russell), W. B. Yeats, and Lennox Robinson, the last of whom eventually married Dowden's daughter. Eileen Garrett moved in circles that included AE, Edward Carpenter, H. G. Wells, Catherine Dawson (the founder of P.E.N.), James Stephens, W. B. Yeats, James Joyce, Aldous Huxley, and, in the early stages of her career, Sir Arthur Conan Doyle. As the editor of *Tomorrow* magazine and the founder of the Creative Age Press (1941–51), Garrett subsequently sponsored the publication of both new literary work and psychical research studies. These connections were especially significant since many women who took up mediumship had literary proclivities. Established authors, moreover, were not averse to trying their hand at automatic writing, as the example of W. B. Yeats clearly illustrates (see Chapter 6). But for the most part, literary interest in spiritual phenomena did not go so far as to recognize mediums *as authors* in their practice of mediumship.

Further from the limelight of literary culture, mediums did, however, frequently facilitate literary production. Poems, plays, stories, and even multivolume novels appeared with some regularity in the works of respected mediums. Known in psychical research circles through her pseudonym "Mrs. Holland," Rudyard Kipling's sister produced long poems, ostensibly dictated by Scots ancestors. Hester Dowden also produced fiction and poems through her automatic writing—some of it doggerel, she admitted, but some "of a very striking nature"; in her own person, however, she herself maintained, she was never "guilty either openly or secretly of writing poetry!" (Hester Travers Smith, *Voices from the Void* 154, 30)—a claim echoed by other mediums. And in one of the most remarkable instances of literature produced through automatic writing, Mrs. John H. Curran, working in the United States between 1913 and 1937, produced six novels, numerous short stories, and one play, as well as more than three thousand poems and countless allegories, maxims, and epigrams, purportedly dictated to her by "Patience Worth," a seventeenth-century Englishwoman.[10]

In general, however, there was little in such literary experiments, only a few of which actually saw wide publication, to force a public discussion of them as something more than ephemera. There was, for ex-

[10] Many of "Patience Worth's" poems were anthologized along with the work of famous writers. Dr. Morton Prince, who investigated Mrs. Curran's mediumship for the SPR, concluded that she lacked "the talent to compose any of Patience Worth's literary works" (Eleanor Touhey Smith, *Psychic People* 107)—a judgment often also formed about other "literary" mediums.

ample, no tradition in Great Britain analogous to the French surrealist experiments that claimed automatic writing as part of the theory and practice of a recognized artistic movement.[11] Even extended investments like those of W. B. and Georgie Yeats, as Chapter 6 demonstrates, appeared too private and idiosyncratic for general application. In fact, in Great Britain, the history of authorship revealed through automatic writing remained largely unexamined, even at the time of its greatest visibility.

Of course, the great bulk of automatic writing in the early twentieth century did not pretend to be "literature." Much of it, as we know from popular representations, consisted in personal communications from departed friends and relatives—often of a quite trivial nature. Much of it, however, as I indicated in Chapter 4, consisted in extended esoteric and metaphysical meditations, ranging uncertainly between scholarly tract and private journal entries. In this, Cummins's *Scripts of Cleophas* was no exception; purporting to be a "A Reconstruction of Primitive Christian Documents" treating the work of the apostles from the death of Jesus to St. Paul's departure for Athens, the scripts were hailed, like the work of other mediums, for their display of "exact knowledge" known only to "serious scholars" and experts (*Scripts* xiv). Such works, however, even at their most scholarly, depended for their effectiveness on literary structures and mechanisms: coherent characterization, stylistic sophistication, vivid dramatizations, convincing dialogue, sustained narrative, and rich intertextuality. Cummins's *Scripts of Cleophas* was celebrated for its novelistic features, which were attributed either to "Cleophas" or to his "chosen medium of communication," the novelist Geraldine Cummins. Thus believers and skeptics alike could classify the *Scripts* as a kind of early Christian "historical novel" (*Scripts* xvi–xvii).

Given these close ties to literature, it is perhaps not surprising that some of the most celebrated cases involving automatic writing were those that claimed authorship in perpetuity for a host of famous literary figures—cases that, with a few notable exceptions, were disclaimed by authors and mediums alike for giving a bad name to their profession. Only years before Cummins's lawsuit, the press had been full of one of these exceptional instances, and Cummins herself was not far from the center of this controversy. For in 1923–24, Hester Dowden, Cummins's friend and mentor in psychical research, received a series of communications purporting to come from Oscar Wilde (then dead for twenty-

---

[11] For further discussions of automatic writing as a part of the surrealist agenda, see Phil Powrie, "Automatic Writing: Breton, Daumal, Hegel," and Cottom, *Abyss*.

three years)—communications for which Cummins frequently served
as a transcriber or recording secretary. Portions of these scripts were
initially published in numbers of the *Occult Review* and *Daily News* in
1923, but they received their most sustained publicity in 1924 when ex-
cerpts were published (along with commentary by the medium) in a
book titled *Psychic Messages from Oscar Wilde* (published under Dowden's married name, Hester Travers Smith).[12] These communications,
transmitted with extraordinary rapidity, consisted of "Wildean" musings and witticisms, as well as contemporary literary criticism—all
written more or less in the style of Oscar Wilde and often in what would
appear a reasonable facsimile of Wilde's handwriting.[13] In a typical display of wit, for example, "Wilde" introduced himself with the following quip: "Being dead is the most boring experience in life. That is if one
excepts being married or dining with a schoolmaster" (Hester Travers
Smith, ed., *Psychic Messages from Oscar Wilde* 9).

Not surprisingly, Dowden's publication caused something of a sen-
sation, both as a psychological and literary curiosity. And while much
of the response consisted of predictable ridicule—the imputation that
Wilde "has not improved in the process of dying"; that the book makes
the reader "unpleasantly aware of how the Beyond stales one's wit";
that the communications "say too little that is not desperately trivial
and imitative"—the work also received much serious attention and respectable notice.[14] Declaring that many of the "literary compositions"
of "the alleged Oscar Wilde" would "not be out of place in any selection
of his acknowledged writings," the *Times Literary Supplement* distinguished this work from "the usual dreary or trivial matter of 'spirit records'" (1 May 1924, 271). Sir Arthur Conan Doyle went even further, de-

[12] Although this and other of her works were published under her married name of
Travers Smith, I have chosen, partly to avoid more confusion, to maintain the name "Hester Dowden" for all references to this medium. According to her biographer, Dowden returned to use of this name even before the Wilde publication, and it was by this name that
she was generally known in psychical research circles. An American edition of *Psychic
Messages from Oscar Wilde* was published under the title *Oscar Wilde from Purgatory* in 1926.
In 1928, a volume of epigrams, also purportedly communicated by Wilde, was published
by an author calling himself "Lazar."

[13] The reproduction of the communicator's handwriting, while not entirely unprecedented, constituted one of the case's more distinctive features, accounting in part for its
importance in the history of automatic writing.

[14] Quoted in *Psychic Messages* 149; *New York Times Book Review*, 9 May 1926; from a review in the Boston *Transcript*, qtd. in "Oscar Wilde Among the Shades" 458. These criticisms were, in fact, typical of long-standing complaints about mediumistic communications. Dowden's responses were equally conventional: that allowances must be made for
the difficulty of communication; for the time elapsed since the author's finest literary
work was completed; and for the negative effects of the experience of "death" on an author's creativity (*Psychic Messages* 95).

claring these compositions not just "adequate Wilde" but "exquisite Wilde," "so beautiful" that they "might be chosen for special inclusion in any anthology of his writings" (345). Even skeptics tended to find the case worthy of interest, if not for its representation of Wilde then for its contribution to psychical research.

The case, however, has additional interest, for Hester Dowden, was, as nearly every recorded mention of her immediately establishes, the daughter of Edward Dowden, an eminent Shakespeare scholar. Although the "Wilde scripts" materialized under a number of conditions—through the joint sittings of "Mr. V." (pseudonym for Mr. S. G. Soal, a University of London lecturer in mathematics) and Hester Dowden at the ouija board; through Mr. V.'s automatic writing, "assisted" by Dowden (and in some instances other mediums, including Dowden's daughter); through the hands of Hester Dowden sitting alone at the ouija board—Dowden readily acknowledges, "so far as I know no literary criticism has come with anyone except myself" (*Psychic Messages* 90). Indeed, the literary criticism generally emerged in an "interview" format, with Wilde's pronouncements prompted by Dowden's questions at the ouija board. Predictably, Dowden was quick to disclaim any originary authority: "I do not hold myself responsible for any of the literary criticism in these scripts—the opinions expressed by 'Oscar Wilde' are not mine" (*Psychic Messages* v).

In fact, those "opinions" might be viewed as rather questionable, both as aesthetic judgments and as "evidence" that they were authentically Wilde's. In these communications, for example, Wilde purportedly declares Galsworthy his literary successor—the only "modern" whose mind appeals to his literary sensibility (*Psychic Messages* 23). But it remains of interest that in "producing" this body of literary criticism relating to the work of a significant man of letters, Dowden achieved a sudden fame through back door access to the world of her father's profession. If as she casually suggested, "the ouija was a method of 'talking' to Wilde" (88), these private conversations, when published, gave Dowden's life a new and controversial public dimension. Moreover, while she could insist that, "The criticisms of modern writers in the script are not my conscious criticisms," and she could readily dismiss the possibility of subconscious influence with the caveat, "but I can hardly imagine that any part of my mind could speak as Wilde does here" (94), it could be argued (whatever one believes about their origin) that the scripts allowed her to do precisely this: to speak *as* Wilde. Representing herself as "editor" of the communications she was chosen to transmit, Dowden (like so many other mediums) put herself in the position of "author" and "interpreter" of some great man's posthumous pronouncements.

Indeed, in the less well publicized sequel to these occurrences, Dowden tests the limits of this editorial position; writing in March 1928, she announces her receipt of a complete posthumous play entitled, "Is It a Forgery?"—a play scheduled for a single performance later that month. Dowden, who never doubted her capacity to be the vehicle for the earlier Wilde scripts, admits that she balked at the possibility of automatic playwriting. In her account of "How I Received Oscar Wilde's 'Spirit Play,'" she observes, "Oscar's next suggestion was that he might write a play—a suggestion which I refused to consider at first. A play written on the Ouija board seemed an impossibility" (*The Graphic*, 10 March 1928). Ultimately, as she explains, however, "urged on by my friend Miss Geraldine Cummins, the writer of the recently published *Scripts of Cleophas*," she agreed to the experiment, with Cummins to serve as "recorder" for the sittings.

As press coverage of the incident makes clear, Dowden's account of the play's inception made satisfying reading for an audience hungry for novelty; except for Wilde's imputed presence, however, little in her representation of the early stages of composition diverged from more traditional narratives of artistic inspiration, where inspiration arrives at a moment of complete discouragement. But in her account of the manuscript's progress (characterized by the reading aloud of the emerging draft for "Wilde's" approval), Dowden effectively reconstructs Wilde as "editor" to the Wildean productions she authors for him, his role reduced to "correcting" the manuscript and "improving the dialogue." Finally, in the last stage of composition, "Wilde" authenticates the text by, as it were, inserting "Wildeicisms" into it, what Dowden calls, crediting Wilde for the expression, "drop[ping] pearls on the text": "Miss Cummins read while I had my hand on the traveller of the Ouija board. Wilde would say 'Stop' when these 'pearls' were to be dropped in, and he dictated them" (*The Graphic*, 10 March 1928).

Dowden's "literary" work subjected her to ridicule and professional marginalization, but it also garnered her unprecedented celebrity, revealing the power to be tapped in becoming the guardian of an established writer's reputation. Her experience was by no means unique in the annals of psychic history. Mrs. Piper claimed to receive automatic communications from, among many others, Longfellow, Johann Sebastian Bach, Walter Scott, and George Eliot. In America in the 1930s and 1940s, Shirley Carson Jenney produced four volumes of posthumous communications from Percy Bysshe Shelley, work she proudly proclaims "has been placed in the Shelley Memorial Library, Rome, Italy, by the Shelley Memorial Library there."[15] In England, Ida M. Everett Keeble, received in the 1930s a series of scripts purportedly dictated by Ivan Turgenev, while Mrs. D. O. Roberts received psychic communications from Shakespeare (and his characters) in the late 1940s. Dowden herself, on at least two separate occasions in the 1940s, also received Shakespearean communications, including new "original" Shakespeare sonnets.[16]

In the 1920s, of course, when the Wilde scripts appeared, a position of such (literary) authority was much more readily available to women as mediums who practiced automatic writing than as writers in their own right or literary critics. For while the ranks of mediums were by no means occupied exclusively by women, mediumship comprised a field where women predominated—so much so, that the phenomenon has begun to attract the serious attention of feminist scholars and critics (see especially Owen, Basham, and Braude). It should come as no surprise, then, that when Cummins names those she considers "great mediums"–the rare geniuses in her field of endeavor—her exemplary figures invariably turn out to be women (*Unseen Adventures* 18). Indeed, on some levels at least, the role of medium could be seen to encapsulate women's traditional training: to be sensitive, self-sacrificing, instrumental—to be, in a word, "other-directed."

Following this logic, women's generally limited formal education made them especially receptive vessels, leaving them with little in their minds to interfere with the communicator's impressions. As "Wilde" explains to Dowden, these qualities make her an ideal vehicle for him: "If I am to speak again as I used, or to use the pen, I must have a clear brain to work with. It must let my thoughts flow through as fine sand might be filtered through a glass cylinder." By contrast, Wilde suggests, the brain of "Mr. V."—the man whose hand first produced the automatic scripts—cannot serve him: "I cannot use it, for ideas would stick there as flies do in a cloyed mass" (*Psychic Messages* 36). Similarly, Dowden herself observes the advantages of a woman's education: "If the actual content of the medium's brain is used, possibly a training in passivity may serve, also the fact that, in my case, there has been a literary training also" (98).

---

[15] This statement appears on the title page of Shirley Carson Jenney's *Some Psychic Experiences with Shelley* (1950), which lists Jenney as the "Shelley Psychic" for *The Fortunes of Heaven, The Great War-Cloud, The Fortune of Eternity,* and *Moments with Shelley.*

[16] Dowden's Shakespeare communications were incorporated into Alfred Dodd, *The Immortal Master* (1943), and Percy Allen, *Talks With Elizabethans: Revealing the Mystery of "William Shakespeare"* (1949).

This training, of course, parallels the double training of the aspiring woman author, and for many educated women of this period, mediumship afforded many of the advantages once reserved for authorship proper. It is probably no coincidence that the ranks of respected mediums were filled with aspiring writers. Alice Kipling Fleming, who produced automatic writing as "Mrs. Holland," also wrote poetry, short stories, and novels, the best known of which include *A Pinchbeck Goddess* (1897) and *Her Brother's Keeper* (1901), published by Heinemann's and Longmans, respectively. Eileen Garrett, after establishing herself as a successful medium, published several novels under the pen name Jean Lyttle. Mabel Collins, who authored numerous "dictated" works on spiritual subjects, and, with Madame Blavatsky, co-edited the Theosophical Society's journal *Lucifer* from 1887–1889, wrote more than a dozen novels, most published between the late 1870s and 1890s; with Charlotte Despard, she was also the author of a collaboratively written novel, *Outlawed* (1908), about women's rights and the suffrage movement.[17]

In much the same way that the authors discussed in Chapter 3 describe falling into (collaborative) writing, many serious mediums record the offhand manner in which they entered this new territory. Cummins, for example, describes her first psychic experience as a typical rainy-day occupation: "One afternoon a thunderstorm broke over Paris; so, unable to go sight-seeing, we retired to a bedroom, and while thunder pealed and the room darkened I was suitably thrilled by Mrs. Dowden's demonstration of her psychic powers" (*Unseen Adventures* 20). Gladys Osborne Leonard, who began her professional life as an actress, recalls the casually exchanged words in a theater dressing room that launched her on her psychic adventures: "[S]hall we try and experiment together?" (27). So natural do such experiments seem for women of a particular class and education that Garrett explains that she participated in her first séance merely out of "indifferent politeness" (*Many Voices* 47).

If mediumship, then, had a particular appeal for those Woolf was to call "the educated man's daughters," not the least of its advantages was the space it allowed for an ambiguous professionalism. Thus despite the rigorous standards they upheld in their practice, many of the most successful and highly respected mediums were quick to dissociate themselves from the taint of the professional, representing their "work"

---

[17] Collins was later expelled from the Theosophical Society for, in effect, making false claims to have received automatic writing from one of Blavatsky's "Masters" (*Encyclopedia of Occultism and Parapsychology* 244).

as a type of glorified hobby.[18] Yet even as they resisted the professional label, they detailed the long "years of hard, often dull, work of the plodding laboratory type" that constituted their training (Cummins, *Unseen Adventures* 20). And even as they clung to their amateur status, they lobbied for professional recognition of mediums. They hoped for a time "when the genuine and conscientious medium is as assured of a permanent livelihood as is any junior civil servant" (135). But for the women who chose to become mediums in the second and third decades of the twentieth century, the ambiguity of their position was not without its compensations. In much the same way that partnership writing had functioned for an earlier generation, mediumship provided middle-class women with a place to be simultaneously amateurs and professionals—a position with distinct advantages for those caught between the lure of a career and conventional gender expectations. Indeed, as Cummins's own case implies, there was something to be said for being a kind of professional amateur, or in her words, "a Jack of all trades and master of none": "Librarian, secretary, novelist, playwright, short-story writer, athlete, agricultural labourer . . . suffragette" (*Unseen Adventures* 18). Contrasting herself to her "four strong-minded sisters" who "broke through all the barriers to a woman's University training," Cummins represents herself as shy and retiring and bound by convention: "I only went up for one examination in my life and that was for shorthand" (*Swan* 150). Mediumship, however, allows the avowedly weak of will to impersonate the "strong-minded woman." For the "degreeless" Cummins, moreover, her "career" as a medium offered her, within a select circle, a center-stage position that could rival her sisters'—a position, moreover, that allowed her to command authority far greater than that accorded any junior civil servant.

When Cummins, then, gives up her literary ambitions to pursue her life as a medium, she exchanges the trials of the public marketplace for the circumscribed celebrity of coterie recognition. As the plaintiff in the *Cummins v. Bond* case, however, and as a publishing medium, she achieved more widespread notice than her fiction ever brought her. If, as Cummins suggests, she first took up "the elusive pursuit of literature" in deference to her mother, whom she describes as "horrified by [her] ardent wish to emulate [her] father" and "qualify as a physician" (*Swan* 150–51), her later decision to devote herself fully to psychical research entailed a commitment to a pursuit equally elusive. And the sacrifice this decision demanded ("to abandon literary work") appears

---

[18] The resistance to professionalization also involved a question of integrity, for without payment, Cummins explains, there could be "no financial incentive to commit fraud" (*Unseen Adventures* 50).

no less a proper act of "daughterly" submission: the fulfillment of a deathbed promise to another woman, her friend, mentor, and house-mate, E. B. Gibbes. Ironically, however, it was as a medium that Cummins received her greatest authorial recognition—not only in her precedent-setting trial but in the judgments advanced regarding her au-tomatic writings. For as the "author" of "transmitted" books, Cummins was regularly credited with creative powers far exceeding those re-vealed in her "original," unaided writings. As one fellow writer put it, describing the "communicator" in the Cummins–Willett scripts: "I've read Geraldine's fiction. She could not possibly have invented Mrs. Wil-lett'" (qtd. in *Swan* lxi).

Such judgments, of course, were marshaled by believers as "proof" of survival in an afterlife; as such, they form a base for the understand-ing of automatic writings as a collaborative undertaking. Cummins, for example, projects the writing process as "a collaboration between two minds, that of the interpreter and that of the discarnate being" (*Unseen Adventures* 133).[19] But as the history of mediumship reveals, this "collaboration" could be configured differently, with considerably less authority accruing to the medium. In a classic model of mediumistic communication, the female medium provides the "matter" for the mas-culine "intelligence," in effect, becoming a speaking/writing body. In Mrs. Piper's trances, for example, one entity would sometimes speak through her mouth, while at the same time, unknown to herself or the initial speaker, her hand would produce writings dictated by another communicator (Sage 10). Such representations would seem to relieve the medium of any deliberative function (hence the idea of "automatic" or "involuntary" writing); in these representations her mind is con-strued as no more than "a borrowed brain mechanism."[20] Accounts of automatic writing frequently represent it as a type of bodily seizure, ex-acting a toll so great as to pose physical or mental danger to the me-dium. The freedom that automatic writing afforded women, then, would seem something other than the "irresponsible pleasure" that Diana Basham imagines, whereby women gained access to authorship with "all its pressures and anxieties removed" (118). It would be safer to say the pressures and anxieties were transferred to other locations.

Significantly, mediums themselves regularly disavowed any respon-

[19] "Interpreter" is Cummins's preferred term for medium. It is also the term Georgie Yeats chooses (see Chapter 6).

[20] The phrase "borrowed brain mechanism" appears in an Editor's note to an essay pub-lished in the *Quarterly Transactions of the British College of Psychic Science*: "[T]he imperfect representations of style may signify the limitation of the powers of a communicating In-telligence in the expression of ideas through a borrowed brain mechanism" ("The Oscar Wilde Script" 309).

sibility for their writings, frequently casting themselves as no more than secretaries: "*I have not written any of this book at all*; I have only taken down as faithfully as I have been able what I have heard" (D. O. Roberts 9); "I have not composed a single sentence of those rapidly written scripts" (Cummins, *Swan* 149). And witnesses to the scenes of automatic writing generally confirm the medium's passive agency in phrases like "the pencil is held," "the pencil writes," and so on. Sometimes, the scripts themselves take up this issue, with the medium, in effect, writing herself out of the picture. In the "Shakespeare" scripts, for example, that Dowden produces for Percy Allen, "Francis Bacon," one of several "Elizabethans" with whom Dowden enables Allen to communicate, converses with Allen about Dowden's lack of authorial agency—a conversation conducted through Dowden's writing.

> P.A. May we regard Mrs. Dowden as *not* responsible for what she writes— her script being what we call "automatic"?
>
> F.B. She is not responsible; not in any manner. She is my pen, and with her I write. My *pen* is not responsible for what I say.
>
> (Allen 33)[21]

Such representations fulfill one version of the writing contract in which the medium's role is relegated to pure instrumentality. Here, Dowden's instrumentality empowers "Shakespeare" to proffer his autobiography and ultimately to write new "original" sonnets, for as "Shakespeare" later tells Allen, "I believe I have, in the hand that holds the pencil, an obedient tool, that will serve us" (Allen 129). In a type of escalating metonymy, "the hand that holds the pencil" (Mrs. Dowden)— becomes the "tool" (pen/pencil)—of the discarnate author. As "an obedient tool," however, the medium lacks even the name of writer.

Cummins's formulation, then, in rendering the medium an "interpreter" and hence "coauthor" of her productions, uneasily resolves the competing claims that mark the medium's ambiguous status vis-à-vis both professionalism and authorship: passive vehicle versus active agency; mind versus matter; conventional secretary versus creative artist. Indeed, as Cummins herself admits on more than one occasion, a medium does bear certain affinities to a stenographer, taking down, as

---

[21] Interestingly enough, this exchange comes about as an effort to explain why in earlier automatic scripts she wrote for Alfred Dodd, Dowden represented Francis Bacon as the "real" Shakespeare; in the Allen scripts, Bacon's authorial role is diminished, with Lord Oxford represented as Shakespeare's most significant "collaborator." "Bacon" explains this discrepancy by attributing the remarks in the earlier work to a "Deputy" who represented him.

from dictation, the words the communicator transmits; shorthand writing, in fact, could be a prerequisite for mediumship, and Cummins deployed her stenographer's skills both in her own automatic writing and in the services she performed as recording secretary for other mediums. As Cummins construes it, however—and this, I would argue, is the ultimate paradox of her trial—the secretarial imagination is not without its shaping influence; a secretary, in other words, within the practice of automatic writing, might well be called an author—a proposition, I argue in the next chapter, Georgie Yeats takes to its limit. When Cummins complains, then, of Frederick Bligh Bond's audacious claims to authorship, her comments belie her own implication in the complexities of the secretarial position.[22]

Reviewing her role as "the central figure in a legal dispute"—the case of *Cummins v. Bond*—Cummins remarks, "A lawyer informed me that if I had lost the case any author's typist could claim, and might successfully establish, that he was the exclusive owner of the book he was employed to type"; and she goes on to offer this caution, "Therefore, when an author does not first write down, but dictates directly to a typist, some immortal poem or story, the typist may, to put it vulgarly, get away with the literary goods. He can publish the poem or story and the author has no legal redress. The copyright of the spoken word belongs to the world" (*Unseen Adventures* 112, 113). As Cummins's case makes clear, however, it belongs to *this* world only. For if one credits an otherworldly author (as Cummins presumably does), Cummins herself might be said to have gotten away with the literary goods, to have established herself as exclusive owner of what was dictated to her, what she was, in the parlance of automatic writing, "employed" to transcribe or copy.

From this perspective, a medium's claim to copyright could be said to rest on the same grounds as the claims of a typist or stenographer; indeed, the construction of automatic or transmitted writings as the medium's literary property would seem to run counter to most spiritualist teaching, exalting the medium over the message she communicates and the originating communicator. As was seen in the preceding chapter, the medium supplies the words for some being that speaks through her. The medium, that is, puts into words (drawn from or pieced out of her own vocabulary) the ideas and impressions she receives, as it were,

[22] It is doubly ironic, then, that "Mrs. Willett," writing through Cummins, will later accuse her having "the mind of a typist secretary" (Cummins, *Swan* 97).

automatically (i.e., reflexively and nonverbally). As one "communicator" confirms for Cummins, "When we converse through a medium and with a medium or automatist we become, as it were, dependent on her thoughts, words and images" (*Swan* 25). The resulting communication, as Cummins's "control" spirit explains, "is like a patchwork quilt. Bits are hers and other patches yours" (32–33).

For Cummins, this situation confers a degree of agency and authority, for, as she argues, in the case of automatists like herself, "the brain and memory of the medium or interpreter are used to a greater extent than the average observer imagines" (*Unseen Adventures* 125). Consequently, the "interest and value of the communications" the medium receives and transmits depend in no small part "on the quality of the instrument"—i.e., the quality of the medium or, as Cummins prefers to put it, the quality of the "interpreter." But for Cummins's communicator—the once-famous medium "Mrs. Willett"—the medium's "interference" now constitutes a source of corruption: "But medium is an incorrect term. They should be called interpreters, and bad ones at that! So often there is mistranslation" (*Swan* 36). Cummins herself admits to the presence in most communications of "what one might call 'padding,'" extraneous material from the medium's subconscious that must be carefully sifted out of the transmitted writings (*Unseen Adventures* 133). In fact, in many instances, the medium's creative input can be seen to produce the anachronisms, errors, and inconsistencies—not to mention the stylistic and grammatical lapses—so characteristic of the scripts of automatic writing.

In the "Cleophas" case, for example, one of the peculiarities of the scripts (and a source of some amusement to skeptical observers) was that the early Christian scribe (whose native tongue would presumably be Greek, Aramaic, or Hebrew) should speak in a markedly "archaic English." Ironically, it was Bond's testimony to this point that made Cummins's case for her. Arguing that the "peculiarity of the scripts" (as in automatic writing more generally) was that "the message is conveyed without words," Bond in effect located authorship in the medium. For his testimony confessed that "the words and the framework of the message are formed in the brain of the medium. The language of the script was not the language of the communicating intelligence. It is the idea which is conveyed." As the *New York Times* account concludes, the Copyright Act of 1911 "protects the language, not the idea; and Mr. Bond had admitted that the communicating intelligence conveys the idea and not the language" (28 August 1926, 4:4).

In settling the claims of the medium in the "language" or "wording" of the communications, *Cummins v. Bond* established the authorship of the medium in the material practice of writing; in doing so, however, it wrote the "spirit" out of the proceedings. But the practice of mediumship, with its insistence on instrumentality, would seem to resist the claims that supported the progressive extension of copyright from the Statute of Anne of 1709 to the 1911 act invoked in the Cummins trial—claims that came increasingly to rely on notions of originality and uniqueness. If the history of copyright records the court's efforts to balance the claims of the public good against the rights of the proprietary author, mediums would seem staunchly identified with the former, with the proponents of the dissemination of "useful knowledge."[23] Certainly, it was on these grounds that mediums most frequently justified putting their works before the public—even works as apparently personal as their autobiographies.

Mediums who published their own life stories regularly disclaimed any desire for the "personal distinction" of authorship, preferring to see publication as an act of selfless public service. When the texts in question were the ones the mediums transmitted for others—the "scripts" that were ostensibly communicated through them in order to make certain knowledge public—the strain on the medium was all the more evident. For the task at hand was incompatible with the self-promotion of authorship. What would be the meaning, then, of a medium's copyright in a case like Cummins's? Certainly, insofar as copyright law favors the construction of a single author/single text model of literary production, it cannot comprehend the nuances of a practice that resists such "commonsense" assumptions. As Dowden makes clear, automatic writings are inherently collaborative; indeed, she prefaces her account of her own mediumship by thanking "the sitters at my circle, who have always been most patient, friendly, and helpful; what I have written is quite as much a record of their work as my own" (Travers Smith, *Voices from the Void* v). Yet it is precisely the claim of a "sitter" to be considered a co-worker—a coauthor or joint writer—that the Cummins trial treats so contemptuously. For to Bond's claim that his presence at the sittings was necessary to the production of the texts—that the communications were, if written in Cummins's hand, nonetheless addressed to him and dependent on his participation—Cummins quotes, with apparent satisfaction, her counsel's heavy-handed irony about "inspiration": "My

[23] Vanden Bossche in "The Value of Literature" characterizes the copyright debate of 1837–1842 as one between competing understandings of print culture: imaginative literature versus useful knowledge. The advancement of knowledge, however, was a rubric that was claimed, at different times, by both promoters and opponents of the extension of copyright. More explicitly than other forms of authorship, mediumship claimed the right to reproduce knowledge from a common site—what might be called the collective unconscious.

counsel retorted that it might just as well be said that the copyright in Keats's *Ode to the Nightingale* was vested in the Nightingale" (*Unseen Adventures* 112). Moreover, what accounts of the trial (including Cummins's published recollections) fail to credit adequately is that Bond was no ordinary sitter. The author of *The Gates of Remembrance* and the editor of the journal *Psychic Science*, he was famous for his architectural work on Glastonbury Abbey—and perhaps even more for the automatic scripts he received from its former inhabitants, scripts transmitted to him through the hands of various mediums, including Hester Dowden. An established architect, scholar, and spiritualist practitioner (three of his Glastonbury scripts had been published at the time of the trial), Bond was held in great repute in the psychical research community and was not simply, as the trial seemed to present it, the "amateur" to Cummins's "professional." When the court, then, dismissed his contributions as a "labour of love" (and therefore not deserving remuneration) and relegated Bond to the role of functionary (a typist/editor whose contribution to the text was to "punctuate, transcribe, and paragraph it"), the court endorsed an inversion of gender codings that produced Cummins's authority through the successful feminization of her adversary (*London Times*, 22 July 1926).

Indeed, despite the trivial cast given to Bond's allegations, all of his claims exist well within available understandings of the collaborative nature of automatic or transmitted writings. When, for example, Bond argues that he had previously published several works of automatic writing and had never before had a copyright claim from a medium, he is being no more than honest. Nor was he alone in this practice. For a "sitter" to publish automatic writings—to put himself in the position of author—was, in fact, more the rule than the exception, and the practice did not cease with Cummins's precedent-setting lawsuit. Dowden published most of her automatic scripts in this format, including a significant body of work produced in the 1940s. In 1941, for example, Peter Fripp, one of Dowden's sitters, published, under his own name, *The Book of Johannes*, the teachings of Dowden's principal "control," with whom Fripp represented himself as collaborating (13). At about this time, Dowden also facilitated the publication of a series of children's books by "Heather," the pen name for the recently deceased daughter of one of Dowden's sitters—a Mrs. Vivian, who held the copyright for "Heather"'s fiction. As Dowden's biographer observes, Mrs. Vivian's role was strictly secretarial, confined to "editing and typing the words which were sent to the publisher unaltered" (Bentley 147), precisely the role Cummins attributed to Bond to discredit his contribution.

Perhaps most tellingly, in 1949, Percy Allen published *Talks with Eliza-bethans*, a text consisting largely of automatic scripts produced for him by Dowden (scripts purporting to come from William Shakespeare and his contemporaries);[24] the text's master stroke, however, was the publication of three new Shakespeare sonnets, "dictated, from another world" to Hester Dowden, written, as notes make clear, "in Mr. Allen's absence, and without his knowledge" ([5]). While, in acknowledgments, editorial comments, and author's notes—indeed, in the text of his own narrative—Allen gratefully acknowledges Dowden as his "gifted amanuensis and collaborator" ([6]), her name does not appear on the title page nor does she ever receive from him the designation "author."[25] Even where Allen most explicitly acknowledges collaboration, he remains "author" to Dowden's "intermediary"—a gendered division of labor reinforced by the communicators, who represent Dowden as a "link" and Allen as a colleague or co-conspirator: "She, the woman, has great affinity with our period; and she acts as a link between you and me; but, my dear sir, you surely know you were one of us, though not conscious of it in this incarnation" (Allen 118).

Even though Cummins's attorneys could slight Bond's participation in the Cleophas scripts, his participation reads differently when contextualized within the professional discourse of automatic writing. Allowing, for example, that "[t]he part which the defendant took at the séances was that he occasionally asked the plaintiff questions and placed his fingers on the back of her hand when she was writing," Cummins's counsel maintained that such interference "was regarded by the plaintiff as a hindrance rather than a help" (*London Times*, 22 July 1926); but other spiritualist practitioners saw such interventions differently, as constitutive of an alternative writing practice, subject to a set of laws incompatible with the conventions of proprietary authorship. Dowden, for example, articulates a theory of "double mediumship": "At the ouija-board, where two persons work together, it is all important to discover mediums whose respective qualities balance and assist each other. The control will generally say he requires 'a negative and a positive'" (Travers Smith, *Voices from the Void* 107). In *Psychic Messages from Oscar Wilde*, she extends this understanding to the production of auto-

---

[24] Although Allen's text includes some materials received through other (female) mediums, the heart of the book rests in Dowden communications.

[25] Dowden's name does appear on the title page of the copy of the book I consulted, penciled in by the university's library staff for the purposes of cataloging. Automatic texts raise a number of bibliographical quandaries, with the sitter, the communicator, and the medium all vying for the position of author.

matic scripts. In the "Oscar Wilde" case, a male medium "Mr. V" produced the actual writing, but only, according to Dowden, when she (or
in some instances her daughter) rested her hands on his: "I could not get
the handwriting without him; he could get nothing without my help"
(*Psychic Messages from Oscar Wilde* 90). For Dowden, this constitutes a
genuine case of collaborative mediumship, and she is quick to insist
that a single "origin" or author cannot be established: "It must be recognized that in cases of double mediumship the communications cannot be attributed to either operator alone." Dowden, moreover, adopts
a position that sheds new light on Bond's claims: "In my experience the
ideas expressed are more definitely connected with the person who lays
his hand on the writer's hand than with the actual automatist. The messages are *definitely* a joint production" (91).

I offer these instances not to determine whether Bond's participation
in the Cleophas scripts qualifies as a genuine case of double authorship
but to suggest that his claims underline a significant difference in the
understanding of authorship that automatic writing permits—a difference Cummins's legal position forces her to resist. In fact, in turning to
the Society of Authors to adjudicate her differences with Bond before
taking her case to court, Cummins committed herself to a proprietary
definition of authorship bound to clash with the orthodoxies of her own
mediumistic profession. This is not to say that practitioners of automatic writing represented a coherent opposition to the legal consolida-
tion of the authorial position; rather, automatic writing represented a
peculiarly charged (although only marginally visible) site where competing understandings of authorship played themselves out in the first
decades of the twentieth century.

In fact, it could be argued that automatic writing (and its related practices, ouija board writing, planchette writing, clairaudience, direct voice
communication) constitutes, above all, a discourse about the practice
and problematics of authorship. While most cases of automatic writing
did not directly invoke famous authors or pass for literature per se,
the scripts often addressed the conditions of their own construction—
exploring issues of origins, composition, transmission, production, inspiration—and hence could be said to constitute a kind of metacom-
mentary on authorship. In this, Cummins's *Scripts of Cleophas* (a kind of
crypto-Biblical writing) could be seen as exemplary, highlighting the
network of "authors" (chroniclers, compilers, scribes) that produce and
transmit the works of divine authority. It highlighted, moreover, the
challenge automatic writing posed to the conventions of publishing.
For scripts such as Cummins's—given their length, repetitiveness, and

lack of formal decorum—could not be published without substantial editing.[26]

Publication conventions only partially cover the way these texts continue to resist legibility. These texts are also linked to what Marlon B. Ross identifies as "scribbling" or "wayward writing," the living remains of earlier scribal practices. In this they might be profitably compared to the Brontës' early writing, which, like the scripts, redefined the channels through which knowledge and creative expression could be accessed. These writing practices share with the Brontë juvenilia distinct affinities to what Peter Jaszi has called "serial collaborations"— "works resulting from successive elaborations of an idea or text by a series of creative workers, occurring perhaps over years or decades" (40); in the case of automatic writing, however, such collaborations might extend over centuries, even millennia. Mediums, moreover, as Cummins surely recognized, often participated, knowingly or not, in serial productions, supplying their individual contributions to the collected posthumous works of some recognized historical figure, such as Oscar Wilde or Shakespeare. Luminaries of the psychical research community also apparently became prolific communicators after death. Cummins, for example, like "Mrs. Willett," received extended communications from F. W. H. Myers, one of the SPR's founders—as did large numbers of other mediums, most famously in the Cross-Correspondence Experiments. This latter instance was quite explicitly a serial collaboration, for a coherent text could only be pieced together by laying side by side the fragmentary messages—most purportedly from Myers—received by a variety of mediums in widely dispersed places.

Thus automatic writing, by breaking down distinctions between the literary and the nonliterary, the original and the copied, the spoken and the written, the product and the process, the spontaneous and the crafted, might be seen to testify to the continued existence of those writing practices, often communal or collaborative in nature, that could not be subsumed under the rubric of the proprietary author. Although certain sensational texts such as the Wilde communications (and, to a lesser extent, the Cleophas scripts) achieved wide readership and public notice, the more typical and obscure examples challenged conventions of

[26] These texts also raise questions about differential modes of publication. While two of Mrs. Curran's "Patience Worth" novels, for example, were published by Henry Holt & Co., other of her works were published by the "Patience Worth Publishing Company." Daisy Roberts's and Ida Keeble's texts were also privately published, although Roberts's original publication was subsequently incorporated into *Elizabethan Episode* (Regency Press).

authorship differently, reopening the question of coterie writing, of the meaning and significance of texts written for small, sometimes closed, communities of readers.

If automatic writing, then, preeminently posed the question, Who writes? it also asked, with new urgency, Who reads? And it asked, in a discourse at once technical and philosophical, How is writing achieved? For responding to a historical transformation in modes of communication, the texts of automatic writing could be said to articulate a new technology of writing—a technology that appears at once a kind of pre-technological throwback and a radical appropriation of the language of science and technology. As *Cummins v. Bond* suggests (in invoking the threatening possibility of a typist's copyright), automatic writing might be read as a particular response to the crisis in authorship prompted by the availability of typewriters and other technologies that sever writing from the hand that writes it. In this respect, it is perfectly in keeping with the history of copyright that a new technology of authorship and publishing would prompt a reexamination of authorial boundaries. Indeed, one of the staples of automatic writing is to present the author as machine (typewriter, telegraph, telephone, radio receiver, radar device, dictaphone), while recalling attention to the manual labor that fuels this operation (hand, pencil, paper). It is also to insist on the ultimate "mystery" of writing, on the spirit that drives the machine. In its inevitably paradoxical positioning, then, automatic writing both extends and undermines a "modern" understanding of authorship.

It would seem no accident, then, that in the historical moment when automatic writing flourished, such writings should often take a particular configuration, the so-called conversations with illustrious authors; for these posthumous communications appear at a historical moment when the modern idea of the proprietary author has been consolidated, as has been the status of long-dead authors as "common" property. That the desire to speak with the dead should so often appear in this particular manifestation bespeaks the cultural authority of authors and their power to legitimate what might otherwise seem an eccentric activity.[27] In this context, the emerging "genre" of posthumous communications

[27] Even today, the institutional authority of Shakespeare continues to make such dreams plausible, as in the famous opening line of Stephen Greenblatt's *Shakespearean Negotiations: The Circulation of Social Energy in Renaissance England*: "I began with a desire to speak with the dead." See also Marjorie Garber, *Shakespeare's Ghost Writers: Literature as Uncanny Causality*, for another discussion of the way "Shakespeare" haunts the modern imagination. Garber provocatively links the thematics of ghosts and ghostwriting in the Shakespeare plays to the continuing controversies surrounding Shakespeare's authorship.

becomes a self-conscious site for debating the nature and status of authorship. Hence the kind of "inside joke" that allows "Wilde" to name his play "Is It a Forgery?"[28] And hence the sustained interest in Shakespeare as the "authority" for alternative understandings of writing.

As both the ultimate example of privileged authorship and a figure whose authorship has always been in question, Shakespeare proved peculiarly susceptible to such interested reconstructions. Indeed, the numerous "Shakespeare" scripts produced through automatic writing generally argue one or both of two things: that Shakespeare was psychic (i.e., he received his plays automatically) and/or that "Shakespeare" wrote collaboratively.[29] Thus the "William Shakespeare" who communicates with Mrs. Roberts admits, "I think I know now I did not write the plays, but they came, with my hand and my pen. I thought that was how everybody wrote—I did not know they were great" (Roberts 72). The larger argument here, however, is the same as the one that Allen argues with more scholarly pretensions, to establish the existence of some "Shakespeare Group" responsible for authorship of the plays and poetry: "'William Shakespeare' was, of course, the official pen-name of the aristocratic group which used Will of Stratford as stage-adviser, playmaker, and, in modern phrase, producer, and also as their official and accredited mask" (70).[30] In Allen's formulation, this group has at its center Lord Oxford—the one of whom William Shakespeare could say, "We two are Shakespeare" (40)—but including at different times and with different degrees and types of input Francis Bacon, Beaumont and Fletcher, and Sir Philip Sidney. Arguing the case for joint authorship (on the "empirical" evidence of Elizabethan observer/participants and the production of new Shakespeare sonnets, dictated to the medium in the 1940s), the scripts elaborate a practice of "ideal collaboration" that reproduces familiar divisions of labor, with Oxford playing "poet" to William Shakespeare's "playwright."[31]

[28] According to Dowden, Wilde initially titled the drama "The Extraordinary Play" but changed the title when informed of objections from the producer. "Call the play Is It a Forgery?," he apparently replied, "and say the author himself is debating the question" (The Graphic, 10 March, 1928, 401).

[29] In addition to Percy Allen, Alfred Dodd, and Daisy Roberts, see C. L'Estrange Ewen, Shakespeare—Automatist or Nothing (1946) and Shakespeare—No Poet? The Story of an Unpublished Volume (1938).

[30] As Garber notes, the Shakespeare Authorship Society, dedicated to promoting the claims of Lord Oxford as the author of "Shakespeare," was formed in 1922; these automatic scripts thus participated in a renewed cultural interest in the Shakespeare authorship controversy.

[31] As Allen's text elaborates, Shakespeare provides the plot and stagecraft, while Oxford provides the "poetry"; Shakespeare provides the broad comedy, while Oxford supplies the tragedy and romance. As Jeffrey A. Masten has argued in "Beaumont and/or Fletcher:

While Allen's reconstructions ensure Shakespeare's proper aristocratic credentials, they participate, like other automatic writings, in the
democratization of authorship. For Allen's scripts, despite their eccentric, even mystical, modes of production, could be said to demystify authorship: in effect, to normalize it. Indeed, by partitioning the "genius"
of Shakespeare into recognizable and discrete components, Allen renders such genius accessible to ordinary practitioners. In this model of
authorship, the medium (or sitter) achieves some kind of parity with the
author/communicator.[32] One of the earliest messages, for example, that
Allen receives is to inform him of the collective nature of his enterprise,
an assessment Allen is quick to credit: "As for the statement that I am
not the only writer of the book, I have long felt this to be true of *all* my
writings on Elizabethan subjects, granted that they were not dictated to
me directly from the beyond. I have stated frequently . . . that I have con-
tinuously felt, during the progress of these writings, the effective urge
of some higher power working through me" (26).

Establishing in his own person a link to more conventional authorship, Allen uses the text at hand to generalize about the practice of writing. Promoting themselves as representative rather than exceptional,
texts such as Allen's remind us that writing is always mediated: all
authorship can be seen as collaborative or collective and as the effect of
"some higher power" working through the hand that holds the pen.
The practices of automatic writing thus address the kind of social con-
structionist arguments that Foucault has popularized; indeed, they argue quite literally that the author does not so much speak as is spoken
through. As such, they contain the potential to radically reconceive authorship, even where one does not believe that the texts are "dictated . . .
directly from the beyond." In fact, as an extended demonstration of "the
author function," these texts ask with intense seriousness, What is an
author? And they pose this question in a context where the answer is
anything but self-evident.[33]

Collaboration and the Interpretation of Renaissance Drama," however, this type of
proprietary and hierarchical division of labor misrepresents the historical practice of
sixteenth-century dramatists who did not labor under our "modern" notions of singular,
individualized authorship.

[32] As "Shakespeare" tells Mrs. Roberts, for example, as recipients of "gifts" not of their
choosing, they both perform similar functions despite apparent disparities: "You only
hold a pencil, I wrote those plays; it is all one, we both received our gifts" (*Shakespeare &
Co. Unlimited* 12). Indeed, Shakespeare's confession, "I thought everyone wrote like that,"
suggests, in effect, that he believed that everyone wrote the way mediums do. This democratization of authorship is also evident in the gendered redistribution of labor that
permits women (often with limited formal education) to transmit the texts of distinguished personages.

[33] Anticipating Foucault's famous inquiry in "What Is an Author?" Peter Fripp writes in
his introduction to the *Book of Johannes*, "Let me confess that I am myself startled in many

Yet if, as I have been arguing, the collaborative nature of authorship is the most distinctive feature of automatic writing, for mediums a gap often remained between theory and practice. Mediums, like other authors, were not exempt from the pull of proprietary ownership that governed the dominant public constructions of authorship at this historical moment. Thus, although Dowden argues that "better results often come through double mediumship than through one person" (*Psychic Messages* 92), and although she scrupulously documents the conditions under which each of the Oscar Wilde scripts was produced, much of *Psychic Messages* (published under Dowden's name alone) seems directed at establishing her primary authorship. As the scripts are represented in her edition, the bulk of them—including most of the instances of original literary criticism—derive from communications she receives when sitting alone at the ouija board. "Mr. V.," by contrast, produces very little without Dowden's assistance. Although Mr. V. was tested with four different persons, according to Dowden, "only one succeeded in getting anything through with him" (90). Moreover, when Mr. V. does produce writing alone, Dowden dismisses it in an offhand manner: "The script was long; not Wilde at his best, I thought" (91). Even for the "five or six automatic scripts" produced by Mr. V. and Dowden working together, Dowden, as the one who lay her hands on the hands of the writing medium, can claim a more central influence, as "Oscar Wilde" confirms in an independent communication.[34]

Of course, this represents only one side of the story. In an account of these occurrences published in the *Proceedings* of the SPR, Eleanor Sidgwick confirms that without partnership of the sort provided by Dowden, Mr. V. "has practically not succeeded in obtaining automatic writing at all—his pencil merely taps the paper"; but she notes, "in the scripts before us three ladies besides Mrs. Travers Smith [i.e., Dowden] have at different times successfully given the necessary help by placing hand or fingers on his wrist" (Sidgwick 187). And while she does not resolve the problematic question of "joint automatism," she gives equal time to the opposing perspective, copying into her report a part of the script not included by Dowden but published in the *Sunday Express* of 5 August 1923, an ostensible communication from Wilde to Mr. V.:

---

ways as this book becomes written, which is perhaps a curious thing for an author to say, but then, who is the author?" (9). Fripp, in fact, comes close to coining the term "author-function": "I am in a way serving that function, but we may come to some other conclusion as it unfolds itself" (9).

[34] See Travers Smith, *Psychic Messages* 13 and 22. "Mr. V.."'s brother, however, after performing an extensive stylistic analysis of the handwriting and literary style of the Wilde scripts, argues that the scripts Mr. V— produces with mediums other than Dowden are of a higher literary quality ("The Oscar Wilde Script" 309).

It is through your temperament that I am able to give my thoughts to the world. You have the curious combination of the literary and scientific temperament which creates a sort of psychic affinity with myself. It is true that one of the ladies here supplies a certain motive force—just as an electronic machine must have its 'starters' or whatever one may call them. But these are merely the accessories and the accessories are not the machine. The machine I use is your human temperament. So please remember that there is only one Oscar Wilde and that you are his prophet. (Sidgwick 195)

Finally, however, Sidgwick offers yet another possibility, culled from the Wilde texts produced with one of the other mediums: that "Oscar Wilde" may not be a single author or entity.[35]

In this context, Cummins's authorial claims take on new complexity. Trained as both a medium and an author (collaborative and otherwise), Cummins could be said to mediate the competing interests of these two distinct but overlapping identities. For if she abandons her career as an author, she never ceases to identify herself as one; she never ceases, moreover, to be sensitive to constructions of her psychical work that would deny her (authorial) agency. She repeatedly notes that she does not like the term "automatic writing," suggesting as it does some unconscious or involuntary procedure; and in her own accounts of her work, she scrupulously designates her productions "transmitted" or "communicated" writings, terms she deems more accurate and representative. Nor does she like the term "control," the generally accepted designation for the spirits Cummins calls, "the guardian caretaker[s] of a medium." "I dislike the word 'control,'" she writes. "Mine, Astor, has never controlled me" (*Swan* 151–52). In fact, the absence of mention of controls in Cummins's copyright case is symptomatic of the way the trial's construction of "automatic writing" necessarily oversimplified a complexly mediated proceeding, confirming Jaszi's thesis that "the extension of copyright protection to new categories of works may entail reimagining them so as to suppress complicating details about their modes of production" (38).

To locate authorship in the hand that holds the pen (as the trial did, apparently with Cummins's blessing) was, as I have tried to suggest, to threaten the entire spiritualist machinery. It was also to deny one of automatic writing's most fundamental features by enforcing the single author/single text model of authorship. Such a model offers little, moreover, that could explain Cummins's own role as a collaborative writer: the author, with Susanne Day, of three plays performed at the Abbey

[35] Asked how he is able to communicate through both Mr. V. and Dowden, "Wilde" suggests that he has multiple manifestations: "Quite possibly our name is legion" (Sidgwick, "The 'Oscar Wilde' Script" 195).

Theatre.[36] And it offers little to suggest the ways mediumship might challenge the fundamental categories of literary production. In fact, even as Cummins made claims for the authorship of a medium, she continued to project the two as mutually exclusive.[37] Thus when she closes her autobiography with the surprising claim that authors of imaginative literature and literary critics should be the ultimate judges of "the mass of evidence so far provided by leading mediums" (*Unseen Adventures* 162), she argues on the basis that "their professional job is the study and expression of human personality in all its aspects" and not on the claims for some deeper structural and stylistic affinities. Reaffirming the principle that good mediumship is "more in the nature of art than science" (132), she nonetheless refuses the more radical claim that *as writing*, literary and mediumistic practices might, in some senses at least, be indistinguishable. Instead, she repeats the act of repression that determined her own career history, harnessing the skills of an author (and literary critic) to the service of psychical research—research that demands that the "author" cease to function as such.

Similarly, in her literary criticism, such as the biography of her friend and compatriot, the author Edith Somerville, Cummins relies on the most conventional authorial configurations. Cummins glosses over Somerville's long-standing interest in spiritualism, although Cummins herself would later be called on to act as her medium. Despite Somerville's insistence, moreover, that after Ross's death, her partner continued to write with her—leaving Somerville feeling that she was often "little more than an earthly secretary taking down dictation" (Robinson 47)—Cummins has little to say about Somerville's automatic writing. "Such a collaboration must remain a debatable point until our darkness is more enlightened" is the most she will venture (*Dr E. Œ. Somerville* 63).[38] Perhaps even more surprisingly, in spite of the status of the Somerville and Ross partnership as one of the most famous and sustained instances of literary collaboration, Cummins produces a biography in which collaboration is seriously underrated. Indeed, treating Somerville as her solo subject and representing her as the "senior partner" in this team, Cummins's biography, in effect, reconstitutes Somerville as *single* author.

Like the structures of authorship foregrounded in her trial, these

---

[36] These plays were *Broken Faith* (1912), *The Way of the World* (1914), and *Fox and Geese* (1917).

[37] Cummins suggests, for example, that as long as she considered herself a fiction writer, she avoided reading any psychical research scholarship, fearing that the "technical jargon would interfere with [her] composition" in her "consciously composed literary work" (*Swan* 156).

[38] Cummins's reserve, however, did not prevent more traditional scholars from dismissing the biography as unprofessional.

public articulations and practical applications of the authorial position confine authorship to its most narrow, and generally acceptable, limits. Leaving little space for forms of authorship that might challenge hegemonic representations, Cummins's authorial constructions could, however, be read as self-defeating. For ultimately they foreclosed the terms of analysis by which competing understandings of authorship (including those Cummins practiced as both "author" and "medium") might be seen as something more than a curious footnote to standard literary histories.

6

Romancing the Medium
The Silent Partnership of Georgie Yeats

In December 1919, a little more than two years after the some-what sudden marriage of the fifty-two-year-old poet W. B. Yeats to the twenty-five-year-old Georgie Hyde-Lees, the couple prepared for a trip to America. "George," WBY wrote to John Quinn, a trusted family friend and literary patron, is "very excited at the thought of America & many people, having been practically alone with me since our marriage, every evening in my study helping me at my work. We shall bring with us the manuscripts."[1] If this portrait of a marriage leaves something to be desired, it does not tell the whole story of those sequestered eve-nings. For as is now widely known (if not always fully credited), the work the Yeatses shared in those evening sessions consisted in George's automatic writing, amounting to some 3600 manuscript pages—the raw material for what was to become W. B. Yeats's *A Vision* (1925; rev. ed. 1937). Indeed, as WBY reveals in the 1937 edition of the text—"four days after my marriage, my wife surprised me by attempting automatic writing" (8)—George's "gift" launched one of the most famous honey-moons in literary history.[2]

Yeats's biographers readily acknowledge that the conditions of that marriage were less than promising; WBY had in the preceding year pro-

---

[1] Quoted in George Mills Harper, *The Making of Yeats's "A Vision": A Study of the Auto-matic Script* 2:386 (hereafter *MYV*). "George" was W. B. Yeats's preferred name for his wife, born Bertha Georgie Hyde-Lees; before her marriage, she generally went by the name Georgie, and this is the name that appears most frequently in Yeats criticism. For the purposes of this chapter, I have chosen to represent W. B. Yeats by the initials WBY in order to avoid, to some degree, the problematic gender hierarchies of treating these his-torical figures as "Yeats" and "Georgie." It is also a way to signify that "Yeats" can name more than one author.

[2] This period of sustained automatic writing lasted until March 1920, when it was largely replaced by "a new method" (practiced through 1922) in which George talked in her sleep and Yeats recorded her communications.

Figure 10. W. B. and Georgie Yeats, during a visit to the United States in 1920. Corbis-Bettmann.

posed to (and been rejected by) both Maud Gonne and her daughter—in the case of the latter, only months before his successful suit to Georgie. By his own account, he was "in great gloom" that he had "betrayed three people" and damaged all their lives irreparably.[3] Against this backdrop, George's sudden discovery of psychic gifts has often been read as her attempt to "romance" an unhappy and distracted husband; by her own admission, George apparently set out to "fake" automatic writing—writing that, over the extended course of the scripts, she threatened to withhold if her husband wasn't sufficiently attentive to her.[4] "The more you keep this medium emotionally and intellectually happy," the communicators announce about a year into the sittings, "the more will script be possible now."[5] "What is important is," they remind them a year later, "that both the desire of the medium and her desire for your desire should be satisfied," for "without *sexual & emotional* satisfaction . . . there is no force" (*YVP* 2:487).[6] Failure to abide by their rules, WBY is told, will not be tolerated. "For every public speech or lecture you give after tomorrow during the next 6 months," George writes at the beginning of one session, "I shall stop script one month—For every occasion you talk system in private conversation one month" (2:222–23).

Although these messages appear in the hand of the medium, the mass of scripts Georgie Yeats facilitated cannot be explained as simple deception, nor, however complex their motivations, as a calculated trade-off between sexual and psychic favors.[7] Sustained for two and a half years and over the course of more than four hundred fifty physically taxing sessions, they represent an extraordinary exercise of wifely "influence" on the career of a major literary figure; as the manuscripts demonstrate, moreover, the scripts can only be understood as a complex partnership production. Indeed, aware of Quinn's censorious views of his occult studies, WBY, in his letter, admits *only* to the partnership—"George . . . [has been] . . . helping me at my work"—without revealing its modus operandi. And he implies that the manuscripts in question are his latest literary productions.

[3] WBY to Lady Gregory, 29 October 1917 (qtd. in *MYV* 1:3).

[4] For George's admission, see Virginia Moore, *The Unicorn: William Butler Yeats' Search for Reality* 253.

[5] *Yeats's "Vision" Papers*, ed. George Mills Harper (general editor) et al. (1992) 2:119 (hereafter *YVP*).

[6] These messages appear in mirror writing, three or four times the size of George's normal handwriting; in these scripts, mirror writing usually signals that the communicators don't want the medium to understand their message.

[7] Almost all the comments in the scripts, including the above threat to withhold communication, appear in the "voice" of one of the ostensible communicators. For an extended reading of the automatic writing in terms of the sexual dynamics of the Yeatses' marriage, see Elizabeth Butler Cullingford, *Gender and History in Yeats's Love Poetry*.

But if WBY assumes the admission of his wife's literary assistance is less compromising than the revelation of his participation in her automatic writing, it is because the "collaboration" he thus projects is of a sort so familiar as not to require notice: the help any wife might give a literary husband—working, presumably, as secretary, typist, editor, or research assistant. As Jack Stillinger suggests, the "practice of spousal collaboration is so common" that it is often "difficult to focus on its consequences for authorial 'authority' in a piece of writing" (50). And in the case of the Yeatses, Georgie Yeats practiced spousal collaboration in its common as well as uncommon manifestations. An obituary notice in *The Times* (26 August 1968), for example, gives these roles equal billing: "She acted as secretary for her husband and typed most of his plays. Like W. B. Yeats she was interested in psychic research and in spiritualism." The unusual collaboration, then, that the Yeatses practiced in the first years of their marriage may be less exceptional than would at first seem apparent; for their writing partnership, for all its esoteric trappings, shares a good deal with the "normal" collaborations, often beginning at home, that go into literary production.

Indeed, when read in the larger context that this book offers, what is most important to note about the Yeatses' nightly experiments is that this is a collaboration structured by marriage—literally as well as figuratively. As such, the Yeatses' practice both extends and revises the patterns exhibited in women's same-sex literary unions—partnerships that also often represented themselves in terms of marriage (see Chapter 2). Certainly, it allows for a more explicit recognition of the erotics of collaboration—an erotics, as Chapter 4 argues, upon which mediumship capitalizes. As the communicators repeatedly inform the Yeatses, their partnership depends on sexual difference—depends, that is, on their particular union of antithetical qualities, producing "the psychic link" that allows a special sympathy between them (*MYV* 1:181).

As a partnership modeled on the married couple, the Yeatses' collaboration, of course, was not without precedent. The Yeatses were not unique, for example, in tying a wife's psychic gifts to her husband's presence; F. W. H. Myers, whose work WBY studied, documents at least one such instance, while the Order of the Golden Dawn, with whose workings WBY was intimately familiar, offered its own examples of mediumistic wives supplementing their husbands' teachings.[8] Nor were the Yeatses unique in enacting a kind of intellectual partnership with impo-

---

[8] For Myers reference, see *MYV* 1:278n. In the Order of the Golden Dawn, Moina Mathers MacGregor, wife of MacGregor Mathers and sister of Henri Bergson, produced automatic writing connected to the Order's teachings, as did Mary Felkin, wife of another Golden Dawn Chief, Dr. R. W. Felkin.

tant significance for literary study. As Stillinger points out, John Stuart Mill regularly credited Harriet Taylor Mill with the "joint production" of many of the works that bear his name—nowhere more so than in the production of *On Liberty* (66). Robert Louis Stevenson also collaborated with his wife, but not always openly, insisting, for example, despite his wife's intimate involvement in the composition, that *Dr. Jekyll and Mr. Hyde* was "his work entirely" (Koestenbaum 150).[9] And in an account that might read like a perverse echo of the Yeatses' honeymoon, Elizabeth Brunazzi documents how Colette's husband of eighteen months, Henry Gauthier-Villars, locked his twenty-one-year-old bride in a room and extracted writing from her, ultimately publishing her autobiographical fictions under his signature.

Whitney Chadwick and Isabelle de Courtivron demonstrate, in the cases they collect in *Significant Others* that the early twentieth century offered many models for combining creativity and intimate partnership beyond those this book has already documented—models that suggest the range of spousal arrangements, with their differential power structures, through which the parties to a couple might articulate their creative aspirations (although not generally through collaborations as substantive as the Yeatses'). They thus put into perspective the intellectual climate in which WBY could romance a prospective bride by offering her a part in a joint intellectual adventure, in the "fine and stirring things" they will do together. For promising his fiancée that "when we are dead our names shall be remembered," WBY, in effect, proposes a reciprocal working arrangement. "My work shall become yours and yours mine," he tells her (qtd. in Dailey 55).

But unlike some contemporaneous unions, the partnership Georgie Hyde-Lees and W. B. Yeats enacted, depended on Georgie's acceptance of her secondary position: her embrace of the role of "wife of the poet."[10] If in fact her role was not reducible to this rubric, George herself was instrumental in maintaining this fiction. Thus in the massive Yeats industry she religiously fostered, a range of her activities has remained invisible—and largely through her own offices. While her part, then, as producer of the automatic scripts—indeed, her contribution to *A Vision*—has been consistently trivialized or underrated, this is not a

[9] In this case, Fanny Stevenson, like Georgie Yeats, worked as a kind of translator and amanuensis, converting the hand signals of her invalid husband into speech and writing. Like WBY, moreover, Stevenson attributed the germ of the novel to a dream vision, involving "unseen collaborators" (Koestenbaum, *Double Talk: The Erotics of Male Collaboration* 150).

[10] So canonical is this position (epitomized in Curtis B. Bradford, "George Yeats: Poet's Wife") that Ann Saddlemyer titles a recent essay (a progress report on her forthcoming biography), "Georgie Hyde Lees: More Than a Poet's Wife."

simple case of male appropriation. For the authorship she practiced was one for which she never sought credit; in fact, both before and after WBY's death, she actively resisted all publicity for her part in their joint undertaking.

That the Yeatses' partnership should reproduce some of the most conventional gendered hierarchies is not, after all, surprising; nor is it surprising that it should be modeled otherwise from the types of collaborations, also taking marriage as their emblem, where the partners shared gender, class, age, experience, and nationality (see Chapters 2–4). Kaplan and Rose, for example, in rejecting a "heterosexual model" for their own collaborative writings, project spousal collaboration as inevitably hierarchical. Taking the late twentieth-century authors Louise Erdrich and Michael Dorris as an example, they suggest that Erdrich, a well-established author in her own right, loses her autonomy—her "rich, original, personal voice"—when she enters into partnership, becoming "a parrot for Dorris's ideas . . . a nearly silent but conspicuously adoring spouse" (559). How much more so would a partnership in the early part of the century between an already famous poet and an unpublished woman, over twenty-five years his junior, be implicated in the traditional structures and hierarchies of marriage. The Yeatses' literary union, moreover, was not one in which both partners contributed the same type of labor. Rather, their roles were represented as mutually exclusive (and implicitly hierarchical), with Georgie playing "psychic" to WBY's "artist."[11]

As a most private and exclusive form of mediumship, their work together was, in addition, both like and unlike the relationship of other mediums to their "sitters"—as Chapters 4 and 5 illustrate. And it was both like and unlike WBY's relation to other mediums, whom he had been frequenting for some time—most intensely in the years immediately before his marriage. Certainly, Georgie Yeats bore little resemblance to the public image of the medium that WBY projected—his "fat old woman in Soho" of "Swedenborg, Mediums, and the Desolate Places" (1922) or the culturally illiterate "Mrs. Henderson" of Words Upon the Window Pane (1934).[12] But Georgie perfected the personal relationship WBY had explored with other highly cultured mediums. Eileen Garrett recalls that when she first became acquainted with Yeats,

[11] Early in the automatic scripts, for example, WBY is informed, "You must not allow yourself to think of development in any sense but artistic you cannot be both a psychic and an artist" (MYV 1:36).

[12] In WBY's play, Mrs. Henderson is a London medium who conveys messages ostensibly from Jonathan Swift; when questioned, she claims not to know "anybody called Swift," recognizing her communicator as only "[t]hat dirty old man" (Yeats, Words 57).

he sought to enlist her in "some experiments to communicate with the fairy people"—experiments that would have required both daily and nightly attention. "There was no doubt in my mind," she observes, "as I thought over the amazing conversations with Yeats, that the man truly believed he was visited by Tibetan lamas and received authentic automatic writing from them" (*Many Voices* 61). WBY was also familiar with the work of Hester Dowden and Geraldine Cummins; Dowden's father, in fact, was a close friend of the family, and WBY consulted the daughter on more than one occasion—both before his marriage and after it. He was privy to the emerging mediumship of his friend Lady Edith Lyttelton ("Mrs. King"), whose psychic development influenced him to cultivate his own powers. In the years before his marriage, moreover, WBY pursued a "special relationship" with Mrs. Chernoweth (a trance medium "specializing in dead poets" [Foster 463]), Mrs. Wreidt, and especially, Miss Radcliffe—the latter, like Georgie, a young, well-educated Englishwoman with a remarkable gift for automatic writing. If, as Arnold Goldman suggests, Radcliffe could be said to have offered WBY "a personal laboratory situation" (121) to investigate the roots of automatic writing, Georgie Yeats extended this position, relocating the "laboratory" in the poet's own chambers and transforming it into a workshop of creation.

If WBY's dealings with other mediums modeled a relationship that ultimately only a wife could satisfy—a relationship that required a medium entirely at his disposal—they also constituted a ground for bringing him and Georgie together. Indeed, WBY courted Georgie by drawing her into his psychical research and inviting her to attend séances with him. After one of their earliest meetings, for example, Georgie assisted WBY by researching information he received in one of his sittings with Elizabeth Radcliffe. The subject, interestingly enough, was a young woman's "influence" on the life and works of a great man of letters. For Radcliffe, who knew no German, produced automatic writing in that language from a person purporting to be Anna Louisa Karsch, a minor German poet and contemporary of Goethe. Although WBY received assurances that Karsch "not only influenced Goethe's poetry greatly but also was responsible for initiating him into the 'Rosy Cross Society,'" Georgie, relying on conventional bibliographic sources, could find "no evidence" to support these assertions (Harper and Kelly 152n). Any influence Karsch had on Goethe, she concluded, "must have been slight" (153n). In her first act of "assistance," then, Georgie Hyde-Lees set the terms for her own subsequent reception; for the roles for which she could find no evidence (literary influence, suppressed coauthor, spiritual mentor and collaborator) were precisely the ones she would play, also without due recognition, in her husband's career. But if the ghostly Karsch prefigured Georgie's unsung influence on a great man's life and letters, Radcliffe held the position that Georgie would most visibly occupy. The episode thus anticipates the improvement on mediumship that Georgie's surprising automatic writing would work, allowing her to play, in her own person, all the parts to a psychic communication: "communicator," medium, and investigator/researcher.

While Georgie's complex writing practice has, until the 1980s, largely eluded notice, this is in part a function of her own fierce protection of her privacy. Numerous commentators have noted that Georgie Yeats has the dubious distinction of being "the least famous of the women in the poet's life" (Margaret Mills Harper, "Message" 35). But the lack of attention to Georgie's authorship is also a function of the problematic status of *A Vision* in the Yeats canon and biography—its place, along with the automatic scripts that facilitated it, as in George Harper's words, the "most maligned and misunderstood *tour de force* in the history of modern literature" (*MYV* 1:xiv). The importance WBY himself attributed to the work has not in fact found ready acceptance. Few have been willing to take the work at face value: as the articulation of a system that explains not only a good deal of WBY's major poetry but the course of Western civilization, the spiritual progress of the soul, the rudiments of Eastern philosophy, and the nature of the creative imagination. When first published in 1925/26 in a limited edition offered through private subscription, WBY's friends and associates were deadeningly silent about it. And when published in a substantially revised edition in 1937, with his wife's initiatory role now publicly acknowledged, the work continued to baffle its readers. Critics, in fact, have never quite known what to make of it, often viewing it as no more than a cumbersome "guide" or "index" to the poetry—the price we pay for Yeats's great lyric achievements—or dismissing it as an embarrassing lapse in the otherwise stunning career of a man of genius: a text so esoteric and abstract as to be, in effect, unreadable. In this context, Georgie's problematic "contribution" to the text is only one factor in rendering it unassimilable.[13]

That contribution, however, as scholarship in the 1980s and 1990s demonstrates, deserves more serious attention than it has traditionally received in literary studies. George Mills Harper, the scholar who has studied the manuscript materials most closely and extensively and has overseen their publication, is unequivocal on this matter: "George Yeats

---

[13] For an illuminating discussion of critical responses to *A Vision*, see Barbara L. Croft, *"Stylistic Arrangements": A Study of William Butler Yeats's "A Vision"* 15–30.

and her Communicators were far more important in the making of *A Vision* than anyone has suggested"; "The book was in truth an unusual collaboration, for which George has received little credit—and she wanted none" (*MYV* 1:18–19). Margaret Mills Harper is even more insistent, arguing that "much of the literary output of one of our century's major poets from the year of his marriage on was directly influenced by a unique imaginative partnership with a highly creative woman" ("Medium" 50). Indeed, she argues, many of the "symbols or concepts (or even turns of phrase) we have come to think of as specifically Yeatsian are in fact not the product of his brain alone" (65). Despite these recognitions, however, the exact nature of Georgie's contribution to the Yeats corpus has remained difficult to pinpoint—even with increasing manuscript evidence to work from.

It is clear that *A Vision*, in all its multiple manifestations, was never a simple transcription from the automatic scripts Georgie Yeats produced in her frequent sittings with her husband. Whatever bits of these communications ultimately found their way into the published version had first to be selected, edited, interpreted, and codified: in card files kept by WBY, notebooks kept by both partners, sleep and dream notebooks to which they both contributed, discussions between the Yeatses in preparation for new sittings, the abandoned dialogues and mini-essays that WBY composed in his first efforts to order and compile the visionary system, the multiple drafts, composed by WBY, of the manuscript of *A Vision*. The scripts themselves, moreover, were often produced in what turned out to be a highly directive question-and-answer format, with the communicators responding only to questions put to them, sometimes offering no more than "yes" or "no" answers. And WBY is generally credited with the composition of the questions. As WBY's letters and journals indicate, *A Vision*, even more so than his other texts (and WBY was a notorious rewriter), was a product of continual reordering and reworking, a repeating and revising of the materials that went into it. It was, in effect, always a re-vision, as the frequent references in the scripts to the going over of the same ground indicate. As WBY perhaps intuited from the first, when he offered "to spend what remained of life explaining and piecing together those scattered sentences" (*A Vision* 8), the project was inherently unfinished and unfinishable. The question, then, of how much Georgie Yeats contributed to the final form of the text we know as *A Vision* does not admit of easy answers.

If we turn to the automatic scripts themselves, the place where Georgie's hand is most clearly visible, the question of authorship is not so much resolved as multiplied. For the scripts articulate an overabundance of authorial positions—not only Georgie and WBY but a host of spirit Controls and Guides (including false spirits who act as Frustrators), the personal Daimons of the Yeatses (and their children), as well as numerous past-life incarnations. Thus the compilation of "[a] complete list of the collaborators in the *Vision* manuscripts," as Margaret Mills Harper explains, is a daunting exercise ("Message" 38). How we understand these positions, moreover, depends on the assumptions we bring to them—assumptions, not surprisingly, that have generally been tied to traditional views of authorship. Not only do most treatments of the automatic writing assume that WBY is the ultimate point of reference, they also reflect a profound uneasiness with the alternative articulations of authorship that mediumship dictates—the types of articulations, for example, that Chapter 5 illustrates.[14] Indeed, divorced from WBY's personal involvement in them, the scripts, George Mills Harper implies, would have no literary interest.

Thus while Harper scrupulously refers to the Yeatses as "collaborators"—and repeatedly insists that Georgie Yeats's contributions be properly recognized—his careful study of the manuscript evidence maintains the hierarchies that presume W. B. Yeats to be the "real" author. In Harper's rendering, then, certain passages can be confidently attributed to George (or her communicators), while others can be seen to reflect WBY's shaping influence. Indeed, demonstrating that WBY provides the language if not the concept for the ideas communicated, Harper attributes to WBY precisely what, as Chapter 5 points out, counts as copyrightable—what would make the scripts his literary property.[15] In this he follows the communicators' famous announcement (interestingly enough not found in any of the manuscripts of the automatic writing): "we have come to give you metaphors for poetry" (*A Vision* 8). For as WBY appears to understand this promise, the spirits will provide a body of ideas to be shaped by the poet. Harper, however, goes even further, repeatedly noting instances where WBY could be said to have originated the concepts; and he follows WBY in suggesting that "the Script and *A Vision* were an outgrowth and extension

[14] In this Richard Ellmann is perhaps typical when he concludes that, whatever Georgie may have contributed, "In the end everything is stamped with his personality and brought into line with his work" (*Yeats: The Man and the Masks* 227–28). K. P. S. Jochum's review of the recently published *Vision Papers*, with its persistent return to the problem of fixing singular and stable authorship, is a perfect example of critical resistance to unfamiliar authorial practices.

[15] See, for example, such claims as, "It is important to note that he is responsible for the language if not the ideas of his Instructors" (*MYV* 1:69). In crediting Georgie Yeats with the "seminal ideas" for *A Vision* ("Medium" 49), Margaret Mills Harper sustains this position, even as she opens George's authorship to new consideration.

of *Per Amica"* (*MYV* 1:79)—a work produced single-handedly by WBY before his marriage.

Harper's narrative, of course, represents a selective reading of a daunting body of materials; it is motivated, moreover, quite self-consciously, by the interests of a "student of literature." Not surprisingly, then, what appears most important in the scripts is what appears to be the "purest" Yeats, what can most fully be credited to him. Harper thus consistently identifies those scripts written in response to direct questions from WBY as the scripts most worthy of study—the ones that illustrate "Yeats's method of inquiry at its best" (*MYV* 2:354). Singling out, for example, an extended series of scripts on the concept of "transference," Harper observes, "To students of literature," these sittings are "perhaps the most provocative if not the most significant series in the entire Script" (2:347). These sittings, I would add, are, not coincidentally, the ones where WBY's questions are "often only statements, and clearly anticipate the answers, demonstrating that the ordering mind was his, not George's or the Guide's" (2:347). Indeed, they represent the place where WBY explores the possibility of dispensing altogether with the services of the medium. Perfecting WBY's Socratic method, the scripts, in fact, become entirely self-reflexive here, endorsing a vision of the artist/poet who, as a kind of superior "medium" retrieves archetypal images from the world's unconscious memory; the "triumphant conclusion," then, toward which the scripts lead turns out to be "a climactic summary of Yeats's theory" (2:354)—an articulation of the "astonishing discoveries—chiefly his own" (2:351) that so captured his imagination.

Harper's account, moreover, of the Yeatses' unusual collaboration can be seen to track the progressive diminishment of George's authority and influence. If George appears the leader in initiating the experiments, by August 1918, Harper represents Yeats as "now the leader, not the recipient" (*MYV* 2:101); by November 1918, he concludes, "In effect, Yeats had become the director, though George continued in spurts to stimulate his thought" (2:168). With the development of a "New Method" in March 1920, moreover, the medium relinquishes her primary role as writer. As WBY explains it, "George speaks while asleap" (*YVP* 3:9)—with Yeats dictating condensed versions of these "sleeps" back to the medium who subsequently records them.[16] As Harper observes, however, the partners' respective authority here is difficult to

---

[16] While many of the Sleep and Dream notebooks are in George's hand, internal evidence makes clear that she is often writing from WBY's dictation. If the "sleeps," moreover, replace written with oral communication, they also sacrifice the specificity of writ-

calculate: "Had he taken notes? Did he alter what she had said in sleep? Did she collaborate in the written record?" (*MYV* 2:396). Finally, WBY announces their decision to dispense with all forms of mediumship: "In I think July we decided to give up 'sleep' 'automatic writing' & all such means & to discourage mediumship, & to get our further thought by 'positive means'" (2:395). While these changes in method were by no means absolute, the story they tell remains compelling: the making of *A Vision* requires the exorcising of the medium. In this narrative, then, George's role can be rechanneled into a more conventional one: an editorial assistant who advises WBY on the manuscript's revisions.[17]

In Harper's reconstruction, however, it could be argued that George's role was never anything but secondary. While WBY, for example, is consistently credited for his contributions to the System, George's contributions, from the start, appear questionable. Indeed, what is attributed to George almost always appears with some qualification, as in "George and the Communicators," "the Control (or the Medium)," or "George and her Control" (*MYV* 1:109, 72, 98). While Harper, then, can argue that WBY depreciates his own role when he insists that he "like the Medium was essentially an instrument of the Communicators" (2:122), he does not appear to question George's analogous self-effacement. If anything, his narrative betrays its own ambivalence as to whether George's authorial input is more suspect for being or not being what it claims to be. In other words, is George less of an author for being a medium or is she less of a medium than she appears to be? Either way, George's mediumship appears problematic. Like WBY, who deleted the line "and after some vague sentences it was as though her hand were grasped by another hand" (2:416) from the published account of his wife's automatic writing, Harper seems intent on undermining George's automatism, repeatedly questioning the extent to which the automatic scripts were indeed automatic.[18]

---

ten transcription, substituting condensations of the communications (recorded after the fact) for verbatim transcriptions.

[17] "Since we gave up the sleeps we have worked at the system by discussion, each bringing to these their discoveries" (*YVP* 3:120). According to Harper, at this stage, "George participated in the selection of materials and organization of their discoveries" (*MYV* 2:404–5).

[18] Harper, indeed, seems almost obsessed with this issue; after posing these questions in the preface to his study—"Did she indeed write automatically? If so, was her entire production automatic? And, finally, how automatic, if at all, was Yeats's part in the production?"—he returns to them less than a page later, "Finally, we need to consider how automatic the writing was—or, at least, how automatic Yeats thought it was" (*MYV* 1:xii, xiii) . Pursuing this argument even further, Jochum questions the general acceptance of the scripts as, in fact, automatic writing, arguing that the editors of Yeats's *Vision Papers* have been lax, or coy, in their treatment of the materials. But like Harper, Jochum works within an overly narrow understanding of the practices of automatic writing.

Noting a striking change in format, whereby, along with a reversion to her regular handwriting and punctuation, the medium ceases to run her words together, Harper represents the scripts as becoming progressively less automatic—that is, progressively less invested in *the appearance* of automatism. As such, the script evidence opens the medium to charges of conscious or unconscious deception. Harper speculates, "[D]id she plan it as a diversion and gradually become a convert to her own deception?" (*MYV* 1:5). Was she, in effect, a victim of what the scripts call the "subliminal romancing of the medium" (*YVP* 1:237)—mistaking subliminal responses from her own unconscious for authentic spirit communications? If so, then her scripts might be seen to lose much of their value. As one communicator explains, the script is "more & more influenced by her will" and has "therefore become less automatic" (*MYV* 2:168)—a situation he presumes to be in need of remedy. For as "willed" writing, the value of the scripts depends on the interest of George's mind (both conscious and unconscious). What such a reading of George's will tends to yield, however, is a narrative more narrowly personal than the scripts' ambitious visionary system: George's desire to divert the scripts from subjects deemed too personal (e.g., WBY's relationships with other women); her efforts to manage her husband's literary career by redirecting his poetic energies; her attempts to rationalize her importance to WBY and the uniqueness of their relationship; her desire to have a child, voiced through the communicators; her efforts to extricate herself from a writing task (the automatic scripts themselves) that had become oppressive. Even more significantly, Harper implies that if George's scripts are less automatic or "authentic" than they initially appear to be, they are consequently more dependent on WBY's shaping direction—more determined by his leading questions. "In this respect," Harper explains, "their Script was only partially automatic, and it is quite unlike much of the automatic writing monitored by representatives of the SPR" (*MYV* 1:245).

Of course, such an admission opens up another possibility. If George's communications are not authentically "automatic," the argument could be made that George is even more of an author (or coauthor) than we have thus far credited her with being.[19] As Margaret Mills Harper suggests, in dispensing with the conventional markers of "automatic writing," George's scripts only make explicit "what none of the participants had denied from the outset: George's mind and character were a necessary influence on the System" ("Medium" 52). Indeed, her account of the scripts' development projects an alternative narrative of progress—

[19] David Pierce makes precisely this argument (*Yeats's Worlds: Ireland, England, and the Poetic Imagination* 60).

one that allows George to claim increasing authority for the communications, a process that culminates with, in George Harper's words, "an announcement that George was 'no longer the medium,' preferring instead a 'different name—interpreter'" (*MYV* 2:223). "*Interpreter*," Margaret Harper explains, "is a far more accurate description of the role George Yeats played in the process than *medium*, implying as it does that she translated ideas into intelligible language" ("Medium" 54). Noting a shift in method in the later stages of the communications, with George now recording both the questions and answers, she observes: "No longer even in procedural details would she be an empty vessel for a male text, a female body bearing the offspring of male minds" ("Message" 47).[20]

If Margaret Mills Harper finds evidence for Georgie Yeats's increasing authority where George Mills Harper reads the story of its diminishment, both critics nonetheless assume that the interest of George's mediumship lies in its exceptionality—in the fact that "the 'medium' was not exactly a medium" ("Message" 37). But as Chapter 5 demonstrates, the counter model they maintain—the medium as "an empty vessel," "a passive or unconscious scribe" ("Message," 47, 37)—rests on a misunderstanding of the historical practice of mediumship. George's writing, then, is of interest, I am arguing, not because it is unique but because it is typical. Like other alternative writing practices, however, it tells a story of authorship informed by contradictions—a story not fully assimilable into either the conventional narrative of male precedence or its feminist revision, as the Harpers respectively articulate it.

If Georgie Yeats's writing was not fully automatic, neither was that of many of the most respected early twentieth-century mediums. The very conception of this writing as "automatic" or "involuntary" was upheld more by its popularizers and their public than by practicing mediums and their scientific investigators. Or, to put it another way, the meaning of these terms was not self-evident. For even those who wrote in the fullest state of trance understood themselves (and were understood by experts) to perform something more than merely passive agency.

[20] As Margaret Mills Harper reads this development, "The experiments were being weaned away from the model of a male source of power and female receptivity with which they began: Yeats asking the questions, the spirits answering, and Georgie passively relaying information between them, her own words effaced" ("Message" 47). If the extent of George's agency, at the start, is open to question, so too is this progressive trajectory—especially as the scripts give way to oral transmissions communicated by George while asleep (and to WBY's independent sleep visions). It is difficult to see how such a development marks an advance in feminine (or feminist) authority. Harper's argument, however, for the way the scripts destabilize all traditional notions of authority and authorship remains compelling.

Rarely, then, did automatic writing correspond with absolute power-lessness for the medium. The term "Interpreter," as a description of the medium's function, was not something Georgie Yeats invented; it was a term, as has already been shown, in common parlance in psychical research circles and favored by many mediums. If, as Margaret Mills Harper suggests, the term is particularly accurate for Georgie Yeats, im-plying as it does that "she translated ideas into intelligible language," this is precisely what all mediums did—whatever name they went by.

Certainly, George's practice corresponds to an understanding of the medium's writerly function that informs much of the literary work then being produced through automatic writing. Edith Somerville, for ex-ample, at about this time, began producing a new body of fictional lit-erature purportedly incorporating "automatic" communications from "Martin Ross," her recently deceased writing partner—communica-tions that like those of the Yeatses apparently worked through a highly directive question-and-answer format and did not require a trance state on the part of "the medium." In the United States, Mrs. Curran, also without going into trance, produced her copious "Patience Worth" fiction—ultimately attracting the SPR's attention. But the question of the nature and extent of a medium's automatic function was also one engaging the SPR in its deliberately chosen subjects. "Mrs. Willett" (see Chapter 4), who first began to produce scripts for the SPR in the years immediately preceding Georgie Yeats's surprising discovery, served the society as a site to explore the workings of a conscious (or partially con-scious) medium—a medium whose writings were not, strictly speak-ing, automatic. As Gerald Balfour explains in his exhaustive study of Mrs. Willett's mediumship, "Save in a single exceptional case I do not think Mrs Willett has ever experienced the feeling that her hand was being *moved for her* by some influence external to herself. Her script-writing is not automatic in that sense" ("Study" 78).

The same, presumably, might be said, however, for parts, if not all, of the script-writings of other mediums. WBY, for example, in his "Prelim-inary Examination" of Elizabeth Radcliffe's mediumship, notes, "She is really automatic in certain states," where, "It is plain that the muscles of her hand can record what her mind's eye sees without the conscious control of the intellect" (Harper and Kelly 157, 156). But as his com-ments imply, she must be less automatic in other states, and in this the production of her automatic writing can be seen as typical. If Georgie Yeats, then, initially experiences her automatic writing *as such*—her hand, to her "utter amazement," acting "as if 'seized by a superior power,'" her mind unaware (and ignorant) of what her hand is writing (Virginia Moore 253)—but later experiences the writing as less involuntary, this does not necessarily disqualify her from ordinary mediumship. Nor does her tendency to interrupt the proceedings "to add her own observations," suggest, as Margaret Mills Harper implies, some dropping of the mask or unusual assertion of conscious authority ("Medium" 52). As Balfour notes of Mrs. Willett, "Her trance sittings abound with remarks describing her own experiences at the moment," as well as occasional comments, "not always complimentary, on the messages she is asked to transmit" ("Study" 60). Indeed, like Mrs. Willett, who at times is deliberately excluded from the communications she transmits, Georgie Yeats appears to fluctuate between being an active and acknowledged participant in her communications and being an unwitting instrument for them.

The contradictory features in George's script-writing thus appear fully consonant with the practice of other mediums. Even the changes in handwriting, which both Margaret and George Harper seize on, are not in themselves definitive; in fact, within the literature of psychical research, such practices might be subject to different readings, with a medium's use or resumption of her ordinary hand not necessarily implying more consciously controlled writing. In the case of Mrs. Willett, for example, whose scripts display two distinct handwritings, Balfour notes a practice that appears counterintuitive: the more closely the medium's handwriting "resembles her normal style, the further removed she has become from the completely normal consciousness" ("Study" 76). "[T]he nearer she is to deep trance the more closely does her script approximate to her ordinary handwriting," with stops inserted and words no longer running together. "Punctuation marks," Balfour suggests, "are also a sign, though not an infallible one, that she is deeply 'under'" (76). Balfour explains this development as a function of the medium's relaxing her concentration on the rules, as dictated by the communicators, for best producing automatic writing; it could be argued, then, that the more her scripts resemble automatic writing, the more they reflect her conscious will to create this effect.

This is not to say that there is nothing distinctive in the Yeatses' automatic writing, but their practice looks different when contextualized in frameworks other than literary studies. In these other contexts, many of the features that might seem peculiar do not in themselves appear unusual. The preponderance of highly personal materials within the scripts (George Harper estimates as much as three-fourths of the manuscript material) corresponds with many other script productions. Balfour notes, for example, that the "bulk of Mrs Willett's automatic output is too private for publication" ("Study" 43). The use of mirror writing, prevalent throughout the Yeats scripts, and the disguising of messages to prevent the medium's comprehension, were features, as has already been suggested, common in contemporary automatic writing. Nor was it unusual for scripts to evolve from the personal to the universal. WBY himself, before he began automatic writing with his wife, engaged other mediums in acutely private matters, first approaching Elizabeth Radcliffe, for example, to confirm whether or not his lover was pregnant. If the personal parts of the scripts the Yeatses produced together— the particularized references to WBY's former lovers, the repeated allusions to the couple's sex life, and the unsolicited advice on family planning—were more personal than usual, this was a difference of degree, not kind, a function of the greater intimacy made possible by spousal mediumship.

Like other texts of automatic writing, moreover, as Chapter 5 documents, the Yeatses' scripts represent a self-conscious intervention into the space of public authorship—an intervention that erodes the distinction between public and private; and like these other texts, their scripts expose the problematic borders that put their authorship in question. For automatic writings, as we have seen, are never "pure" or uncontaminated. Indeed, even the staunchest believers in the supernatural recognize, in dealing with automatic scripts, the inevitably mixed nature of the product: its balance between what comes from the medium's own mind (and from its different levels of consciousness) and what comes from some external agency (something outside of her). As the Yeats communicators explain, "automatic writing is two," part "definite spirit thought," part "subliminal" messages from the medium (*YVP* 1:237). Automatic writing thus simultaneously exemplifies and problematizes the possible meanings of collaborative authorship. Beyond the most evident problems, it poses the further difficulty of distinguishing "true" spirit communications from telepathy with someone living. Insofar as one might argue, then, that George Yeats's automatic scripts reflect W. B. Yeats's mind and influence, this would be the case, to some extent, in any mediumistic situation. For it is part of the medium's function to mirror the mind of the sitter—hence the history, as we have seen in Chapter 5, of sitters claiming authorship for a medium's productions.

WBY made little effort to disguise the self-serving aspects of his interest in mediumship: his desire to find confirmation for his aesthetic intuitions, his search for a comprehensive system on which to anchor his poetry. George's automatic writings, then, did not appear in a void but as part of the history of WBY's self-conscious experiments with other mediums. Geraldine Cummins, for example, probably some time in 1917, met WBY at the home of Hester Dowden in Dublin, where he attended one of their sittings. Cummins recalls how, while sitting at the ouija board, her "control" spelled out "a romantic story of old times," the plot of the play on which WBY was currently working. For Cummins, as for other respectable mediums, such telepathic communications stood as warnings of the "leakage" from other minds—including the medium's own subconscious—that can compromise the authenticity of communications. But from the perspective of the Yeatses, this "curious instance of telepathy" offers peculiar insight into the function mediumship may have served for the poet: as a place to give his works-in-progress a dress rehearsal. When WBY, then, invites Cummins to extend the dialogue, addressing her control in "picturesque language"— "Astor, I will now paint my thoughts upon the air and you will interpret them for me!" (*Unseen Adventures* 32)—he defines the mediumistic role George would perfect for him: the privileged interpreter of the poet's musings.

Although the Yeatses' automatic scripts, then, undoubtedly had a distinctive imprint, the elements upon which they played their variations were part of the common practice of mediumship. Unlike the automatic scripts produced for the SPR under "test conditions," however, the Yeatses' experiments involved a deliberate mixing of conscious and unconscious proceedings. Indeed, within the closed circle of their home mediumship, they both produced the scripts and "investigated" them, dispensing with the usual machinery to ensure objectivity. The Yeatses, however, were not attempting to prove the authenticity of their communications. For them, the scripts were not ends in themselves but material to be worked on; more so, then, than the "official" mediums discussed in Chapter 5, they could exploit the literary nature of automatic writing, turning it into a resource for conscious literary productions. Ultimately, then, whatever its "involuntary" origins, their automatic script served a larger writing project that, like other artistic creations, was highly controlled and directed (even if its logic has often eluded its readers).

If the Yeatses' automatic writing, however, was only one piece of the apparatus that ultimately went into *A Vision*, it is worth remembering that it also had an existence independent of it. Viewed as an instance of Georgie Yeats's writing, the automatic scripts have a story to tell apart from W. B. Yeats and his literary reputation: the story, variations of which have appeared in earlier chapters, of how a woman asserts agency without explicitly claiming authorship. For however surprising the Yeatses found it, George's automatic scripts did not come out of thin air. They belong to a history of women's "secret writing"—even if George was not conscious of this fact. Like other mediums (and like other women who wrote outside established structures), George chose to write under cover of secrecy, and secrecy, in turn, fueled her operation, much as it had for the Brontë siblings. Significantly, then, it was George who maintained an investment in keeping the matter private. Indeed, exceeding the strictures of other mediums, George, when she wrote, adamantly refused to allow observers. In doing so, I would argue, she was not simply protecting herself (and her husband) from embarrassing personal revelations (although this was undoubtedly a motivation). She was also protecting a mode of literary production—hence her desire that WBY appear "sole author." Not only was she, as WBY acknowledged, "unwilling that her share should be known" (*A Vision* 19), she was also insistent that they not go public about their supernatural collaborators.

The reasons for secrecy are not hard to come by. This was, after all, writing that issued from the couple's honeymoon. And as the scripts remind us, it was writing that depends on the most complete union of its partners.[21] As a form of women's secret writing, however, with a history behind it, the scripts also remind us of the erotic potential in all automatic and collaborative writing. Indeed, as writing practiced under the auspices of marriage, the scripts license what other mediumistic performances often only hint at. But like other mediumistic productions, they also remind us how much this erotic energy has been directed toward the acquisition and display of knowledge. Like the work of Mrs. Willett, Geraldine Cummins, and Hester Dowden, for example, George's scripts provided access to secret sources of knowledge—knowledge, in her case, of esoteric lore and arcane matters. And as with these other mediums, they allowed her to speak with an authority she could scarcely command in her ordinary existence. Indeed, her script pronouncements belie the common perception of George as neophyte to WBY's expert, as in, WBY's words, "a student in all my subjects" (*MYV* 1:57).

Instead, the scripts open the possibility that in some instances at least George was WBY's teacher—through her "ghosts" and through her own considerable reading.[22] Originally debarred by the communicators, for example, from reading philosophy, WBY later takes up this study by following a list of George's readings. Representing his wife's reading, however, as scattered and eclectic—"two or three volumes of Wundt, part of Hegel's *Logic*, all Thomas Taylor's *Plotinus*, a Latin work

---

[21] In the "Sleeps," occurring in the late stages of their psychical experiments, WBY was encouraged to make love to the medium in order to facilitate the transmission of messages.

[22] WBY acknowledged this fact, if only half facetiously, when he told Olivia Shakespear that "George's ghosts have educated me" (qtd. in Connie K. Hood, "The Remaking of *A Vision*" 67). He makes a similar claim in the introduction to *A Vision* (8).

of Pico della Mirandola, and a great deal of medieval mysticism" (*A Vision* 19–20)—WBY at once acknowledges this debt and minimizes it. But as Susan Ramsay Dailey argues, George's library confirms that "her readings were more extensive and more varied" (16). And the scripts give ample evidence of widespread knowledge of literature and philosophy, some of it at least traceable to the medium. Indeed, where WBY maintained that "[w]hen the automatic script began, neither I nor my wife knew, or knew that we knew, that any man had tried to explain history philosophically," Georgie corrected him, penciling a notation in the margins, "X untrue. GY had read Hegel's philosophy of history" (Finneran, "On Editing" 132n). As Ann Saddlemyer explains, moreover, George "was far more familiar with contemporary poetry than her husband, and much more conversant with other literary forms" ("Georgie Hyde Lees" 199).

If George, then, was not a conventional intellectual, neither was she, any more than other mediums, simply a bored housewife. In making sense of her mediumship, however, critics have had very little to go on; consequently, they have been inclined to take as canonical the few remarks in the official record. In the 1937 edition of *A Vision*, for example, WBY fixes the image we have largely inherited, "my wife bored and fatigued by her almost daily task and I thinking and talking of little else" (9). In challenging this perception, I do not mean to quarrel with the facts of the matter; George did, indeed, frequently claim to be bored by the communications—communications that increasingly left her irritable and exhausted. But we may not want to take these claims entirely at face value. As the experience of other mediums suggests, a profession of boredom may be formulaic, providing a cover for women to express and enact interest in subjects outside their ordinary inclinations. Thus in the Cummins–Willett scripts, for example, "Mrs. Willett" does a turnaround, admitting that she was "deeply interested" in precisely those aspects of the scripts she had previously claimed bored her.[23]

When WBY married, Ezra Pound wrote to John Quinn, "Yeats might have done a great deal worse: the young woman seemed attractive and sensible and capable of counteracting some of Yeats's tendencies to

---

[23] Even if we don't credit "Mrs. Willett's" return in these communications, the claim for the medium is practically identical, since it comes from the hand of another distinguished medium, Geraldine Cummins. In the voice of "Mrs. Willett," Cummins makes her strongest claims for the medium's active and engaged participation in her mediumistic activity, insisting that mediumship is "not all one-way traffic." The Cummins-Willett scripts thus stand as a corrective to the view that mediums took no interest in the process in which they participated—a view perpetuated by their, largely male, investigators; instead, the scripts claim "process" as the medium's professional territory—what medium's choose to talk about with each other.

spookiness" (qtd. in Reid 307). WBY's sister Lily echoed these sentiments, "She is that comfortable and pleasant thing, a good woman with
brains, and no axe of her own to grind" (qtd. in W. Murphy, *Prodigal Father* 484). Together, these representations promote the ruling image of
Georgie Yeats as intelligent but harmless. Of course, on one level at least,
George turned out to be the exact opposite of what Pound imagined; in
the first years of her marriage, it could be said, she played the part of
spookiness embodied. But if George fed WBY's spooky inclinations, she
did so, quite literally, by lending him her hand and putting her brains
at his disposal. For her story suggests that "a good woman with brains,"
"attractive and sensible," "with no axe to grind" requires an outlet for
her intelligence. As with other contemporary women who turned to
mediumship, her automatic writing allowed her to put her brains on
display for the only audience she cared to cultivate.

If Georgie Yeats had no axe to grind in the traditional sense of personal self-aggrandizement, she had an axe to grind, I would suggest, in
the practice of self-effacement;[24] this practice extended well beyond her
veiled contributions to *A Vision*. In later years she assisted WBY with
his selections for *The Oxford Book of Modern Verse* (choosing, among
other things, the "Michael Field" poems anthologized there), edited
AE's letters for the Cuala Press, and oversaw other Cuala publications—
all without proper recognition. "There is evidence," Saddlemyer argues,
"that she herself wrote at least two plays and one novel, but vowed to
publish under a pseudonym if she published at all" ("Georgie Hyde
Lees" 199–200). These acts appear of a piece with the practice she established in her automatic writing—a practice that, as was typical of such
writings, had something other than proprietary authorship as its signature. From the beginning, the scripts reveal, she exercised a subtle but
persistent influence to promote authorial values not sponsored by the
mainstream—in particular, the value of coterie publication. In a diary
entry for 13 September 1922, WBY notes George's opposition to commercial publication of *A Vision*: "She does not want me to write system
for publication—not as exposition—but only to record & to show to a
few people" (*MYV* 2:405). George can be seen to act here not simply as
the agent for self-censorship but as the publicist for an alternative configuration of the public nature of writing. Indeed, the publishing practice she consistently promoted was one in keeping with the distribution
of other mediumistic manuscripts—writings that often circulated privately among sympathetic readers or were shared exclusively by initi-

---

[24] Ellmann, for example, suggests that the Yeatses had their "first and only serious quarrel of their marriage" over the introduction to the second edition of *A Vision*, where Yeats
announces George's part in the System (*Identity* xvii).

ates. If published at all, such texts were more often than not published through private publication. The 1925 edition of *A Vision*, with its somewhat larger than usual private press run, represented something of a compromise, with six hundred copies, privately printed by T. Werner Laurie, issued to subscribers on 15 January 1926.[25]

If, in the public record, George Yeats did not want her part in the automatic scripts to be known, this was a reluctance shared by many mediums. It was not uncommon for prominent mediums to use pseudonyms, as was the case with Mrs. Willett and Mrs. Holland. Elizabeth Radcliffe similarly shunned publicity (a desire WBY honored in his unpublished study of her), although she apparently contemplated publishing "a small anonymous book" on her automatic writing (Harper and Kelly 136). Similarly, within the "anonymous" forum of the scripts, George was not shy about asserting her authorship. Indeed, the scripts disclose her consistent assertion of authority within the conditions of mediumship.

One can find in the scripts, then, a counternarrative to the one of WBY's definitive influence, a record of George's resistance to WBY's conscious (and unconscious) efforts to direct the production. On several occasions, for example, George refers to WBY as an impediment to her writing, affirming, as did other mediums, the professional necessity of having a clear brain to work with: "[T]hat is why I cant write because you influence me" (*YVP* 2:24); "when you muddle me I cant get my words if you are thinking your own idea you don't give me a free mind to work on" (*MYV* 1:72). In effect, she asserts that she will not write to his dictation: "I don't like writing when you are trying to work out script for me" (*YVP* 2:143). She will not write simply to satisfy him; thus Harper notes her response "in letters two or three times the normal size" to one of WBY's persistent questions: "*no*—please accept no when I say it" (*MYV* 2:100). And when WBY still persists, she tells him, "Not today," and then "now stop"—after which, according to Harper, "[t]here was no further writing for three full weeks" (*MYV* 2:102).

Most significantly, in places at least, the scripts suggest that it is WBY's role as poet—the authorship he claims before coming to these writings—that compromises his authority. Noting, for example, WBY's tinkering with various phases in the system, George complains, "you take away the whole significance of the system because you prefer the idea as poet" (*YVP* 2:11). Reversing the traditional hierarchies that value the work of the artist over that of the psychic, moments like these allow George to claim for herself the more authentic authorship. Mediumship, indeed, lets her be an author because she is not one.

[25] The title page of this edition bears the date 1925.

Read from Georgie Yeats's perspective, then, the scripts supply a discourse for affirming her place in their shared operation. She does not, however, claim authority in place of her husband; more typically, she casts her role as necessary supplement. When WBY asks, for example, whether the control is satisfied with their method of questioning, he is informed that any omissions on his part will be filled in by the medium (*MYV* 1:191). And it is this complementarity that George consistently underlines, stressing the "double force" (1:201) that comes from their working together. The scripts, indeed, can be read as a tract in defense of collaboration—an articulation of a collaborative aesthetic. For the message they consistently return in different contexts is that "automatic writing is two." When WBY sporadically suggests that he do all or most of the writing, the communicators summarily dismiss the suggestion: "[W]e cant use you alone—must have you & medium *equally*" (*YVP* 2:152). And when they concede the possibility of WBY or the medium working alone, they reject out of hand the notion that either could work with another partner (*YVP* 2:269).

Insofar, then, as the automatic scripts affirm collaboration, they also affirm the specific partnership of WBY and his wife as the best collaboration possible—indeed, the only collaboration worth crediting as such (*YVP* 1:199). Thus the scripts reject the notion of a "practical" collaboration between the couple in favor of the higher, more intellectual collaboration their work embodies—a collaboration that taps the entire being of·the partners. And the scripts dismiss WBY's earlier collaborations, real and imagined, as, in effect, not of the same order. Thus WBY's long history of collaboration with Lady Gregory is written off in a sentence, "Imbalanced—you created she transferred—not real colaboration" (*YVP* 1:199), while a hypothetical collaboration with Maud Gonne is represented as essentially unworkable. In invoking these collaborations, however, the scripts put them on the table, opening to investigation the history of WBY's reliance on other silent partners. They thus make explicit what rarely attracts notice: the conditions that establish George, before she ever puts pen to paper, as a-partner-in-the-making.

Long before he ever paid court to Georgie, WBY had, indeed, dabbled with other literary partners. His collaboration with George Moore in 1900, for example, over the play *Diarmuid and Grania* was notoriously turbulent, while, less problematically, his collaboration with Ezra Pound—at once more loosely configured and more profoundly far-reaching—flourished, as James Longenbach has argued, in the years the poets spent together at Stone Cottage in Ashdown Forest in Sussex, in the winters of 1913–1916. When WBY, then, brought his young bride to Ashdown Forest for their honeymoon, he was bringing her to the site of a fruitful creative coalition—one that began, significantly enough, with "the idea that Pound would serve as Yeats's secretary" (Longenbach xi); and it was at Stone Cottage (where the Yeatses repaired about a month into their marriage) that Georgie produced a good deal of her early automatic writing.

George's role, moreover, was to some extent anticipated in the relationships WBY formed with his other lovers, women like herself with highly developed sensibilities, who recognized that to love WBY they had to collaborate with him—at least to the extent of entering into his interests. Thus while Maud Gonne may have remained for WBY the most resistant to incorporation, she played a consistent role as literary inspiration, and she played a more material part in the Abbey Theatre, starring in its production of *Cathleen ni Houlihan*. More extensively, Florence Farr, also an actress, collaborated with WBY on several projects for the theater, most notably his experiments with the oral reading of poetry, while Olivia Shakespear, a novelist, was joined to WBY by "occult interests and literature" (Foster 153).

Closer to home, WBY had also entertained partnerships of sorts with his two sisters. In Lily, the "psychic daughter" of the household, WBY found a repository of visionary insight and personal memory he could tap for his writing, spinning poems from her letters and, in the autobiographical *Reveries Over Childhood and Youth*, drawing on *her* memories to reconstruct *his* childhood. In a sense, then, Lily could be said to have auditioned the part Georgie Yeats made her own: the psychic contact point for WBY's artistry. With Elizabeth (Lolly), the beleaguered publisher of the Cuala Press, WBY entered a partnership at once more pragmatic and oppositional; he struggled with her for editorial control of the press's publications. Here, too, WBY's sister prefigured one of George's functions. For not only would George eventually take over the Cuala operation, she would also manage the Yeats literary "property," serving as a kind of personal business adviser and private copy editor: often, in the case of literary anthologies, she made his selections for him. With both his sisters, then, as with his other collaborators, WBY assumed the privileges of a "man of letters," setting the terms, if not the limits, for the more far-reaching union he would form with his wife, what Saddlemyer has described as "one of the most extraordinary and creative partnerships in the literary world" ("Georgie Hyde Lees" 191).

But it was with Lady Augusta Gregory, with whom WBY collaborated in the two decades preceding his marriage, first on folklore collections and then on plays for the Abbey Theatre, that he practiced writing in ways that most closely anticipated his writing relationship with George. It is perhaps not surprising, then, that Lady Gregory would be the first to whom he confided the secret of his wife's automatic writing—

only a few days after it started; when he wrote to Lady Gregory, more-over, extolling his young wife's virtues, he did so in terms that make clear her role as Lady Gregory's stand-in: "My wife is a perfect wife, kind, wise and unselfish. I think you were such another young girl once" (qtd. in Dailey 61). If, as seems likely from what we now know of WBY's psychic experiments, what makes George seem so perfect to WBY is her selfless capacity for (automatic) writing, this is another way she invokes a younger Lady Gregory. For like George, Lady Gregory, despite her substantial share in WBY's writings, colluded with the pro-moters of Yeats who relegated her to the role of "accessory to genius" (Pethica, "Our Kathleen" 3).[26]

Even today it remains difficult to see these women as autonomous au-thors, largely because of the way they occupied gendered positions, embracing rather than resisting the writing parts assigned to them. If, for example, Lady Gregory initially recognized her part in her work with WBY as "limited to a role as amanuensis and folklore gatherer" (Pethica, "Our Kathleen" 5), this was also the role George assumed for herself. For as WBY clearly recognized, a medium was something of a folklorist, collecting the speech of beings who belong to a culture no longer accessible to us.[27] And George, like Lady Gregory, was content to supply the quality WBY was conspicuously lacking: a "mastery of speech that purported to be of real life" (*Plays* 429). Neither woman, moreover, at least at first, appears to have questioned WBY's literary prerogative—his right to reserve to himself the "actual shaping and writing" of their materials. Indeed, although Lady Gregory suggests that WBY was "slow in coming to believe" that she had "any gift for writing" but eventually recognized her as "a fellow writer," their part-nership does not readily display this implied equality (Gregory, *Seventy Years* 390). For Lady Gregory, who began her playwrighting career by suggesting "a sentence here and there" as she took dictation from WBY (Saddlemyer, *Defence* 17), did not relinquish her role as amanuensis, even as the sentences she contributed to the plays increased with her

---

[26] For discussions of the extent of Lady Gregory's share in the plays written with WBY, see James Pethica, "'Our Kathleen': Yeats's Collaboration with Lady Gregory in the Writ-ing of *Cathleen ni Houlihan*" and Daniel J. Murphy, "Lady Gregory, Co-Author and Some-times Author of the Plays of W. B. Yeats." For a fuller discussion of WBY's complex rela-tionship with Lady Gregory, see also James Pethica, "Patronage and Creative Exchange: Yeats, Lady Gregory, and the Economy of Indebtedness."

[27] It would seem, then, no accident that WBY's most sustained discussion of medium-ship is embedded in a book of folklore—a book "coauthored" with Lady Gregory, *Visions and Beliefs of the People of Western Ireland*. Unlike earlier folklore ventures which WBY pub-lished under his name, this one bears Lady Gregory's signature. WBY, however, provides the text with scholarly credentials, including two essays and the footnotes.

talents. The trajectory of her career does not therefore maintain the tidy progress John Kelly implies, with Lady Gregory beginning as "half editor, half amanuensis," and "gradually work[ing] her way into the position of collaborator, and finally creator in her own right" (Kelly 211); rather, her career calls into question the integrity of these very categories. Like George's then, the story of her coming to authorship is not so much the classic narrative of awakening—from amanuensis, or author's assistant, to author—but a rearticulation of these categories: the story, as it were, of an amanuensis's authorship.

Lady Gregory's authorship has been easy to trivialize, as with other women collaborators, in terms that depend on gender hierarchies. Thus in the standard account of her contribution to the "collaborative" plays, Lady Gregory is credited with improving the dialogue—serving as a kind of dialect coach who provides the type of "local color" women writers excel at. And while WBY, at times at least, was insistent that Lady Gregory be properly credited, he relegates his official acknowledgments to notes and prefaces, making it easy for critics to write this off as no more than "courteous gratitude." In fact, while in other contexts, Lady Gregory's responsibility for the style and wording of the plays would be seen to earn her authorial status (see Chapter 5), here her contributions are represented as "editorial" rather than "creative," or as WBY implies, mere craftsmanship. Thus WBY says in a note to *The Unicorn from the Stars*, the only play in *Plays in Prose and Verse* he officially lists as "in collaboration with Lady Gregory," "The result is a play almost wholly hers in handiwork, which is so much mine in thought that she does not wish to include it in her own works" (*Plays* 435).

But if the work of Lady Gregory's hands can thus be relegated to the margins, the problem is compounded in the case of George Yeats's handiwork. George, indeed, is even more aggressive than Lady Gregory in relinquishing the name of author. But are her scripts, any more than Lady Gregory's, any less her own because she does not wish to claim them? Following WBY's distinction, are her scripts hers in thought or are they only the work of her hand? Is the distinction itself even operative—in her case or Lady Gregory's—and what are its implications for our understanding of authorship? WBY's comments, contrary to the proprietary view of authorship underwritten by copyright law, locate primary authorship in the conception of a work as opposed to its wording. Thus he claims authorship for *Cathleen ni Houlihan*, a play where Lady Gregory's hand is everywhere evident, on the grounds that it came to him in "a dream almost as distinct as a vision" (*Plays* 427)—a claim Lady Gregory appears to respect, although, in private she insists that she wrote "all but all of it." Following this logic, however, what is one to make of the plays Yeats wrote shortly after his marriage (*The Only Jealousy, Calvary,* etc.)—plays almost wholly his in handiwork but having their origins in George Yeats's automatic writing? What is one to make, moreover, of the automatic writing? To put it bluntly, whose vision is it?

This irreducible element of collaboration is at once dramatized and obscured in the practice of dictation. And here too, Lady Gregory's practice illuminates George's innovations, for if Lady Gregory was, as Murphy suggests, the "sometimes author" of WBY's plays, she was also his sometime secretary, writing "their" plays from his dictation. Richard J. Finneran complains, "[I]t seems essentially impossible to assign a particular passage to one or the other" since "a manuscript in Lady Gregory's hand, for instance, could have been dictated by Yeats" (*Editing Yeats's Poems* 136). "Short of being actually in the library at Coole with them," Elizabeth Coxhead maintains, "one cannot put one's finger on what is his and what is hers" (68). But their collaboration, I would argue, poses an even more fundamental challenge to proprietary authorship, undermining the very categories of "his" and "hers." For it posits "dictation" not as fixed but interactive, involving a necessary gap between what "he" says and what "she" writes. At the least, Lady Gregory's part was to "translate" as WBY spoke, to fill in the gaps—both literally and figuratively; but at times her contribution was so extensive that WBY was forced to admit that, when dictating, his imagination could not always keep pace with hers (*Plays* 434–35).

If Lady Gregory's work with WBY opened up the subject, George's practice pushed to the limits the question of the authorship of an amanuensis. George, indeed, never claimed authorship outside this structure; the authorship she practiced as a medium, however, is even more resistant than Lady Gregory's to available categories, challenging as it does the authority of the visible. To follow Coxhead, then, even if we were in the library with WBY and George during the automatic writing sessions, it is not clear that this could help us fix authorial responsibility. For George at least believed that her hand wrote to the dictation of authors whose existence could not be empirically verified. And she wrote in response to questions set by her husband. If her scripts facilitated WBY's subsequent creations, they cry out, in their insistent literalization, for a reassessment of such traditionally gendered categories as wifely "influence."

George's career, moreover, opens to investigation the conditions under which women traditionally render "literary assistance." For on the surface, at least, after the first flurry of psychic activity, George would appear to have assumed more conventional responsibilities: indeed, it might seem that she moved from being the "author" of the automatic scripts to being her husband's secretary, or put another way, she moved from being the secretary to her husband's "communicators" to being her husband's secretary. From March 1920, when the automatic writing effectively ceased, until WBY's death in 1939, George served WBY in a variety of practical capacities: she prepared his literary manuscripts, writing and typing from dictation; corrected WBY's notoriously bad spelling and punctuation; and, on numerous occasions, checked his references and did research for him. She served as recorder, moreover, for their "sleeps" and "dreams," sometimes taking down from WBY's dictation the words *she* spoke in her sleep. And while she no longer communicated messages from the beyond, she may have supplied WBY with proxies; Dolly Travers Smith, for example, the daughter of Hester Dowden, while a house guest of George's, apparently conveyed messages to Yeats from their original communicators assuring him he would have time to complete his new version of *A Vision*.

But despite this apparent shift in function, George's roles as a medium and as a secretary/assistant were not in fact mutually exclusive. Only a few days into their marriage George was already writing letters to WBY's dictation. And WBY's gift of a typewriter soon after their wedding—"to help [George] with her work" (Dailey 63)—suggests the part George assumed when she agreed to the marriage; for "her work" here was clearly helping WBY with *his* work. For George, indeed, there was no clear break between being WBY's personal medium and being his personal secretary. And she succeeded at both for largely similar reasons: her capacity to anticipate WBY's particular requirements.[28] In both functions, moreover, she proved her capacity to bring order to WBY's messy creativity. Thus A. Norman Jeffares, no friend to George's mediumship, concedes this housewifely dimension: "It is possible considering how untidy his mind was, and how tidy that of Mrs Yeats is, that his thought may have, in passing through her mind, received order and precision" (Jeffares 206). If as a full-time companion, then, who knew WBY intimately, George could do more for him than other mediums, she could also do more than other secretaries, allowing WBY to achieve "amazing results" through the methods of revision he developed with her (Bradford 396).

What George's mediumship opens up, then, is the identity between her various functions, the agency involved in her "secretarial" activi-

---

[28] According to Bradford, "George Yeats was the only secretary with whom Yeats worked easily. He liked to dictate directly to the typewriter, reading from his manuscript, and was thrown off by secretaries who either repeated his words or asked him to repeat" (396); as secretary, then, George fulfilled the part of a nearly silent typist, in effect, collapsing typist and typewriter.

ties. It thus tells a story with bearing on the work of other mediums. For as Chapter 5 suggests, mediumship, by definition, blurs the lines between author and editor, creator and amanuensis, agent and instrument. In fact, as the automatic scripts articulated their positions, George was the "interpreter" and WBY the "recipient." What WBY "received" through George's "interpretation," he subsequently dictated back to her in more conventional secretarial structures. For the manuscripts George prepared for WBY and took from dictation were, to a large extent, the plays and poems that had their preliminary articulations in the automatic writing. And the secretarial tasks she performed with such dexterity were perhaps nowhere more dramatically displayed than in the preparation of the manuscript for the 1937 edition of *A Vision*.[29]

If, after WBY's death, the editorial license George exercised brought her under suspicion, her mediumship reminds us that the borders she allegedly transgressed were already permeable. For the automatic scripts demonstrate what the history of mediumship consistently preaches: that literary production is always mediated—the product of many hands, both seen and unseen. The role George would play, moreover, as WBY's posthumous spokesman was one she had rehearsed in the first years of their marriage, when she transmitted messages from the dead for him. Indeed, I would argue, George never ceased to be W. B. Yeats's private medium. When Frank O'Connor wrote to her over an arrangement for WBY's funeral, "[T]his is the last big job you will do for him," George gratefully acknowledged his recognition of her unseen services: "That phrase will be in my mind for ever. It is the first time anyone has written such a sentence to me" (qtd. in Dailey 154). But her services did not cease with WBY's death; rather, they became more visible. Connie Hood, for example, argues that "both before and after Yeats died, [George] felt competent and free to make changes in his work" (63); but it was after his death that these changes came under scrutiny. As Finneran puts it, "Yeats died on 28 January 1939. He had not been long in his temporary resting-place . . . before the process began of—not to put too fine a point on it—corrupting the texts which he had worked so hard to perfect" (*Editing Yeats's Poems* 39)—corruption Finneran attributes to "collaborative revision" in the practice of editing. In Finneran's melodrama, George Yeats is one of the central villains. But the corruption Finneran charges is not easy to verify, given the Yeatses' intimate working conditions, with WBY often dictating revisions to George but leaving no written record of them.

The perfection Finneran celebrates was never the product of WBY's sole labor. The roles George performed after WBY's death—most no-

[29] For a full discussion of George's role in this process, see Hood.

tably, in producing authorized editions of his work, as in the *Collected Poems* and the New York edition of *A Vision*—were an extension of the services she rendered in his lifetime. Indeed, in making George his literary executrix, WBY made her an extension of his authority: the "authority for the 'author's final revisions'" (Hood 66). In a sense, then, he was endorsing her role as his personal medium, for it was through her interventions that "Yeats" could now speak from beyond the grave. As with her mediumship, the tasks she took on problematically combined the roles of author, editor, and interpreter. For in the posthumous editions of Yeats's works, George could be seen both to authorize approved emendations and introduce unapproved ones—a situation not without its ironies. As Finneran himself recognized, there is something almost unseemly in representing George, whom WBY considered a "part author" of *A Vision*, as an unauthorized collaborator in the text. But the irony here may be no greater than that in Finneran's larger argument; for given the long history of the Yeatses' creative partnership, is the question of whether "we are indeed reading . . . 'Yeats's words in Yeats's order'" (Finneran, "On Editing" 129) even a meaningful one for works other than *A Vision*? Or is the question only relevant if we assume that Yeats's voice is singular and if we assume the name "Yeats" has only one referent?

If the partnership the Yeatses formed in the first years of their marriage puts these assumptions into question, George's stewardship, after WBY's death, of the Yeats name and reputation brought her collaboration out of the closet. Indeed, one might say, it gave her the vehicle to most visibly perform her part as the "Yeats medium." Presiding over her husband's literary relics, she became, both literally and figuratively, the doorkeeper to his study, controlling access to the poet's manuscripts; controlling access to personal reminiscences, moreover, she exerted her authority over the "life" as well as the letters. In perhaps her greatest performance as a medium, she became the living voice of the dead poet. As Curtis B. Bradford suggests, she could project Yeats's voice expertly: "Her verbal memory was astonishing and, in spite of the difference of sex and hence of vocal quality, I found her by far the most convincing imitator of Yeats talking or reading poetry" (398). But it was as editor, literary caretaker, and assistant to scholars and researchers—in effect, as manager of the Yeats industry—that she gave her mediumistic part its most significant dimension: controlling how "Yeats" would speak to future generations. I want to suggest that in doing so she performed another service equally important for literary study by providing future generations with a privileged means to reassess the very nature and practice of authorship. Margaret Mills Harper has argued that "we need to find new ways of discussing literary creation" when faced with such a "unique collaboration" as that between the Yeatses ("Medium" 69). We can find the terms for such a discussion in a history of which George Yeats is the most famous exemplar: the history of women who wrote otherwise.

Afterword

Ghostwriting; or,
The Afterlife of Authorship

As I write these concluding remarks at the turn of another century, the future of "the author" has emerged once again as a question of some urgency. While mediumship would seem today no more than a fringe phenomenon—the provenance of new age disciples and telemarketing operators—collaborative authorship, understood more broadly, has been enjoying a new respect and something of a revival. Indeed, bemoaning the loss of "real" authors in a culture of ghostwriting, Jack Hitt, in a 1997 *New York Times Magazine* article, complains, "Most ghosts are out of the attic and prefer names like 'collaborator' or 'co-author'" (39); if Hitt sees little to celebrate in this new development, his remarks nonetheless reveal the extent to which collaboration is now out of the closet, has become a means to legitimate new authorial practices. The last decades of the twentieth century have thus seen increasing numbers of works that identify themselves, implicitly or explicitly, as multiauthored, including computer-generated texts and cybertext fictions. And they have seen a proliferation of postmodernist genres that self-consciously experiment with the "death" or "dispersal" of the solitary author. At the same time, we have witnessed a growing body of revelations about the communal or collective nature of writing relationships, even "relationships" once considered solitary. In fact, it has been argued that in a postmodern age defined by new electronic technology, all authorship will soon be recognized as collaborative.

Such an outcome, celebrated by some for its utopian possibilities, has been derided by others as the end of authorship as we know it. For what new technologies—and new publishing practices—render most visible is the impossibility of fixing authorship to some single, stable act or image. But, as I have been arguing in this book, authorship has always had its multiple histories, and these histories can be liberating, reminding us that authorship itself has more than one configuration. Although automatic writing has not for the most part survived as a serious authorial practice in the late twentieth century, it has produced some notable collaborative writing experiments: the Ouija board poems of Sylvia Plath and Ted Hughes, as well as those of James Merrill and David Jackson. If these instances remain exceptional, they point nonetheless to automatic writing's legacy, for the questions early twentieth-century mediumship raised—indeed performed so flamboyantly—continue to resonate in other late twentieth-century venues. The earlier mediumistic practices, moreover, continue to speak to our current preoccupations with authorship, illuminating the possibilities for new paths as well as the inevitability of resistance. One lesson, then, we might take from these stories is of the enduring afterlife of certain cherished images of the author, images that appear all the more powerful as they cease to correspond to any material practice.

Take, for example, the case of Raymond Carver, whose death in 1988, followed by the sale of Gordon Lish's papers to Indiana University, has unleashed a heated controversy over the skeletons in Carver's closet.[1] On one side is Lish himself, Carver's longtime editor—and, some would argue, suppressed coauthor—whose extensive input into Carver's early writings is documented in his archives; on the other is Carver's widow and literary executor, the poet Tess Gallagher, who has been fierce in protecting her husband's literary legacy and, hence, in keeping this "collaboration" from becoming too public. The story has an added twist, for while resisting one collaboration, Gallagher has introduced another: her own creative partnership with her husband—a partnership at once more intimate and pervasive but less easy to pinpoint, for less dependent on the claim that she literally wrote Carver's words for him.

When the *New York Times Magazine* chose to make this its cover story (9 August 1998), what was implied was that the life and death of a literary icon was at stake. But for readers of this book what may be most unsettling is not the contenders lining up for a share of Carver's posthumous reputation (even his first wife has claimed a piece of the credit) but the intensity with which the idea of the solitary author is being protected—even in the face of evidence to the contrary. Carver, as his letters to Lish document, struggled to free himself from Lish's editorial influence, worrying about his name even as he was making it. And when Lish first considered going public about his "editing," Don De-Lillo warned him that the public, preferring to keep their idea of the au-

---

[1] My discussion here follows D. T. Max's "The Carver Chronicles," or, as the title appears on cover of the *New York Times Magazine*, "Raymond Carver's Afterlife."

thor uncomplicated, would not accept his revelations. "Even if people knew, from Carver himself, that you are largely responsible for his work," he told him, "they would immediately *forget it*" (qtd. in Max 40). Gallagher, allegedly, has gone even further, effectively blocking publication of an article drawing on the Lish manuscripts. Moreover, Gallagher herself admits that she kept her own collaboration private, because of people's "fixed" and "unimaginative" ideas about literary authorship "when it comes to what really happens when two writers live together" (qtd. in Max 51).

What "really happens," I have argued in this book, is richer and more complicated than we have generally recognized. If ghostwriting stands as the emblem of our postmodern condition, this position need not be seen as degrading any more than today's telephone and television psychics should blind us to the fact that mediumship has other histories—histories, indeed, that might put ghostwriting into new perspective. Among the ghosts, moreover, that we now contend with are the ghosts of an authorship that perhaps never existed. If this book, then, has indulged in its own ghostwriting—retrieving from obscurity some long forgotten authors and their writing practices—it has done so to haunt our imagination with new possibilities, to produce, as we stand poised at the turn of a new century, a new afterlife for authorship.

Works Cited

Abel, Elizabeth. "(E)merging Identities: The Dynamics of Female Friendship in Contemporary Fiction by Women." *Signs* 6 (1981): 413–35.
——. "Reply to Gardiner." *Signs* 6 (1981): 442–44.
Alexander, Christine. *A Bibliography of the Manuscripts of Charlotte Brontë.* The Brontë Society in Association with Meckler Publishing, 1982.
——. *The Early Writings of Charlotte Brontë.* Oxford: Basil Blackwell, 1983.
——, ed. *An Edition of the Early Writings of Charlotte Brontë.* 3 vols. Oxford: Basil Blackwell, 1987, 1991.
Allen, Percy. *Talks with Elizabethans: Revealing the Mystery of "William Shakespeare."* London: Rider & Co., 1949.
Altick, Richard D. "The Sociology of Authorship: The Social Origins, Education, and Occupations of 1,100 British Writers, 1800–1935." *Bulletin of the New York Public Library* 66 (1962): 389–404.
Azim, Firdous. *The Colonial Rise of the Novel.* New York: Routledge, 1993.
Baldwin, A. W. *The Macdonald Sisters.* London, Peter Davies, 1960.
Balfour, Gerald. "The Ear of Dionysus." *Proceedings of the Society for Psychical Research* 29 (1917): 197–286.
——. "A Study of the Psychological Aspects of Mrs. Willett's Mediumship, and of the Statements of the Communicators concerning Process." *Proceedings of the Society for Psychical Research* 43 (1935): 43–318.
Barker, Juliet. *The Brontës.* New York: St. Martin's Press, 1994.
Barnard, Marjorie. "The Gentle Art of Collaboration." In *Ink No. 2.* 126–28. Sydney: Society of Women Writers, 1977.
——. "Marjorie Barnard." In *Yacker 2: Australian Writers Talk About Their Work,* edited by Candida Barker, 28–41. Sydney: Pan Books, 1987.
——. "Marjorie Barnard *talking with* Zoe Fairbairns." In *Writing Lives: Conversations Between Women Writers,* edited by Mary Chamberlain, 37–44. London: Virago Press, 1988.
Barthes, Roland. "The Death of the Author." In *Image—Music—Text,* translated by Stephen Heath. New York: Hill and Wang, 1977.

Basham, Diana. *The Trial of Woman: Feminism and the Occult Sciences in Victorian Literature and Society.* New York: New York University Press, 1992.

Bauer, Dale M. "The Politics of Collaboration in *The Whole Family.*" In *Old Maids to Radical Spinsters: Unmarried Women in the Twentieth-Century Novel,* 107–22. Urbana: University of Illinois Press, 1991.

Belenkey, Mary Field, et al. *Women's Ways of Knowing: The Development of Self, Voice, and Mind.* New York: Basic, 1986.

Bell, Quentin. *Virginia Woolf: A Biography.* 2 vols. New York: Harcourt Brace Jovanovich, 1972.

Bendixen, Alfred. "It Was a Mess! How Henry James and Others Actually Wrote a Novel." *New York Times Book Review* 27 April 1986: 3+.

Benstock, Shari. *Women of the Left Bank: Paris, 1900–1940.* Austin: University of Texas Press, 1986.

Bentley, Edmund. *Far Horizon: A Biography of Hester Dowden, Medium and Psychic Investigator.* London: Rider & Co., 1951.

Besant, Walter. *Autobiography of Sir Walter Besant.* London: Hutchinson & Co., 1902.

——. "On Literary Collaboration." *New Review* 6:33 (1892): 200–209.

Black, Helen C. *Pen, Pencil, Baton, and Mask: Biographical Sketches.* London: Spottiswoode & Co., 1896.

Bloom, Harold, ed. *The Brontës.* New York: Chelsea House, 1987.

Bock, Carol. *Charlotte Brontë and the Storyteller's Audience.* Iowa City: University of Iowa Press, 1992.

Bonetti, Kay. "An Interview with Louise Erdrich and Michael Dorris." *Missouri Review* 11:2 (1988): 79–99.

Bonham-Carter, Victor. *Authors by Profession.* London: Society of Authors, 1978.

Bradford, Curtis B. "George Yeats: Poet's Wife." *Sewanee Review* 77 (Summer 1969): 385–404.

Braude, Ann. *Radical Spirits: Spiritualism and Women's Rights in Nineteenth-Century America.* Boston: Beacon, 1989.

Brontë, Charlotte. "Author's Preface." *The Professor and Emma, a Fragment.* London: J. M. Dent, 1985.

——. "Biographical Notice of Ellis and Acton Bell." 1850. In *Wuthering Heights: Authoritative Text, Backgrounds, Criticism,* by Emily Brontë. Edited by William M. Sale, Jr., and Richard J. Dunn. 3d ed. New York: W. W. Norton, 1990.

Brontë, Charlotte, and Patrick Branwell Brontë. *The Miscellaneous and Unpublished Writings of Charlotte and Patrick Branwell Brontë.* Edited by A. J. Symington and T. J. Wise. 2 vols. Oxford: 1936; 1938.

Brunazzi, Elizabeth. "The Question of Colette and Collaboration." *Tulsa Studies in Women's Literature* 13 (1994): 281–91.

Castle, Terry. *The Apparitional Lesbian: Female Homosexuality and Modern Culture.* New York: Columbia University Press, 1993.

Chadwick, Whitney, and Isabelle de Courtivron, eds. *Significant Others: Creativity and Intimate Partnership.* London: Thames and Hudson, 1993.

Childers, Mary, and bell hooks. "A Conversation about Race and Class." In

Conflicts in Feminism, edited by Marianne Hirsch and Evelyn Fox Keller, 60–81. New York: Routledge, 1990.

Cixous, Hélène. "Interview with Hélène Cixous." By Catherine Anne Franke and Roger Chazal. *Qui Parle: A Journal of Literary and Critical Studies* 3:1 (1989): 152–79.

Cixous, Hélène, and Catherine Clément. *The Newly Born Woman*. Translated by Betty Wing. Minneapolis: University of Minnesota Press, 1986.

Clarke, Norma. *Ambitious Heights: Writing, Friendship, Love—The Jewsbury Sisters, Felicia Hemans, and Jane Welsh Carlyle*. London: Routledge, 1990.

Coghill, Sir Patrick. "Opening Address." *Somerville and Ross: A Symposium*. Belfast: Institute of Irish Studies, Queen's University, 1968.

Collins, Robert G., ed. *The Hand of the Arch-Sinner: Two Angrian Chronicles of Branwell Brontë*. Oxford: Oxford University Press, 1993.

Collis, Maurice. *Somerville and Ross: A Biography*. London: Faber and Faber, 1968.

Coltelli, Laura. "Louise Erdrich and Michael Dorris." Interview. In *Winged Words: American Indian Writers Speak*. Lincoln: University of Nebraska Press, 1990.

Conan Doyle, Arthur. "The Alleged Posthumous Writings of Great Authors." *Bookman* 66 (December 1927): 342–49.

Corrigan, Maureen. "20th Century Foxes: Feminists Rewrite Modernism." *Village Voice* 26 April 1988: 53–54.

Cottom, Daniel. *Abyss of Reason: Cultural Movements, Revelations, and Betrayals*. New York: Oxford University Press, 1991.

Coxhead, Elizabeth. *Lady Gregory: A Literary Portrait*. London: Macmillan, 1961.

Croft, Barbara L. *"Stylistic Arrangements": A Study of William Butler Yeats's "A Vision."* Lewisburg: Bucknell University Press, 1987.

Cronin, John. "Dominant Themes in the Novels of Somerville and Ross." *Somerville and Ross: A Symposium*, 8–18. Belfast: Institute of Irish Studies, Queen's University, 1968.

Cross, Nigel. *The Common Writer: Life in Nineteenth-Century Grub Street*. Cambridge: Cambridge University Press, 1985.

"Crossriggs." *The Spectator* 18 April 1908: 624

Cullingford, Elizabeth Butler. *Gender and History in Yeats's Love Poetry*. Cambridge: Cambridge University Press, 1993.

Cummins, Geraldine. *Dr E. Œ. Somerville: A Biography*. London: Andrew Dakers, 1952.

———. *The Scripts of Cleophas: A Reconstruction of Primitive Christian Documents*. 2d ed. London: Rider & Co., 1928.

———. *Swan on a Black Sea: A Study in Automatic Writing: The Cummins-Willett Scripts*. 1965. Rev. ed. Edited by Signe Toksvig. New York: Samuel Weiser, 1970.

———. *Unseen Adventures: An Autobiography Covering Thirty-four Years of Work in Psychical Research*. London: Rider and Company, 1951.

———. "W. B. Yeats and Psychical Research." *Occult Review* 66 (April 1939): 132–39.

Dailey, Susan Ramsay. "'My Delight and Comfort': The Influence of Georgie Hyde-Lees on the Life of W. B. Yeats and the Aesthetic Development of His Work." Ph.D. diss. Catholic University of America, 1987.

Dever, Maryanne. "'No Mine and Thine but Ours': Finding 'M. Barnard Eldershaw.'" *Tulsa Studies in Women's Literature* 14 (1995): 65–75.

Doane, Janice, and Devon Hodges. "Writing from the Trenches: Women's Work and Collaborative Writing." *Tulsa Studies in Women's Literature* 14 (1995): 51–57.

Dodd, Alfred. *The Immortal Master.* London: Rider & Co., 1943.

Dooley, Allan C. *Author and Printer in Victorian England.* Charlottesville: University Press of Virginia, 1992.

Douglas, Alfred. *Extra-sensory Powers: A Century of Psychical Research.* London: Victor Gollancz, 1976.

Dowden, Hester. "The Case for Psychical Research." *North American Review* 218 (Nov. 1923): 686–94.

——. "A Page from My Life: 'Is It a Forgery?': How I Received Oscar Wilde's 'Spirit Play.'" *The Graphic,* 10 March 1928, 401.

Eldershaw, M. Barnard. *A House Is Built.* South Yarra: Lloyd O'Neil, 1929.

——. *Tomorrow & Tomorrow & Tomorrow.* 1947. Rev. ed. Garden City, N.Y.: Dial Press, 1984.

——. "The Writer and Society." In *M. Barnard Eldershaw: Plaque With Laurel, Essays, Reviews & Correspondence,* edited by Maryanne Dever, 222–26. St. Lucia: University of Queensland Press, 1995.

Eliot, Simon. "'His Generation Read His Stories': Walter Besant, Chatto and Windus and *All Sorts and Conditions of Men.*" *Publishing History* 21 (1987): 25–67.

Ellmann, Richard. *The Identity of Yeats.* London: Faber, 1964.

——. *Yeats: The Man and the Masks.* New York: E. P. Dutton & Co., 1948.

Encyclopedia of Occultism and Parapsychology. Edited by Leslie A. Shepard. 2d ed. Detroit: Gale Research Co., 1984.

Erkkila, Betsy. *The Wicked Sisters: Women Poets, Literary History, and Discord.* New York: Oxford University Press, 1992.

Ewen, C. L'Estrange. *Shakespeare—Automatist or Nothing.* [Privately published] 1946.

——. *Shakespeare No Poet?: The Story of an Unpublished Volume.* [Privately published] 1938.

Faderman, Lillian. *Surpassing the Love of Men: Romantic Friendship and Love between Women from the Renaissance to the Present.* New York: William Morrow & Co., 1981.

Feather, John. *A History of British Publishing.* London: Croom Helm, 1988.

——. "Publishers and Politicians: The Remaking of the Law of Copyright in Britain 1775–1842, Part II: The Rights of Authors." *Publishing History* 25 (1989): 47–72.

Feltes, N. N. *Literary Capital and the Late Victorian Novel.* Madison: University of Wisconsin Press, 1993.

Field, Michael. *A Selection from the Poems of Michael Field*. Edited by T. Sturge Moore. London: Poetry Bookshop, 1923.

———. *Works and Days: From the Journal of Michael Field*. Edited by T. & D. C. Sturge Moore. London: John Murray, 1933.

Findlater, Mary, and Jane Findlater. *Beneath the Visiting Moon*. London: Hurst & Blackett, 1923.

———. *Crossriggs*. 1908. New York: Penguin Books, 1986.

———. *Penny Moneypenny*. London: Smith, Elder, 1912.

Finneran, Richard J. *Editing Yeats's Poems: A Reconsideration*. New York: St. Martin's Press, 1990.

———. "On Editing Yeats: The Text of *A Vision* (1937)." *Texas Studies in Literature & Language* 19 (Spring 1977): 119–34.

Flanagan, Thomas. "The Big House of Ross-Drishane." *Kenyon Review* 28 (January 1966): 54–78.

Foster, R. F. *W. B. Yeats: A Life. Vol. 1: The Apprentice Mage, 1865–1914*. New York: Oxford University Press, 1997.

Foucault, Michel. "What Is an Author?" In *Textual Strategies: Perspectives in Post-Structuralist Literature*, edited by Josué V. Harari. Ithaca: Cornell University Press, 1979.

Fripp, Peter. *The Book of Johannes*. London: Rider & Co., 1941.

Fritschner, Linda Marie. "Publishers' Readers, Publishers, and Their Authors." *Publishing History* 7 (1980): 45–100.

Gallop, Jane. "Annie Leclerc Writing a Letter, with Vermeer." In *The Poetics of Gender*, edited by Nancy K. Miller, 137–56. New York: Columbia University Press, 1986.

———. *Around 1981: Academic Feminist Theory*. New York: Routledge, 1992.

Gallop, Jane, et al. "Criticizing Feminist Criticism." In *Conflicts in Feminism*, edited by Marianne Hirsch and Evelyn Fox Keller, 349–69. New York: Routledge, 1990.

Garber, Marjorie. *Shakespeare's Ghost Writers: Literature as Uncanny Causality*. New York: Methuen, 1987.

Gardiner, Judith Kegan. "The (US)es of (I)dentity: A Response to Abel on '(E)merging Identities.'" *Signs* 6 (1981): 436–44.

Garrett, Eileen J. *Many Voices: The Autobiography of a Medium*. New York: G. P. Putnam's Sons, 1968.

———. *My Life as a Search for the Meaning of Mediumship*. London: Psychic Book Club, 1939.

Gaskell, Elizabeth. *The Life of Charlotte Brontë*. 1857. Harmondsworth: Penguin, 1975.

Gerard, E. D. *Beggar My Neighbour*. Edinburgh: William Blackwood and Sons, 1882.

———. *Reata: What's in a Name*. Edinburgh: William Blackwood and Sons, 1880.

———. *A Sensitive Plant*. London: Kegan Paul, 1891.

———. *The Waters of Hercules*. Edinburgh: William Blackwood and Sons, 1886.

Gérin, Winifred. *Branwell Brontë*. London: Thomas Nelson, 1961.

——. *Charlotte Brontë: The Evolution of Genius*. Oxford: Clarendon Press, 1967.

——. *Emily Brontë: A Biography*. Oxford: Clarendon Press, 1971.

Gilbert, Sandra M. "A Conversation with Sandra M. Gilbert." By Garrett Hongo and Catherine Parke. *Missouri Review* 9.1 (1985–86): 89–109.

Gilbert, Sandra M., and Susan Gubar. "An Interview with Sandra M. Gilbert and Susan Gubar." By Elizabeth Rosdeitcher. *Critical Texts* 6.1 (1989): 17–38.

——. "Gilbert and Gubar." By Laura Shapiro. *Ms.* Jan. 1986: 59+.

——. *The Madwoman in the Attic: The Woman Writer and the Nineteenth-Century Literary Imagination*. New Haven: Yale University Press, 1979.

——. *No Man's Land*. 3 vols. New Haven: Yale University Press, 1988, 1989, 1994.

Goldman, Arnold. "Yeats, Spiritualism, and Psychical Research." In *Yeats and the Occult*, edited by George Mills Harper, 108–29. Toronto: Macmillan of Canada, 1975.

Graves, C. L. "Martin Ross." *National Review* 71 (May 1918): 23+.

Greenblatt, Stephen. *Shakespearean Negotiations: The Circulation of Social Energy in Renaissance England*. Berkeley: University of California Press, 1988.

Gregory, Lady Augusta. *Seventy Years: Being the Autobiography of Lady Gregory*. Gerrards Cross: Colin Smythe Limited, 1974.

——. *Visions and Beliefs in the West of Ireland: Collected and Arranged by Lady Gregory with Two Essays and Notes by W. B. Yeats*. New York: Oxford University Press, 1970.

Gwynn, Stephen. "Lever's Successors." *The Edinburgh Review* 234 (October 1921): 346–57.

Harper, George Mills. *The Making of Yeats's A Vision: A Study of the Automatic Script*. 2 vols. Houndmills: Macmillan, 1987.

——, ed. *Yeats and the Occult*. Toronto: Macmillan of Canada, 1975.

——, gen. ed. *Yeats's "Vision" Papers*. 3 vols. Iowa City: University of Iowa Press, 1992.

Harper, George Mills, and John S. Kelly. "Preliminary Examination of the Script of E[lizabeth] R[adcliffe]." In *Yeats and the Occult*, edited by George Mills Harper, 130–171. Toronto: Macmillan of Canada, 1975.

Harper, Margaret Mills. "The Medium as Creator: George Yeats's Role in the Automatic Script." *Yeats: An Annual of Critical and Textual Studies* 6 (1988): 49–71.

——. "The Message Is the Medium: Identity in the Automatic Script." *Yeats: An Annual of Critical and Textual Studies* 9 (1991): 35–54.

Harwood, John. "Olivia Shakespear and W. B. Yeats." *Yeats Annual* 4 (1986): 75–98.

Haynes, Renée. *The Society for Psychical Research, 1882–1982: A History*. London: MacDonald & Co., 1982.

Hepburn, James. *The Author's Empty Purse and the Rise of the Literary Agent*. London: Oxford University Press, 1968.

Herrmann, Anne. Review of *No Man's Land*, vols. 1 and 2, by Sandra Gilbert and Susan Gubar. *Criticism* 31:4 (1989): 507–12.

Hirsch, Marianne, and Evelyn Fox Keller. "Conclusion: Practicing Conflict in Feminist Theory." In *Conflicts in Feminism* 370–85. New York: Routledge, 1990.

——. "Introduction: January 4, 1990." In *Conflicts in Feminism*, 1–5. New York: Routledge, 1990.

——, eds. *Conflicts in Feminism*. New York: Routledge, 1990.

Hitt, Jack. "The Writer is Dead. But His Ghost is Thriving." *New York Times Magazine* 25 May 1997: 38–41.

Hood, Connie K. "The Remaking of *A Vision*." *Yeats: An Annual of Critical and Textual Studies* 1 (1983): 33–67.

Howe, Susanne. *Geraldine Jewsbury: Her Life and Errors*. London: George Allen & Unwin, 1935.

Irigaray, Luce. *This Sex Which Is Not One*. Translated by Catherine Porter. Ithaca: Cornell University Press, 1985.

"Isabella MacDonald Alden." In *American Women Writers: A Critical Reference Guide from Colonial Times to the Present*, 1:33–41. New York: Ungar, 1979.

James, Henry. *The Complete Notebooks of Henry James*. Edited by Leon Edel and Lyall H. Powers. New York: Oxford University Press, 1987.

Jaszi, Peter. "On the Author Effect: Contemporary Copyright and Collective Creativity." In *The Construction of Authorship*, edited by Martha Woodmansee and Peter Jaszi, 29–56. Durham, N.C.: Duke University Press, 1994.

Jay, Karla. *The Amazon and the Page: Natalie Clifford Barney and Renée Vivien*. Bloomington: Indiana University Press, 1988.

Jeffares, A. Norman. *W. B. Yeats: Man and Poet*. London: Routledge and Kegan Paul, 1949.

Jenney, Shirley Carson. *The Fortune of Eternity*. [By Percy Bysshe Shelley.] New York: William-Frederick Press, 1945.

——. *Some Psychic Experiences with Shelley*. London: A. H. Stockwell, 1950.

Jochum, K. P. S. "Yeats's *Vision Papers* and the Problem of Automatic Writing: A Review Essay." *English Literature in Transition* 36 (1993): 323–36.

Kaplan, Carey, and Ellen Cronan Rose. "Strange Bedfellows: Feminist Collaboration." *Signs* 18 (1993): 547–61.

Keeble, Ida M. Everett. *Beyond Earth's Fears*. [Dictated by Ivan Sergevitch Turgenev.] Ipswich: Published for the Author by W. E. Harrison & Sons, 1936.

Kelly, John. "'Friendship is all the House I Have': Lady Gregory and W. B. Yeats." In *Lady Gregory, Fifty Years After*, edited by Ann Saddlemyer and Colin Smythe, 179–257. Irish Literary Studies 13. Gerrards Cross, Buckinghamshire: Colin Smythe, 1987.

Kennard, Jean E. *Vera Brittain and Winifred Holtby: A Working Partnership*. Hanover, N.H.: University Press of New England, 1989.

Koestenbaum, Wayne. *Double Talk: The Erotics of Male Collaboration*. New York: Routledge, 1989.

Krementz, Jill. *The Writer's Desk*. New York: Random House, 1996.

Kunitz, Stanley J., ed. *British Authors of the Nineteenth Century*. New York: H. W. Wilson, 1936.

Laird, Holly. "Contradictory Legacies: Michael Field and Feminist Restoration." *Victorian Poetry* 33 (Spring 1995): 111–28.

——, ed. "Forum: On Collaborations, Parts 1 and 2." *Tulsa Studies in Women's Literature* 13 and 14 (1994–95): 231–40, 7–18.

Lane, Margaret. *The Drug-Like Brontë Dream*. London: John Murray, 1980.

Leichtman, Robert L. *Eileen Garrett Returns*. [Through the mediumship of D. Kendrick Johnson]. Columbus, Ohio: Ariel Press, 1980.

Leonard, Gladys Osborne. *My Life in Two Worlds*. 1931. London: Cassel & Co., 1992.

Leonardi, Susan J., and Rebecca A. Pope. "Screaming Divas: Collaboration as Feminist Practice." *Tulsa Studies in Women's Literature* 13 (1994): 259–80.

Lewis, Gifford. *Somerville and Ross: The World of the Irish R. M.* 1985. Harmondsworth: Penguin, 1987.

——, ed. *The Selected Letters of Somerville and Ross*. London: Faber & Faber, 1989.

Longenbach, James. *Stone Cottage: Pound, Yeats, and Modernism*. New York: Oxford University Press, 1988.

Lowell, Amy. "To Two Unknown Ladies." *North American Review* (June 1919): 837–42.

Lucas, E. V. "The Two Ladies." *Spectator* (1 January 1916): 9–10.

Lunsford, Andrea, and Lisa Ede. *Singular Texts/Plural Authors: Perspectives on Collaborative Writing*. Carbondale: Southern Illinois University Press, 1990.

Lyons, F. S. L. "The Twilight of the Big House." *Ariel* 1:3 (1970): 110–22.

Mackenzie, Eileen. *The Findlater Sisters: Literature and Friendship*. London: John Murray, 1964.

Mannocchi, Phyllis F. "Vernon Lee and Kit Anstruther-Thompson: A Study of Love and Collaboration Between Romantic Friends." *Women's Studies* 12 (1986): 129–48.

Masten, Jeffrey A. "Beaumont and/or Fletcher: Collaboration and the Interpretation of Renaissance Drama." In *The Construction of Authorship*, edited by Martha Woodmansee and Peter Jaszi, 361–82. Durham, N.C.: Duke University Press, 1994.

Maurat, Charlotte. *The Brontës' Secret*. Translated by Margaret Meldrum. London: Constable & Co., 1969.

Max, D. T. "The Carver Chronicles." *New York Times Magazine* (9 August 1998): 34–40+.

Maynard, John. *Charlotte Brontë and Sexuality*. Cambridge: Cambridge University Press, 1984.

McClintock, Anne. *Imperial Leather: Race, Gender and Sexuality in the Colonial Contest*. New York: Routledge, 1995.

McDonald, Jan. "'Disillusioned Bards and Despised Bohemians': Michael Field's *A Question of Memory* at the Independent Theatre Society." *Theatre Notebook* 31.2 (1977): 18–29.

McDowell, Deborah E. "Transferences: Black Feminist Thinking: The 'Practice' of 'Theory.'" In *"The Changing Same": Black Women's Literature, Criticism, and Theory*, 156–75. Bloomington: Indiana University Press, 1995.

McGann, Jerome. "The Rationale of Hypertext." In *Electronic Text: Investigations in Method and Theory*, edited by Kathryn Sutherland, 19–46. Oxford: Clarendon Press, 1997.

Meredith, Isabel. *A Girl among the Anarchists*. 1903. Lincoln: University of Nebraska Press, 1992.

Meyer, Susan. *Imperialism at Home: Race and Victorian Women's Fiction.* Ithaca: Cornell University Press, 1996.

Michie, Elsie B. *Outside The Pale: Cultural Exclusion, Gender Difference, and the Victorian Woman Writer.* Ithaca: Cornell University Press, 1993.

Michie, Helena. "Not One of the Family: The Repression of the Other Woman in Feminist Theory." In *Discontented Discourses: Feminism/Textual Intervention/Psychoanalysis,* edited by Marleen S. Barr and Richard Feldstein, 15–28. Urbana: University of Illinois Press, 1989.

——. *Sororophobia: Differences among Women in Literature and Culture.* New York: Oxford University Press, 1992.

Miller, D. A. *The Novel and the Police.* Berkeley: University of California Press, 1988.

Miller, Nancy K., ed. *The Poetics of Gender.* New York: Columbia University Press, 1986.

——. *Subject to Change: Reading Feminist Writing.* New York: Columbia University Press, 1988.

Mitchell, Hilary. "Somerville and Ross: Amateur to Professional." In *Somerville and Ross: A Symposium,* 20–37. Belfast: Institute of Irish Studies, Queens University, 1968.

Moglen, Helene. *Charlotte Brontë: The Self Conceived.* 1976. Madison: University of Wisconsin Press, 1984.

Moore, Lisa. "'Something More Tender than Friendship': Romantic Friendship in Early-Nineteenth-Century England." In *Lesbian Subjects,* edited by Martha Vicinus, 21–40. Bloomington: Indiana University Press, 1996.

Moore, Virginia. *The Unicorn: William Butler Yeats' Search for Reality.* New York: Macmillan, 1954.

Moriarty, David. J. "'Michael Field' (Edith Cooper and Katherine Bradley) and Their Male Critics." In *Nineteenth-Century Women Writers of the English-Speaking World,* 121–42. New York: Greenwood Press, 1986.

Mortimer, Raymond. Review of *Beneath the Visiting Moon,* by Mary and Jane Findlater. *New Statesman* 12 May 1923: 146.

Murphy, Daniel J. "Lady Gregory, Co-Author and Sometimes Author of the Plays of W. B. Yeats." In *Modern Irish Literature: Essays in Honor of William York Tindall,* edited by Raymond J. Porter and James D. Brophy, 43–52. New York: Iona College Press, 1972.

Murphy, William M. *Family Secrets: William Butler Yeats and His Relatives.* Syracuse: Syracuse University Press, 1995.

——. *Prodigal Father: The Life of John Butler Yeats (1839–1922).* Ithaca: Cornell University Press, 1978.

O'Brien, Conor Cruise. *Writers and Politics.* London: Chatto and Windus, 1965.

Oppenheim, Janet. *The Other World: Spiritualism and Psychical Research in England, 1850–1914.* Cambridge: Cambridge University Press, 1985.

Ormrod, Richard. *Una Troubridge: The Friend of Radclyffe Hall.* London: Jonathan Cape, 1984.

"Oscar Wilde among the Shades." *Current Opinion* 77 (October 1924): 458–459.

"The Oscar Wilde Script: A Critique by the Brother of Mr. V———." *Quarterly Transactions of the British College of Psychic Science* 3 (January 1924): 299–326.

Owen, Alex. *The Darkened Room: Women, Power and Spiritualism in Late Victorian England.* Philadelphia: University of Pennsylvania Press, 1990.

Patterson, Lyman Ray. *Copyright in Historical Perspective.* Nashville: Vanderbilt University Press, 1968.

Pethica, James. "'Our Kathleen': Yeats's Collaboration with Lady Gregory in the Writing of *Cathleen ni Houlihan.*" *Yeats Annual* 6 (1988): 3–31.

———. "Patronage and Creative Exchange: Yeats, Lady Gregory, and the Economy of Indebtedness." In *Yeats and Women,* edited by Deirdre Toomey, 168–204. Houndmills: Macmillan, 1997.

Pierce, David. *Yeats's Worlds: Ireland, England, and the Poetic Imagination.* New Haven: Yale University Press, 1995.

Porter, Mrs. Gerald. *Annals of a Publishing House: John Blackwood.* New York: Charles Scribner's Sons, 1898.

Powell, Violet. *The Irish Cousins: The Books and Backgrounds of Somerville and Ross.* London: Heinemann, 1970.

Power, Ann. "The Big House of Somerville and Ross." *The Dubliner* (Spring 1964): 43–53.

Powrie, Phil. "Automatic Writing: Breton, Daumal, Hegel." *French Studies: A Quarterly Review* 42:2 (1988): 177–93.

Prince, Walter Franklin. *The Case of Patience Worth: A Critical Study of Certain Unusual Phenomena.* Boston: Boston Society of Psychic Research, 1927.

Prins, Yopie. "A Metaphorical Field: Katherine Bradley and Edith Cooper." *Victorian Poetry* 33 (Spring 1995): 129–48.

———. "Sappho Doubled: Michael Field." *Yale Journal of Criticism* 8 (1995): 165–86.

Ratchford, Fannie Elizabeth. *The Brontës' Web of Childhood.* New York: Columbia University Press, 1941.

———, ed. *Gondal's Queen: A Novel in Verse by Emily Jane Brontë.* Austin: University of Texas Press, 1955.

Reid, Benjamin L. *The Man from New York: John Quinn and His Friends.* New York: Oxford University Press, 1968.

Roberts, D[aisy]. O. *Shakespeare & Co. Unlimited.* London: [Privately published], 1950.

Roberts, Daisy O., and Collin E. Woolcock. *Elizabethan Episode: Incorporating Shakespeare and Co., Unlimited.* London: Regency Press, 1961.

Robinson, Hilary. *Somerville and Ross: A Critical Appreciation.* New York: St. Martin's Press, 1980.

Rose, Mark. *Authors and Owners: The Invention of Copyright.* Cambridge: Harvard University Press, 1993.

Ross, Marlon B. "Authority and Authenticity: Scribbling Authors and the Genius of Print in Eighteenth-Century England." In *The Construction of Authorship,* edited by Martha Woodmansee and Peter Jaszi, 231–58. Durham, N.C.: Duke University Press, 1994.

Saddlemyer, Ann. "Georgie Hyde Lees: More than a Poet's Wife." In *Yeats the*

European, edited by A. Norman Jeffares, 191–200. Princess Grace Irish Library: 3. Savage, Md.; Barnes & Noble Books, 1989.

——. *In Defence of Lady Gregory, Playwright*. Dublin: Dolmen Press,1966.

Sage, M. *Mrs Piper and the Society for Psychical Research*. Translated by Noralie Robertson. Abridged edition. Preface by Sir Oliver Lodge. New York: Scott-Thaw, 1904.

Sassoon, Siegfried. *Meredith*. New York: Viking Press, 1948.

Saunders, David. *Authorship and Copyright*. London: Routledge, 1992.

Saunders, J. W. *The Profession of English Letters*. London: Routledge and Kegan Paul, 1964.

Schiff, Stacy. "The Genius and Mrs. Genius: The Very Nabokovian Marriage of Vladimir and Véra." *New Yorker*, 10 February 1997, 41–47.

Shelley, Mary. *Frankenstein; or, The Modern Prometheus: The 1818 Text*. 1974. Chicago: University of Chicago Press, 1982.

Showalter, Elaine. *A Literature of Their Own: British Women Novelists from Brontë to Lessing*. Princeton: Princeton University Press, 1977.

Sidgwick, Eleanor Mildred. "The 'Oscar Wilde' Script." *Proceedings of the Society for Psychical Research* 34 (1924): 186–96.

Smith, Eleanor Touhey. *Psychic People*. New York: William Morrow, 1969.

Smith, Susy. *The Mediumship of Mrs. Leonard*. New Hyde Park, N.Y.: University Books, 1964.

Smith-Rosenberg, Carroll. "The Female World of Love and Ritual: Relations Between Women in Nineteenth-Century America." *Signs* 1:1 (1975): 1–29.

Somerville, E. Œ., and Martin Ross. *Further Experiences of an Irish R.M.* London: Longmans, Green, 1908.

——. *Irish Memories*. New edition. London: Longmans, Green, 1925.

——. *The Real Charlotte*. London: Ward and Downey, 1894.

——. *Some Experiences of an Irish R.M.* London: Longmans, Green, 1889.

——. "Two of a Trade." Reprinted in *Dr. E. Œ. Somerville*, by Geraldine Cummins, 180–86. London: Andrew Dakers, 1952.

——. *Wheel-Tracks*. London: Longmans, Green, 1924.

Stevenson, Lionel. *The Ordeal of George Meredith: A Biography*. New York: Charles Scribner's Sons, 1953.

Stewart, Susan. *On Longing: Narratives of the Miniature, the Gigantic, the Souvenir, the Collection*. Baltimore: Johns Hopkins University Press, 1984.

Stillinger, Jack. *Multiple Authorship and the Myth of Solitary Genius*. New York: Oxford University Press, 1991.

Sturgeon, Mary. *Michael Field*. New York: Macmillan, 1922.

——. *Studies of Contemporary Poets*. London: George G. Harrap & Co., 1920.

Sutherland, J. A. *Victorian Novelists and Publishers*. Chicago: University of Chicago Press, 1976.

Sword, Helen. "H.D.'s *Magic Ring*." *Tulsa Studies in Women's Literature* 14.2 (1995): 347–62.

——. "Modernist Mediumship." In *Modernism, Gender, and Culture: A Cultural Studies Approach*, edited by Lisa Rado, 65–77. New York: Garland, 1997.

——. "Necrobibliography: Books in the Spirit World." *Modern Language Quarterly* 60.1 (1999): 85–112.

Taylor, Ina. *Victorian Sisters: The Remarkable Macdonald Women and the Great Men They Inspired.* Bethesda, Md.: Adler & Adler, 1987.

Travers Smith, Hester. *Voices from the Void: Six Years' Experience in Automatic Communications.* 1919. London: Psychic Book Club, 1954.

——, ed. *Psychic Messages from Oscar Wilde.* London: T. Werner Laurie Ltd., 1924.

Trollope, Anthony. *An Autobiography.* 1883. Edited by Michael Sadlier. London: Oxford University Press, 1923.

Tuchman, Gaye. *Edging Women Out: Victorian Novelists, Publishers, and Social Change.* With Nina Fortin. New Haven: Yale University Press, 1989.

Vanden Bossche, Chris R. "The Value of Literature: Representations of Print Culture in the Copyright Debate of 1837–1842." *Victorian Studies* 38:1 (1994): 41–68.

Vicinus, Martha. Introduction to *Lesbian Subjects: A Feminist Studies Reader,* 1–12. Bloomington: Indiana University Press, 1996.

——, ed. *Lesbian Subjects: A Feminist Studies Reader.* Bloomington: Indiana University Press, 1996.

Weintraub, Stanley. *Four Rossettis: A Victorian Biography.* New York: Weybright and Talley, 1977.

White, Christine. "'Poets and Lovers Evermore': Interpreting Female Love in the Poetry and Journals of Michael Field." *Textual Practice* 4.2 (1990): 197–212.

Wiggin, Kate Douglas Smith. *My Garden of Memory.* Boston: Houghton Mifflin, 1923.

Wiggin, Kate Douglas Smith, et al. *The Affair at the Inn.* Boston: Houghton, Mifflin, 1904.

——. *Robinetta.* Leipzig: Tauchnitz, 1911.

Williams, David. *George Meredith: His Life and Lost Love.* London: Hamish Hamilton, 1977.

Willis, J. H., Jr. *Leonard and Virginia Woolf as Publishers: The Hogarth Press, 1917–41.* Charlottesville: University Press of Virginia, 1992.

Winnifreth, Tom. *The Brontës.* New York: Collier Books, 1977.

——. *The Brontës and Their Background: Romance and Reality.* 2d ed. Houndmills: Macmillan, 1988.

Wong, Hertha D. "An Interview with Louise Erdrich and Michael Dorris." *North Dakota Quarterly* 55:1 (1987): 196–218.

Woodmansee, Martha. "The Genius and the Copyright: Economic and Legal Conditions of the Emergence of the 'Author.'" *Eighteenth Century Studies* 17 (1984): 425–48.

——. "On the Author Effect: Recovering Collectivity." In *The Construction of Authorship: Textual Appropriation in Law and Literature,* edited by Martha Woodmansee and Peter Jaszi, 15–28. Durham, N.C.: Duke University Press, 1994.

Woodmansee, Martha, and Peter Jaszi. Introduction to *The Construction of Authorship: Textual Appropriation in Law and Literature,* edited by Martha Woodmansee and Peter Jaszi, 1–13. Durham, N.C.: Duke University Press, 1994.

——, eds. *The Construction of Authorship: Textual Appropriation in Law and Literature*. Durham, N.C.: Duke University Press, 1994.

Woolf, Virginia. *Orlando*. San Diego: Harcourt Brace Jovanovich, 1928.

——. "Professions for Women." In *The Death of the Moth and Other Essays*. New York: Harcourt, Brace and Company, 1942.

——. *A Room of One's Own*. New York: Harcourt, Brace, Jovanovich, 1929.

Worth, Patience. *The Sorry Tale: A Story of the Time of Christ*. New York: Henry Holt, 1924.

Yeats, W. B. *Plays in Prose and Verse*. New York: Macmillan, 1930.

——. "Swedenborg, Mediums, and the Desolate Places." In *Visions and Beliefs in the West of Ireland*, by Lady Augusta Gregory, 311–36. New York: Oxford University Press, 1970.

——. *A Vision*. 1937. New York: Collier Books, 1966.

——. *The Words upon the Window Pane*. Dublin: Cuala Press, 1934.

——. *Yeats's "Vision" Papers. Vol. 1: The Automatic Script: 5 November 1917–18 June 1918*. Edited by Steve L. Adams et al. General Editor, George Mills Harper. Iowa City: University of Iowa Press, 1992.

——. *Yeats's "Vision" Papers. Vol. 2: The Automatic Script: 25 June 1918–29 March 1920*. Edited by Steve L. Adams et al. General Editor, George Mills Harper. Iowa City: University of Iowa Press, 1992.

——. *Yeats's "Vision" Papers, Vol. 3: Sleep and Dream Notebooks, Vision Notebooks 1 and 2, Card File*. Edited by Robert Anthony Martinich and Margaret Mills Harper. General Editor, George Mills Harper. Iowa City: University of Iowa Press, 1992.

Index

Abel, Elizabeth, 74n19, 75
Alcott, Louisa May, 38, 105
Alden, Isabella MacDonald ("Pansy"), 112
Alexander, Christine, 34n2, 36, 37–39, 44–45, 49, 50–52, 55, 57
Allen, Percy, 164, 169, 173–74
Altick, Richard D., 7, 97n6, 103
Authorship:
    and the canon, 4, 7, 29–30, 172
    as career for women, 20, 24–25, 29, 92–95
    conventional attitudes toward, 3, 23, 25–27, 30, 34, 97, 135, 154, 188, 212
    and copyright, 150–52, 154, 165–70, 172, 188
    feminist approaches to, 1–2, 8, 24, 28, 31, 75–76
    as mediumship, 24–25, 59–61, 152–53, 174, 211
    professionalization of, 31, 91–92, 96–99, 103–4, 107–13
    poststructuralist critique of, 2–3, 174, 210
    solitary, 3, 7, 23, 30, 61–62, 73–74, 88, 111–12, 210–12
    See also Collaborative writing
Automatic writing:
    classical and scriptural allusions in, 6, 127, 156, 132–35, 170
    communications from illustrious authors, 6, 29, 132, 156–60, 164, 169–70, 171–76, 185–86
    Cross-Correspondence Experiments, 7, 128, 129n13, 171
    mechanics of, 14–18, 127–29, 131, 139–41, 153, 165–66, 170, 189, 193–94

and modernist movements, 152n5, 154–56
and proprietary authorship, 25–26, 150–52, 154, 165–72, 175, 177–78
as secret writing, 22, 127, 171–72, 196–97
as stenography, 23, 26, 150, 163–65, 177, 192, 206–7
stylistic unconventionality of, 128, 140, 153, 166, 170–71, 194
    See also Mediumship and entries for individual mediums
Azim, Firdous, 35n5, 39n9

Baldwin, A. W., 105n15
Balfour, Gerald, 131, 132n17, 133–35, 136–37, 140n23, 147, 193, 194
Barker, Juliet, 33n1, 36, 37n6, 38, 40, 42n10, 43–44, 47, 48n14, 49, 51n16, 119
Barnard, Marjorie, 27, 67, 68n7, 69–70, 71n16, 76n22, 89, 104, 107–8
    See also Eldershaw, M. Barnard
Barney, Natalie, 81
Barrie, James, 69
Barthes, Roland, 2
Basham, Diana, 8n3, 28n9, 163
Bauer, Dale M., 107n18
Belenkey, Mary Field, et al., 74n19
Bendixen, Alfred, 107n18
Benstock, Shari, 81–82
Besant, Walter, 69n11, 70, 108, 109, 111–12
    collaboration with James Rice, 4, 116n31, 117
Binding, Paul, 106n17
Black, Helen, 96, 104, 121, 122
Blavatsky, Madame, 161, 145n28

Bloom, Harold, 40
Bock, Carol, 41
Bond, Frederick Bligh. *See* Cummins v.
    Bond
Bonetti, Kay, 194n4
Bonham-Carter, Victor, 97n6
Bradford, Curtis B., 183n10, 206n28, 208
Bradley, Katherine. *See* Michael Field
Braude, Anne, 8n3, 28n9
Brittain, Vera, 19, 113n27
Brontë juvenilia:
    as analogous to automatic writing, 46,
        59–60
    as challenge to conventional author-
        ship, 36, 59–62
    Charlotte-Branwell collaboration, 34,
        41, 44–49
    Charlotte-Emily collaboration, 34n3, 40,
        41–43, 55–56
    and colonialism, 35, 54
    editing of, 36, 39, 50, 52, 54–59
    Emily-Anne collaboration, 34n3, 40,
        41–43, 55–56
    as fantasy, 35–37, 40, 42–43, 48, 53
    as "juvenile" writing, 34, 37–40, 44, 48,
        51
    as literary apprenticeship, 36, 39–41,
        47–49, 54
    as miniatures, 39, 49–50, 52–55
    normalization of, 37, 40, 51–52, 58
    as pathology, 35–38, 40, 48
    as private publication, 34, 37, 50, 52, 54,
        61, 67
    and professional authorship, 37–39;
        43–44; 49, 51–52, 54
    and reception history, 35–41, 44–52,
        61–62
    as secret writing, 35–37, 46–47, 49–50,
        53, 59, 62
The Brontës:
    and idea of genius, 35, 39–41, 61–62,
        119
    as separate authors:
        Anne, 33–34, 49
        Branwell, 34, 43, 55, 57–58, 60,
            101–2
        Charlotte, 33–34, 40–44, 47–49, 55,
            59–60, 101–2
        Emily, 33–34, 43–44, 49, 55–56
    considered as single author, 33, 40
    as exotics, 54, 119–20
    See also Brontë juvenilia
Brunazzi, Elizabeth, 183

Carlyle, Jane, 19, 106
Carver, Raymond, 211–12

Castle, Terry, 64, 81, 130n16
Chadwick, Whitney, and Isabelle de
    Courtivron, 3n2, 21, 82n32, 183
Childers, Mary, and bell hooks, 79, 82,
    125
Cixous, Hélène, and Catherine Clément,
    78
Clarke, Norma, 106n16
Clément, Catherine, and Hélène Cixous,
    78
Coghill, Sir Patrick, 11, 76n23
Colette, 183
Collaborative writing:
    and amateurism, 9, 28, 38, 96, 98, 101–6,
        114–15
    conversational method of, 26–27, 71,
        75–77, 79–80, 126–27
    cross-class and cross-race, 27–28, 85,
        86–87, 120, 125–26, 136
    as curiosity, 7, 26, 29, 68–69, 107–8, 117
    domestication of, 11, 28, 64, 66, 68
    as double-handedness, xiv (fig. 1), 1–2,
        18, 20, 71–72, 85–86, 108, 113
    erotics of, 5, 21–22, 63–68, 72, 181–82,
        197
    and exoticism, 5, 27–28, 31, 119–27
    familial, 5, 19–21, 28, 31, 38, 63–64,
        105–6, 110, 115–16
    invisibility of, 8–9, 18, 22, 68, 74, 111
    as literary apprenticeship, 4, 9, 29, 36,
        37, 39–40, 48–49, 61–62, 104–5
    male, 4, 20–22, 65–66, 68, 70–71, 74, 89,
        108–9, 111–12, 117
    and middle-class solidarity, 27–28, 31,
        86–88, 122–23, 125
    problematic boundaries of, 3, 9, 18–22,
        26–27, 75
    and professionalism, 22, 29, 38–39, 49,
        51–52, 54, 91–92, 96–101, 106–13
    representations of, 2, 9–17, 26–27, 180
    resistance to, 3, 18–19, 27, 63–64, 72, 84,
        210–12
    as secret writing, 9, 21, 35, 37, 49–50, 68
    spousal, 20, 30, 182–84, 197, 211
    theories of, 3–4, 8, 18, 20–22, 65–66, 71,
        78–79, 84–88
    tropes for, 69–70, 71–73, 80, 84
    and voyeurism, 67–68, 72–73, 74, 114
    See also Authorship, Lesbianism,
        Mediumship
Collins, Mabel, 161
Collins, Robert G., 34, 50n15, 52, 55–58, 61
Collis, Maurice, 64n3, 71, 73, 114, 127
Coltelli, Louise, 19n4
Conrad, Joseph, 4, 108
Control spirits, 6, 27, 28, 128–29, 136–47

Cooper, Edith. *See* Michael Field
Corrigan, Maureen, 80
Cottom, Daniel, 152, 156n11
Coxhead, Elizabeth, 205
Croft, Barbara L., 186n13
Cronin, John, 123n8, 124
Cross, Nigel, 108n21
Cullingford, Elizabeth Butler, 181n7
Cummins, Geraldine:
　as author, 6, 135, 150, 153–54, 162–63,
　　176–78
　as biographer of Edith Somerville, 6,
　　64n2, 96, 135, 177
　and Hester Dowden, 129n13, 138–39,
　　156–57, 159, 161, 195
　and Irish identity, 128, 135–36, 153
　as medium, 6, 15 (fig. 7), 127–28, 130,
　　137, 138–39, 152–53, 160, 161–70,
　　172, 176–78, 197
　Scripts of Cleophas, 29, 132–33, 135, 150–
　　51, 153–54, 156, 165–70, 170, 171
　and "Mrs. Willett," 128–31, 135–36,
　　139–40, 148, 163, 165n22, 166, 198
　and W. B. Yeats, 185, 195–96
　See also Cummins v. Bond
Cummins v. Bond, 150–52, 154, 165–68,
　170, 172, 176
Curran, Mrs. John H. ("Patience Worth"
　medium), 132–33, 155, 171n26,
　193

Dailey, Susan Ramsay, 198
de Courtivron, Isabelle, and Whitney
　Chadwick, 3n2, 21, 82n32, 183
Dever, Maryanne, 64n4, 73n18, 89n38,
　95n5
Dickinson, Emily, 19
Doane, Janice, and Devon Hodges, 81n29
Dodd, Alfred, 160n16, 173n29
Dooley, Allan C., 100
Dorris, Michael, 18–19, 184
Douglas, Alfred, 129n13
Dowden, Hester (Hester Travers Smith):
　and collaborative mediumship, 158,
　　160, 170, 175–76
　communications with "Oscar Wilde," 6,
　　29, 156–60, 169–76
　communications with "Shakespeare,"
　　164, 169, 173–74
　and control spirits, 137–39, 145, 146
　and Geraldine Cummins, 129n13, 138–
　　39, 156–57, 159, 161, 195
　as medium, 6,14, 16 (fig. 8), 18, 129n13,
　　132, 137–39, 145, 146, 155, 164, 167,
　　168–69, 185, 195, 197
Doyle, Sir Arthur Conan, 155, 157–58

Ede, Lisa, and Andrea Lunsford, 3
Eldershaw, M. Barnard (Marjorie Barnard
　and Flora Eldershaw), 5, 64, 67,
　69–70, 72n17, 89, 95, 104, 107–8,
　120
Eliot, Simon, 116n31
Ellmann, Richard, 188n14, 199n24
Erdrich, Louise, 18–19, 184
Erkkila, Betsy, 19

Faderman, Lillian, 69, 82n32, 83, 92n2
Feather, John, 151n3
Feltes, N. N., 97n6, 112n25
Feminist literary criticism, 1–4, 8, 24–25,
　28–29, 74–90
Field, Michael (Katherine Bradley and
　Edith Cooper):
　as aesthetes, 4, 99, 100–101
　as collaborative authors, 4, 10 (fig. 2),
　　63–67, 69–74, 75n20, 83, 86, 89, 99–
　　103, 199
　critical reception of, 4, 29, 99, 101–2
　and lesbianism, 22, 63–65, 79, 82n32,
　　83
　and private publication, 66–67, 99–101
　and professionalism, 99–103
　and Sapphic poetry, 4, 63, 79
　seamlessness of collaboration, 69–74
Findlater, Mary, and Jane Findlater, 5,
　10–12 (figs. 3–4), 71, 73, 94–95,
　97, 103–4, 106n17, 120
Finneran, Richard J., 205, 207–8
Flanagan, Thomas, 122, 123n6
Ford, Ford Madox, 4, 108
Foucault, Michel, 2, 174
Freeman, Mary Wilkins (collaboration on
　The Whole Family), 107
Fripp, Peter, 174n33–175n33
Fritschner, Linda, 20n6, 113n26

Garber, Marjorie, 172n27, 173n30
Gallagher, Tess, 211–12
Gallop, Jane, 84–88
Gardiner, Judith Kegan, 74n19
Garrett, Eileen, 128, 129nn13–14, 138,
　140, 143, 144n26, 145n29, 155, 161,
　184–85
Gaskell, Elizabeth, 20, 35, 37–38, 47,
　50–51, 119
Gerard, E. D. (Emily and Dorothea Ger-
　ard), 5, 31, 93–94, 104, 105, 121–22
Gérin, Winifred, 24, 33n1, 34, 37, 39, 40,
　41, 43n11, 47, 48, 60
Gilbert, Sandra M., and Susan Gubar, xiv
　(fig. 1), 1–2, 76–82, 119n1
Graves, C. L., 125n9

Gregory, Lady Augusta, 123, 201–5
Greenblatt, Stephen, 172n27
Gubar, Susan, 66n6, 69n10
and Sandra M. Gilbert, xiv (fig. 1), 1–2,
76–82, 119n1
Gwynn, Stephen, 123, 125n9

H. D., 19, 130
Haggard, Rider, 4, 108, 111
Hall, Radclyffe, 6, 20, 63n1, 130, 141
Harper, George Mills, 179n1, 181n5,
186–94, 200
and John S. Kelly, 185
Harper, Margaret Mills, 186–88, 191–94,
208–9
Haynes, Renée, 129n13
Hepburn, James, 97n6
Herrmann, Anne, 79, 82
Hirsch, Marianne, 74n19
and Evelyn Fox Keller, 88
Hitt, Jack, 210
Hodges, Devon, and Janice Doane, 81n29
"Holland, Mrs.," 128, 129n13, 155, 161, 200
as Alice Kipling Fleming, 38, 105–6.
See also Kipling family collaborations
Holtby, Winifred, 19, 113n27
Hood, Connie K., 197n22, 207, 208
hooks, bell, and Mary Childers, 79, 82,
125
Hope, Anthony, 108
Howe, Susanne, 106n16
Howells, William Dean (collaboration on
The Whole Family), 106–7
Hughes, Ted, 211

James Henry, 112, 98n8
and The Whole Family, 106–7
Jaszi, Peter, 176
and Martha Woodmansee, 3n2, 30,
151n3
Jay, Karla, 81
Jeffares, A. Norman, 206
Jenney, Shirley Carson (the Shelley Psy-
chic), 132, 159–60
Jewsbury, Geraldine, 19, 20n6, 106
Jochum, K. P. S., 188n14, 190n18

Kaplan, Carey, and Ellen Cronan Rose,
78n26, 184
Keeble, Ida M., 160, 171n26
Keller, Evelyn Fox, 88
Kelly, John, 204. See also Harper, George
Mills, and John S. Kelly
Kennard, Jean, 113n27
Kipling family collaborations (Rudyard
Kipling, Alice "Trixie" Kipling,

Alice Macdonald Kipling, and
John Kipling), 38, 105–6
See also "Mrs. Holland" and Macdonald
family collaborations
Koestenbaum, Wayne, 3n2, 4, 21–22, 65–
66, 68, 69n9, 70n13, 71–72, 108n21,
183
Krementz, Jill, 3

Laird, Holly, 3n2, 8, 18, 69n12, 70n13,
74n19, 75nn20–21, 78, 83, 84
Lane, Margaret, 36
Lang, Andrew, 4, 107, 108, 111
Lee, Vernon (Violet Paget), 113n27
Leonard, Gladys Osborne 6, 17 (fig. 9),
128–29, 130n16, 138, 141–45, 161
Leonardi, Susan J., and Rebecca A. Pope,
25, 66, 78n26
Lesbianism:
and feminist criticism, 31, 79–85
and homophobia, 31, 72–74, 80, 114
and homosocial bonding, 22, 130
instability of category of, 68–69, 83
and lesbian writing, 22, 65–66, 79,
81–83, 85
and mediumship, 130
and romantic friendship, 21, 69, 82–83,
92–93, 114
as specter, 64, 65, 74, 81, 85
and women's collaborative writing, 5,
21–22, 63–69, 72, 74, 78–80, 82–84,
114–15
See also entries for individual collaborative
authors
Lewis, Gifford, 64n3, 89, 102n13, 109n22,
114–15
Lish, Gordon, 211–12
Longenbach, James, 201–2
Lowell, Amy, 20, 81n30, 115
Lucas, E. V., 103n14, 126
Lunsford, Andrea, and Lisa Ede, 3
Lyons, F. S. L., 130

Macdonald family collaborations (Louisa
Macdonald Baldwin, Georgiana
Macdonald Burne-Jones, and Alice
Macdonald Kipling), 105
See also Kipling family collaborations
Mackenzie, Eileen, 71, 73, 96
Mannocchi, Phyllis F., 113n27
Martin, Violet ("Martin Ross"). See Som-
erville, E. OE., and Martin Ross
Masten, Jeffrey A., 173n31
Maurat, Charlotte, 36
Max, D. T., 211n1
Maynard, John, 37

McClintock, Anne, 146
McDowell, Deborah, 87
McGann, Jerome, 57n21
Mediumship:
 and agency, 23–25, 27, 131, 134, 148,
  152, 163–66, 176, 192–94
 as authorship, 7–8, 23, 30, 32, 128, 151–
  55, 163, 165–67, 170–72, 174–79,
  188, 191–93, 196, 200, 205
 as collaboration, 6–7, 13, 18, 22–26, 128,
  154, 163, 167–70, 175–76, 182–84,
  187–88, 194, 201
 as deception, 142, 162n18, 181, 190–91
 erotics of, 129–32, 134, 145–46
 and exoticism, 14, 27–28, 31, 128–29,
  136, 138–49
 and female empowerment, 7–8, 25, 28,
  132, 152–53
 and gender conventions, 25, 28, 130,
  132, 160, 162–63
 as intellectual adventure, 132–35,
  146–48
 literary aspects of, 132–33, 151–61,
  168–70, 173–74, 186–93, 196
 and professionalism, 23, 28, 152, 160–
  62, 164–65
 representations of, 13–18, 180
 and women's education, 131, 133–35,
  144, 160–61, 197–99
 See also Automatic writing and entries for
  individual mediums
Meredith, Isabel (Helen and Olivia Rossetti), 105, 120
Merrill, James, 24, 211
Meyer, Susan, 35
Michie, Elsie, 20
Michie, Helena, 40, 84, 86n35
Mill, John Stuart, and Harriet Taylor Mill,
  183
Miller, D. A., 49
Miller, Nancy K., 2
Mitchell, Hilary, 102n13, 106, 109n22,
  111n23, 126n11
Moglen, Helene, 37, 40, 42n10, 48–49
Moore, Lisa, 83n33
Moore, T. Sturge, 100n10, 101
Moore, Virginia, 181n4, 193
Moriarty, Daniel J., 101n11
Mortimer, Raymond, 97
Murphy, Daniel J., 203n26, 205
Myers, F. W. H., 131, 140n23, 171, 182

Nabokov, Vladimir, and Vera Nabokov, 20

O'Brien, Conor Cruise, 123n8
Oppenheim, Janet, 8n3

Ormrod, Richard, 130n16
Owen, Alex, 8n3, 138n21

Pethica, James, 203
Pierce, David, 191n19
Pinker, J. B., 110–11
Piper, Mrs., 128, 137, 139n22, 159
Plath, Sylvia, 211
Pope, Rebecca A., and Susan J. Leonardi,
  25, 66, 78n26
Powell, Violet, 71, 102n13
Powrie, Phil, 156n11
Pound, Ezra, 4, 198–99, 201–2
Prince, Walter Franklin, 128, 133n18
Prins, Yopie, 70n13, 79n27

Ratchford, Fannie, 35–36, 37, 39, 44, 51,
  55–56
Rice, James (collaboration with Walter
  Besant), 4, 116n31, 117
Rieger, James, 20n7
Roberts, Mrs. D. O., 160, 164, 171n26, 173,
  174n32
Robinson, Hilary, 64n3
Rose, Ellen Cronan, and Carey Kaplan,
  78n26, 184
Ross, Marlon B., 171
Rothenstein, Sir William, 74
Rossetti family collaboration (Michael
  Rossetti, Dante Gabriel Rossetti,
  Christina Rossetti, and Maria
  Rossetti), 105
 Helen and Olivia Rossetti (Isabel Mere-
  dith), 105, 120

Sackville-West, Vita, 19
Saddlemyer, Ann, 183n10, 198, 199, 203
Sassoon, Siegfried, 101, 102n12
Saunders, David, 151n3
Saunders, J. W., 97n6
Schiff, Stacy, 20
Shakespeare, William (spirit communica-
  tions), 160, 164, 169, 172–74
Shelley, Mary, 20, 24
Showalter, Elaine, 74n19
Sidgwick, Eleanor, 175, 176n35
Smith, Eleanor Touhey, 155n10
Smith, Logan Pearsall, 101n11
Smith, Susy, 141, 142, 144
Smith-Rosenberg, Carroll, 69
Society for Psychical Research (SPR), 6,
  128, 134, 141, 193
Somerville, E. OE. (Edith), and Martin
  Ross (Violet Martin):
 and automatic writing, 5–6, 70n15, 71,
  116–18, 126–27, 177, 193

as collaborative authors, 4–5, 13–14
  (figs. 5–6), 31, 67–68, 73, 75–76, 86,
  95–96, 103–4, 106–11, 113–18
  collaborative method, 26, 70, 75–76,
  108, 109–10, 116–17, 126–27
  critical reception of, 4–5,29, 91–93,
  116–17
  as Irish writers, 5, 91–93, 112–27
  imputations of lesbianism, 64, 82n30,
  114–15
  literary works, 92–93, 111, 122
  and professionalism, 68, 89, 91–93,
  103–4, 106–7, 109–11, 113–18
  seamlessness of collaboration, 70–71,
  73, 113
  "Two of a Trade," 26, 86, 70, 92, 114–15,
  117–18
Stein, Gertrude, and Alice B. Toklas, 18,
  20, 82
Stevenson, Lionel, 101n11, 112
Stevenson, Robert Louis, 4, 108, 183
Stewart, Susan 53–55, 58–59
Stillinger, Jack, 3, 4, 20, 182, 183
Sturgeon, Mary, 63–65, 69n10, 71, 73, 96,
  100, 102
Sutherland, J. A., 112
Sword, Helen, 130n16, 152n5
Symonds, John Addington, 65n5

Taylor, Ina, 105n15
Tenant, Winifred Coombe. See "Mrs.
  Willett"
Travers Smith, Hester. See Dowden,
  Hester
Trollope, Anthony, 51, 98
Troubridge, Una, 140, 141, 144, 145
Tuchman, Gaye, 97n6, 98

Vanden Bossche, Chris R., 151n, 167
Verrall, Mrs., 128, 131, 132, 137
Vicinus, Martha, 74, 83n33
Vivien, Renée, 81

Walker, Alice, 24
White, Christine, 79, 83
Wiggin, Kate Douglas, 94n4, 104–5
Wilde, Oscar (spirit communications), 6,
  29, 156–60, 169–76
"Willett, Mrs." (Winifred Coombe Tenant), 6–7, 128–37, 139–40, 148, 171,
  193–94, 197, 198, 200
  and Geraldine Cummins, 128–31, 135–
  36, 139–40, 148, 163, 165n22, 166,
  198
Williams, David, 102n12

Winnifreth, Tom, 38n8, 39
Wise, Thomas James, 35
Woodmansee, Martha, 151n3, 152n7
  and Peter Jaszi, 3n2, 30, 151n3
Woolf, Virginia, 24–25, 38, 94, 97, 100,
  105, 161
"Worth, Patience." See Curran,
  Mrs. John H.

Yeats, George (Bertha Georgie Hyde-
  Lees):
  as author, 4, 187–88, 191, 196–97,
  199–201
  degree of automatism in automatic
  writing, 181, 190–94
  erasure of authorship, 183–86, 188–90,
  196–99
  intellectual and spiritual interests of,
  182, 197–98
  as literary assistant, 20, 181–82, 185–86,
  199, 202, 205–6
  as manager of the Yeats industry, 183,
  202, 207–8
  as medium, 163n19, 182, 184, 186–98,
  201, 205, 207
  as secretary, 182, 190, 205–7
  as wife, 20, 183, 198–99, 203
Yeats, George, and W. B. Yeats:
  and automatic writing, 4, 29, 128, 155,
  181, 186–98, 200–201, 205, 207
  erotics of collaboration, 179–86, 197,
  200
  collaboration as contribution to A Vision, 179, 183, 186–90, 198, 199, 207,
  208
  collaboration as secret writing, 196–97,
  199–200
  portrait of, 180 (fig. 10)
  sleep and dream writing, 189–90, 206
Yeats, W. B.:
  collaboration with Lady Augusta Gregory, 123, 201–5
  collaboration/friendship with Ezra
  Pound, 198–99, 201–2
  collaborations with other women, 181,
  197n 22, 199, 201–2
  relationships with mediums, 184–85,
  193, 195–96, 200
  as solitary author, 4, 183–84, 188–89,
  197

Reading Women Writing

A SERIES EDITED BY

Shari Benstock
Celeste Schenck

Tainted Souls and Painted Faces: The Rhetoric of Fallenness in Victorian Culture
by Amanda Anderson
Greatness Engendered: George Eliot and Virginia Woolf
by Alison Booth
The Madwoman Can't Speak: Or Why Insanity Is Not Subversive
by Marta Caminero-Santangelo
Talking Back: Toward a Latin American Feminist Literary Criticism
by Debra A. Castillo
Articulate Silences: Hisaye Yamamoto, Maxine Hong Kingston, and Joy Kogawa
by King-Kok Cheung
H.D.'s Freudian Poetics: Psychoanalysis in Translation
by Dianne Chisholm
From Mastery to Analysis: Theories of Gender in Psychoanalytic Feminism
by Patricia Elliot
Feminist Theory, Women's Writing
by Laurie A. Finke
Colette and the Fantom Subject of Autobiography
by Jerry Aline Flieger
Autobiographics: A Feminist Theory of Women's Self-Representation
by Leigh Gilmore
Going Public: Women and Publishing in Early Modern France
edited by Elizabeth C. Goldsmith and Dena Goodman
Cartesian Women: Versions and Subversions of Rational Discourse in the Old Regime
by Erica Harth
Borderwork: Feminist Engagements with Comparative Literature
edited by Margaret R. Higonnet
Narrative Transvestism: Rhetoric and Gender in the Eighteenth-Century English Novel
by Madeleine Kahn

The Unspeakable Mother: Forbidden Discourse in Jean Rhys and H.D.
by Deborah Kelly Kloepfer
*Recasting Autobiography: Women's Counterfictions in
Contemporary German Literature and Film*
by Barbara Kosta
Women and Romance: The Consolations of Gender in the English Novel
by Laurie Langbauer
Nobody's Angels: Middle-Class Women and Domestic Ideology in Victorian Culture
by Elizabeth Langland
Penelope Voyages: Women and Travel in the British Literary Traditions
by Karen R. Lawrence
Autobiographical Voices: Race, Gender, Self-Portraiture
by Françoise Lionnet
Postcolonial Representations: Women, Literature, Identity
by Françoise Lionnet
Writing Double: Women's Literary Partnerships
by Bette London
Woman and Modernity: The (Life)styles of Lou Andreas-Salomé
by Biddy Martin
In the Name of Love: Women, Masochism, and the Gothic
by Michelle A. Massé
Imperialism at Home: Race and Victorian Women's Fiction
by Susan Meyer
*Outside the Pale: Cultural Exclusion, Gender Difference, and
the Victorian Woman Writer*
by Elsie B. Michie
Dwelling in Possibility: Women Poets and Critics on Poetry
edited by Yopie Prins and Maeera Shreiber
Reading Gertrude Stein: Body, Text, Gnosis
by Lisa Ruddick
Conceived by Liberty: Maternal Figures and Nineteenth-Century American Literature
by Stephanie A. Smith
Kassandra and the Censors: Greek Poetry since 1967
by Karen Van Dyck
From the Margins of Empire: Christina Stead, Doris Lessing, Nadine Gordimer
by Louise Yelin
Beyond Consolation: Death, Sexuality, and the Changing Shapes of Elegy
by Melissa F. Zeiger
Feminist Conversations: Fuller, Emerson, and the Play of Reading
by Christina Zwarg

1 2 25

ADZ-4356